CELTIC NIGHT

*Compiled by
members of the
Northumbria Community*

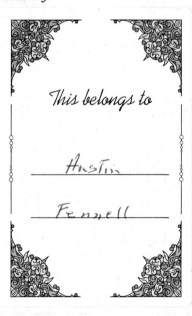

This belongs to

Austin

Fennell

Marshall Pickering
An Imprint of HarperCollins*Publishers*

Marshall Pickering is an Imprint of
HarperCollins*Religious*
Part of HarperCollins*Publishers*
77–85 Fulham Palace Road, London W6 8JB

First published in Great Britain
in 1996 by Marshall Pickering

10   9   8   7   6   5   4   3   2

A catalogue record for this book is
available from the British Library

ISBN 0 551 02974-9

Printed and bound in Great Britain by
Caledonian International Book Manufacturing Ltd, Glasgow, G64

*To those of our community who have
lived and prayed so much of this material.*

*May the Lord
bless and keep
you and your dear ones
this night and every night.*

Contents

The title of this volume is *Celtic Night Prayer*, partly so that it will be recognizable as a companion volume to *Celtic Daily Prayer, a Northumbrian office.*

In what sense is it Celtic?

In and amongst the material here you will find prayers, stories and illustrations drawn from the Celtic Christian tradition. Some of this material is very old, and some quite modern. We make no apology for this. If the early Celtic saints (and those they taught to follow in similar well-trodden ways of prayer and courageous mission) have much to say to us in our generation and culture, then it must be interpreted within our life today.

The present revival of interest in things Celtic may eventually pass. The startling testimony remains that men and women who simply loved God and followed Jesus wherever the Spirit impelled and empowered them to go, lit a fire in the so-called dark ages that brought warmth and culture, learning and most of all faith to vast numbers of people.

The prayers and simple liturgies or rituals (call them what you will!) that we present here seek to recreate the relevance and immediacy of 'Celtic' prayer. We are *not* saying that these are precisely what was done in years long past.

What do we mean by night prayer?

The last-thing-at-night time of prayer is traditionally the Office of Compline, blending familiar psalms of protection amidst hostile spiritual powers with prayers of love and trust as sleep beckons. The person of prayer needs rest, and a heart at peace with itself, with God and with others.

But there are times of vigil and silence, to watch and wait with Christ while all around is sleeping. In the busyness of daylight many things clamour for our attention and easily distract us. When night closes in we have to look at things differently. There are many sorts of night – the long nights of wintertime, nights of difficulty or unanswered questions, times of loneliness and the apparent absence of God.

When prayer seems to be getting us nowhere it is then we need most of all to pray longer. Even a cursory look at the psalms of Scripture assures us that all we experience is only echoing what praying people always have been through.

My God is He who 'even gives me songs in the night'.

How to use this book

1 Some people will want to use this book each night, making use of the year's supply of daily readings and Scriptures. It will live on their coffee-table or next to the bed, preferably with a well-used note pad or journal in which the most important thoughts or feelings are recorded.

(The daily readings were compiled to be used as part of Morning Prayer or Evening Prayer for our community. Those who already have *Celtic Daily Prayer* will find here a further year's supply of readings.)

2 Some people will use this as a source-book for prayers, stories or ideas.

3 Some people will want to keep the book to dip into from time to time. Even if you generally like to read a book from cover to cover, this may be one which will invite you to pause every now and then before continuing.

'Shall we say Compline tonight?'

A perfect end to the day! On retreats it can be used to bring time together to a close as the whole household goes into quiet until next morning. It can be helpful also when loved ones are separated by distance to gather them into God's arms in prayer. These prayers are not lengthy and can be offered in just a few moments.

Some people have recollections of praying at the bedside as a small child. Here is just this kind of ritual:

'I am going now into the sleep', says one of the prayers, leaning confidently back into the arms of the all-loving One.

Examples of life fully lived

Introducing some of you to the stories of these saints is a joy. It is with the easy familiarity experienced with members of a very close family. 'Oh, and did you hear about the time when …?'

The recklessness of Brigid, the humility of the young king Oswald, the vision and steadfastness of Aidan, Chad's willingness to adapt without complaint, the obedience and commitment of Hild and the prayerfulness of Cuthbert – what a colourful and amazing family this is.

The stories have been set to one side so that the prayers can be applied to our own life and story directly, and not just when reflecting upon the life, character and example of the particular saint. '*Brigid* – a Call to Recklessness' is used to pray the blessing of God on the home. Celtic spirituality is nothing if not practical.

The *Oswald* service challenges us to find God in the daily tasks of ordinary life.

With *Aidan* we are sent out again in the power of

the Spirit to shine as lights in the darkness of our day.

Chad is about journeying and reminds us that our final journey is the most important. In the light of that ultimate destination all other chances and changes seem to matter very little. Here is joy *and* a sense of proportion.

The *Hild* meditations, 'in the right place', centre around *not needing* to be anything at all, and are about finding the right seat. There can be no experience of community without the recognition that each is prepared to take the lowest seat.

'*Cuthbert* – a Call to Prayer' is broken into sections to be lived with one at a time. One of these is 'reconciliation', and before moving on, if we have spent time in prayer, we may have to write a letter or even go to the person we never made peace with.

Rites of passage

This selection of prayers has helped us as a community to confess those significant times in our lives of birth, marriage and dying. Such moments are profound, bringing with them a closer awareness of the presence of God in our humanity.

'Hatches, matches and despatches' (christenings, weddings and funerals) represent most people's only experiences of establishment Christianity for better or worse. That contact will be crucial in shaping the individual's perception of the relevance or irrelevance of 'church'.

Giving back the child

The prayers here reflect the desire of parents to thank God for a safe delivery, and to offer the child up to be blessed. The distinct prayers for girl or boy child's naming ceremonies are not at all sexist in their content. Any or all of them can be used if particularly preferred. This was just an attempt to acknowledge that it *is* different and important to be male or female, and, however arbitrarily, that distinction needs honouring and blessing.

The mystery of marriage: a circle with no end

'A Marrying Prayer' is taken from *Carmina Gadelica* with very little change of wording. It is in the spirit of all the other prayers and writings about such relationships in the Celtic tradition. This is the prayer we have used for various weddings in the Community. It has not been used for this purpose for hundreds of years continuously, but we love it, and it says what needs to be said. This is re-creating liturgy – in a living context.

One resource not included elsewhere in the text is the words of a song entitled 'Thigpen's Wedding' from the album *The Vigil* by Kemper Crabb. We include it here as it may be exactly appropriate for use in some wedding services.

Here I set my face unto you.
Here I speak my heart's true vow.
Here I choose to walk beside you,
loving only you,
my heart speaks true,
for evermore from now.

I will love you in the dawning
and in the bright noon-day.
I will love you in the even.
Every day I live,
my heart I'll give.
I'll love you from my grave.

I have heard God in your laughter.
I have seen Him on your face.
And it's clear now what He's after,
for He wrote your name
on my heart in flame;
It's a wound I'll not erase.

We will mount the wings of morning.
We will fly before the wind.
We will dwell within the mystery
of the glories of
Jehovah's love:
a circle with no end.

We will pitch our tents towards Zion
in the shadow of His love.
We will covenant between us.
We will covenant with the earth below
and with heaven up above.
We will covenant with the dust below
and the Spirit up above.

It is important that we affirm the Christian belief in marriage, that bodies and passion and relationship and commitment are good, that promises are made to keep. We can believe in man's love for woman, and hers for him, and in the fervour of this exchange can hear the voice of God.

Marriage involves a commitment to be reconciled, however long it takes. It is sad that in our generation so many Christian marriages are able to disintegrate, leaving wounded lives hoping, perhaps against hope, that they can love again. Sometimes the ex-spouse is gone for good, even remarried, and there is no hope of reconciliation – even God cannot unscramble an egg. But He is able to help us live beyond pain with renewed hope.

Saying farewell

We need to find ways of saying goodbye to those close to us, and not close enough, who leave us to journey through death. Most of the prayers here are for someone who already is in relationship with God through trust in Jesus.

But experience proves time and time again that dying is often the opportunity for real experiences of God touching the life of the most hardened unbeliever. Be prepared to listen, and take seriously such encounters. (The workers in the vineyard hired late in the day are generously given just as much as the others.)

Remember none of us *deserve* to be treated well by God, but because Jesus was treated so badly the way back home is open to whoever is willing to trust Him.

Christmas

The Christmas Eve and Christmas Morning liturgies are recent to us but based on the old Gaelic prayers. The tune for the sung part is 'Away in a Manger' if you wish to sing it. These are simple traditions which can be used year after year and grow in familiarity.

In Ireland on Christmas Eve a candle always burned after dark in the window. (Sometimes this would be standing in a large hollowed out 'bagie' or turnip.)

New Year

The Opening Door literally opens the door to welcome Jesus into the home at the blessing of the year ahead.

The Covenant service is a good Methodist tradition for early in the New Year, but has been important to us from the earliest days as a community. It belongs here as a way of honouring differing traditions and is a way of enriching you with what has been of great value to us.

Maundy Thursday

The footwashing on Maundy Thursday goes back to the very beginning of the Community.

At the first Easter workshop, a towel and basin appeared. After getting over the initial embarrassment, the handful present washed one another's feet. No sentimentalism is intended in this service, but rather the willingness to embrace the foolishness of laying down one's own life daily in community.

The Way of the Cross

The 'stations' on the journey of Jesus to Calvary and beyond are another tradition we have valued as a community. Often we have walked through a city (or place of pilgrimage) carrying a large cross and stopping at different stages of the journey to read and pray. Sometimes the crucifixion has been danced by different men in the group to the slow singing of 'Lift Jesus higher'. The journey culminates not in the tomb, but in the promise fulfilled, the reality of resurrection.

What we are about to receive

Yes, there are several traditional Celtic 'graces' before eating. But we want to explain that if this book were to be compiled in another year or five years it would be different. Prayers grow out of life, and the old sources are discovered and reinterpreted as we go. Who knows what we are about to receive! But if you visit us we will share with you what we do have, and hope you will find nourishment here.

COMPLINE: LATE NIGHT PRAYER

Ita

Ita, who died about AD 570, was Abbess of a women's community at Killeedy, Co. Limerick in Ireland. She ran a school for boys where she taught:

Faith in God
with purity of heart;
simplicity of life
with religion;
generosity
with love.

Among those schooled by Ita was Brendan who honoured her as his foster-mother and adviser. The compline that follows is named for her because of its emphasis on examination of the heart, and the prayers of care and protection for each soul who crosses our path.

Sunday – The Ita Compline

(All say together the sections in bold type)
* Indicates a change of reader
Each in turn say the lines in the boxes

+ *You may silently make the sign of the cross*

The sacred three
to save
to shield
to surround
the hearth
the home
this night
and every night

*Search me O God and know my heart.
Test me and know my thoughts.
*See if there is any wicked way in me
and lead me in the way everlasting.

**O Father, O Son, O Holy Spirit,
Forgive me my sins.
O only begotten Son of the heavenly Father,
forgive.
O God who is one,
O God who is true,
O God who is first,
O God who is one substance,
O God only mighty,
in three Persons, truly merciful,
forgive.**

* O God of life, this night,
O darken not to me thy light.

* O God of life, this night,
close not thy gladness to my sight.

* Keep your people, Lord,
in the arms of your embrace.
Shelter them under your wings.

* Be their light in darkness.
Be their hope in distress.
Be their calm in anxiety.

* Be strength in their weakness.

* Be their comfort in pain.

* Be their song in the night.

> In peace will I lie down, for it is you, O Lord,
> you alone who makes me to rest secure.

---

* Be it on your own beloved arm,
O God of grace, that I in peace shall awake.

**Be the peace of the Spirit mine this night.
Be the peace of the Son mine this night.
Be the peace of the Father mine this night.
The peace of all peace be mine this night.**

+ *You may make the sign of the cross*

**In the Name of the Father, the Son
and the Holy Spirit. Amen.**

Aidan

Aidan came to Lindisfarne from Iona in AD 635 at the request of King Oswald. He was a man of deep prayer who meditated on the words of Scripture, equipping himself in quiet for an active and highly effective apostolate. He remained at Lindisfarne for 16 years.

In AD 651, Aidan was taken ill at Bamburgh and died. Cuthbert, who was at that moment looking after his flock of sheep on the Lammamuir hills, saw a vision of angels taking Aidan's soul to Heaven.

Monday – The Aidan Compline

(All say together the sections in bold type)
* Indicates a change of reader
Each in turn say the lines in the boxes

+ *You may silently make the sign of the cross*

* O Christ, son of the living God,
may Your holy angels guard our sleep,
may they watch us as we rest
and hover around our beds.

* Let them reveal to us in our dreams
visions of Your glorious truth,
O High Prince of the universe,
O High Priest of the mysteries.

* May no dreams disturb our rest
and no nightmares darken our dreams.
May no fears or worries delay
our willing, prompt repose.

* May the virtue of our daily work
hallow our nightly prayers.
May our sleep be deep and soft
so our work be fresh and hard.

**I will lie down and sleep in peace
for You alone, Lord,
make me dwell in safety.**

> My dear ones, O God, bless Thou and keep,
> in every place where they are.

* Into Your hands I commit my spirit;
I give it to You with all the love of my heart.

* How precious to me are Your thoughts, O God!
How vast is the sum of them!
Were I to count them,
they would outnumber the grains of sand.
When I awake,
I am still with You.

I make the cross of Christ upon my breast,
   (+ *You may make the sign of the cross*)
**over the tablet of
my hard heart,
and I beseech the
Living God of the universe —**

may the Light of Lights come
to my dark heart from Thy place;
may the Spirit's wisdom come
to my heart's tablet
from my Saviour.

* Christ without sin,
Christ of wounds,
I am placing my soul and my body
under Thy guarding this night,
Christ of the poor,
Christ of tears.
Thy cross be my shielding this night,
O Thou Son of tears, of the wounds,
of the piercing.

I am going now into the sleep:
O be it in Thy dear arm's keep,
O God of grace, that I shall awake.

* My Christ!
my Christ!
my shield,
my encircler,
each day, each night,
each light,
each dark.

* My Christ!
my Christ!
my shield,
my encircler,
each day, each night,
each light, each dark.
Be near me,
uphold me,
my treasure,
my triumph.

> Circle me, Lord,
> keep protection near
> and danger afar.

* Circle me, Lord,
keep light near
and darkness afar.

* Circle me, Lord,
keep peace within,
keep evil out.

The peace of all peace be mine this night.

+ *You may make the sign of the cross*

**In the Name of the Father, the Son
and the Holy Spirit. Amen.**

Cuthbert

Cuthbert's angelic vision, which coincided with the death of Aidan, convinced him that he was to follow the vocation of the beloved founder of Lindisfarne Abbey.

Cuthbert became a monk at Melrose Abbey, under the guidance of Boisil, the Prior. Cuthbert succeeded him as Prior before becoming Bishop of Lindisfarne in later life. He died in AD 687.

Tuesday – The Cuthbert Compline

(All say together sections in bold type)
* Indicates a change of reader
Each in turn say the lines in the boxes

+ *You may silently make the sign of the cross*

* I will lie down and sleep in peace
for You alone, Lord,
make me dwell in safety.

O God, and Spirit, and Jesu,
  the Three,
From the crown of my head,
  O Trinity,
To the soles of my feet
  mine offering be,
Come I unto Thee, O Jesu, my King –
O Jesu, do Thou be my sheltering.

> My dear ones, O God, bless Thou and keep,
> in every place where they are.

* Whoever has chosen to make the shelter of
the Most High their dwelling place will
stay in His over-shadowing.

* He alone is my refuge, my place of safety;
He is my God, and I am trusting Him.

* He will rescue you from the traps laid for
your feet, and save you from the destroying
curse.

* His faithful promises are your armour.
You need no longer be afraid of any terror by
night, or the death-arrow that flies by day.

* The Lord Himself is your refuge; you have
made the Most High your stronghold.

* Be my strong rock, a castle to keep me safe,
for You are my crag and my stronghold.

* How precious to me are Your thoughts, O God!
How vast is the sum of them!

Were I to count them,
they would outnumber the grains of sand.
When I awake,
I am still with You.

I will not lie down tonight with sin, nor shall
sin nor sin's shadow lie down with me.

O God of life, this night
O darken not to me Thy light.
O God of life, this night
close not Thy gladness to my sight.
O God of life, this night,
Thy door to me, O shut not tight,
O God of life, this night.

* Be it on Thine own beloved arm,
O God of grace, that I in peace shall waken.

Hymn for optional use

As the bridegroom to his chosen,
as the king unto his realm,
as the keep unto the castle,
as the pilot to the helm,
so, Lord, art thou to me.

As the fountain in the garden,
as the candle in the dark,
as the treasure in the coffer,
as the manna in the ark,
so, Lord, art thou to me.

As the music at the banquet,
as the stamp unto the seal,
as the medicine to the fainting,
as the wine-cup at the meal,
so, Lord, art thou to me.

As the ruby in the setting,
as the honey in the comb,
as the light within the lantern,
as the father in the home,
so, Lord, art thou to me.

As the sunshine in the heavens,
as the image in the glass,
as the fruit unto the fig-tree,
as the dew unto the grass,
so, Lord, art thou to me.

* Jesu, Son of Mary!
 My helper,
 my encircler.
 Jesu, Son of David!
 My strength everlasting.
 Jesu, Son of Mary!
 My helper,
 my encircler.

The peace of all peace be mine this night.

+ *You may make the sign of the cross*

**In the Name of the Father, the Son
 and the Holy Spirit. Amen.**

Felgild

Felgild lived in the late 7th century. After Cuthbert
died Aethilwald took his place as hermit of the Inner
Farne. Twelve years later, having never left the island,

he also died. Felgild was the next hermit to come there, but the rigours of his life in the cell aggravated a swelling on his face. The condition was suddenly healed, allowing him to continue the life of a solitary.

The Compline that follows is dedicated to him because he represents so many whose names we never hear who faithfully follow the example of good men and women of old, continuing their battle against the powers of evil, and their devotion to prayer.

Wednesday – The Felgild Compline

(All say together sections in bold type)
* Indicates a change of reader
Each in turn say the lines in the boxes

+ *You may silently make the sign of the cross*

Calm me, O Lord, as you stilled the storm.
Still me, O Lord, keep me from harm.
Let all the tumult within me cease.
Enfold me, Lord, in Your peace.

* Father, bless the work that is done
And the work that is to be.

* Father, bless the servant that I am
And the servant that I will be.

Thou Lord and God of power,
Shield and sustain me this night.

I will lie down this night with God,
And God will lie down with me;
I will lie down this night with Christ,
And Christ will lie down with me;

I will lie down this night with the Spirit,
And the Spirit will lie down with me;
God and Christ and the Spirit,
Be lying down with me.

* The peace of God
be over me to shelter me

* under me to uphold me,

* about me to protect me,

* behind me to direct me,

* ever with me to save me,

The peace of all peace be mine this night.

+ *You may make the sign of the cross*

In the Name of the Father, the Son
and the Holy Spirit. Amen.

Ebba

Ebba died in AD 683. She was the sister of Oswald and
Oswy, joint Kings of Northumbria. She founded and ruled
the double monastery at Coldingham, situated on St
Abb's Head, which was subsequently named after her.

Ebba was consecrated a nun by Aidan. Bede described
her as 'a pious woman and a handmaid of Christ'.

Thursday – The Ebba Compline

(All say together sections in bold type)
* Indicates a change of reader
Each in turn say the lines in the boxes

+ *You may silently make the sign of the cross*

* Find rest O my soul in God alone: my hope comes
    from him.

Come I this night to the Father,
Come I this night to the Son,
Come I to the Holy Spirit powerful:
Come I this night to God.
Come I this night with Christ,
Come I with the Spirit of kindness.
Come I to Thee Jesus.
Jesus, shelter me.

* I will lie down and sleep: I wake again, because the
    Lord sustains me.

* By day the Lord directs his love, at night his song is
    with me – a prayer to the God of my life.

* Be strong and take heart, all you who hope in the
    Lord.

This dwelling, O God, by Thee be blest
And each one who here this night does rest.

---

* May God be in my sleep, may Christ be in my
    dreams.
May the Spirit be in my repose, in my thoughts, in my
    heart.
In my soul always may the Sacred Three dwell.

* May the Father of Heaven, have care of my soul, his
    loving arm about my body,
through each slumber and sleep of my life.

The Son of God be shielding me from harm.
The Son of God be shielding me from ill,
The Son of God be shielding me with power,
The Son of God be shielding me this night.

* Sleep, O sleep in the calm of each calm.
Sleep, O sleep in the guidance of all guidance.
Sleep, O sleep in the love of all loves.
Sleep, O beloved in the Lord of life.
Sleep, O beloved in the God of life.

The peace of all peace be mine this night.

+ *You may make the sign of the cross*

**In the Name of the Father, the Son
    and the Holy Spirit. Amen.**

Boisil

Boisil, Prior of Melrose Abbey, died in AD 661. Bede
described Boisil as 'a priest of great virtue and
prophetic spirit'; Boisil, on his first meeting with
Cuthbert – one of his pupils – exclaimed 'behold, the
servant of the Lord,' recognizing in him the call of
God.

Friday – The Boisil Compline

(All say together sections in bold type)
* Indicates a change of reader
Each in turn say the lines in the boxes

+ *You may silently make the sign of the cross*

* O Lord, you will keep us safe and protect us forever.

**I am placing my soul and my body
In Thy safe keeping this night, O God,
In Thy safe keeping, O Jesus Christ,
In Thy safe keeping, O Spirit of Perfect Truth.
The Three who would defend my cause
Be keeping me this night from harm.**

* I call on you, O God, for you will answer me,
give ear to me and hear my prayer.

* Show the wonder of your great love, you who save
by your right hand those who take refuge in you from
their foes.

* Keep me as the apple of your eye,
hide me in the shadow of your wings.

Lighten my darkness, Lord. Let the light of your
presence dispel the shadows of night.

* Christ with me sleeping, Christ with me waking,
Christ with me watching, each day and each night.

* Save us Lord, while we are awake,
Guard us while we are asleep,
That awake we may watch with Christ,
And asleep may rest in his peace.

God with me protecting
The Lord with me directing
The Spirit with me strengthening
Forever and forever more.

* In the name of the Father precious,
And of the Spirit of healing balm.
In the name of the Lord Jesus,
I lay me down to rest.

The peace of all peace be mine this night.

+ *You may silently make the sign of the cross*

In the Name of the Father, the Son
and the Holy Spirit. Amen.

Patrick

Patrick (AD 389–461) was a Briton, and a former slave
in Ireland. He became the 'Apostle to Ireland',
travelling widely, evangelizing tirelessly and
organizing the churches and monasteries. He
established his episcopal seat in Armagh, which
became the centre of Christianity for the whole
of Ireland.

Patrick was fearless in pursuit of his aim, to destroy
paganism and exalt the name of the Triune God.

Saturday – The Patrick Compline

(All say together sections in bold type)
* Indicates a change of reader
Each in turn say the lines in the boxes

+ *You may silently make the sign of the cross*

In the name of the King of life
In the name of the Christ of Love
In the name of the Holy Spirit
The Triune of my strength.

* I love you, O Lord my strength. The Lord is my Rock,
 my fortress and my deliverer.
My God is my Rock in whom I take refuge.

* I will praise the Lord who counsels me: even at night
my heart instructs me.

* I have set the Lord always before me.
Because he is at my right hand, I shall not be shaken.

I am placing my soul and my body
 under Thy guarding this night, O Christ.
May Thy cross this night be shielding me.

---

* Into Your hands I commit my spirit;
redeem me, O Lord, the God of Truth.

*The God of life with guarding hold you,
The loving Christ with guarding fold you,
The Holy Spirit, guarding, mould you,
Each night of life to aid, enfold you,
Each day and night of life uphold you.

**May God shield me,
May God fill me,
May God keep me,
May God watch me,
May God bring me this night,
To the nearness of his love.**

*The peace of the Father of joy,
The peace of the Christ of hope,
The peace of the Spirit of grace.

The peace of all peace be mine this night.

+ *You may silently make the sign of the cross*

**In the Name of the Father, the Son
and the Holy Spirit. Amen.**

FOLLOW THE EXAMPLE

Brigid (c. 450 – 523)

Many legends and few facts survive about this Irish woman who founded a community at Kildare primarily for women. Famed for her generosity and hospitality, her influence was widespread, but she remained eminently practical.

As a young woman, Brigid was in the habit of giving freely of her father's possessions and food to the poor and needy. Her father became so frustrated he decided to sell her to the king and bundled her into his chariot. He left her at the castle gate while he consulted with the king, and Brigid was approached by a beggar asking for alms. She gave him her father's sword. Brigid's father and the king were amazed, and the king said he could not buy her from her father: 'she is too good for me – I could never win her obedience.'

Once Brigid was the guest at a house when lepers came begging for food. Brigid could find no one about but a young dumb boy. So she asked him for the key to the kitchen. He turned to her and said 'I know where it is kept,' and together they fetched food and attended to the guests.

Brigid led a group of women who had decided to become holy nuns, and asked Bishop Mel to bless their taking of the veil. Brigid held back out of humility, but the bishop saw the Spirit of God descend upon her and called her forward. Laying hands upon her, he said 'I have no power in this matter. God has ordained Brigid.' And so it came to pass that by the intervention of the Holy Spirit the form of ordaining a bishop was read over Brigid.

A poor leper came to Brigid one day and asked her for a cow. Brigid looked at him and asked 'Which would you rather, to take a cow or be healed of your leprosy?' The man chose: 'I would rather be healed than own all the cows in the world.' So Brigid prayed, stretched out her hand, and the leper was made whole.

'May God our Father, our strength and light bless you with what you most need beyond even all you would ask. For the weather is always right for the sowing of good seed.'

Brigid – in welcoming

A Call to Recklessness

This form of prayer may be used

- on Brigid's day – February 1 – to pray a blessing on the home (a group of friends or neighbours may even go from one house to the next)
- whenever a Brigid's cross or other cross is put up by the door or on the wall
- on moving into a new house or blessing a house at any time (the prayers can be taken out and used singly as often as you like)

You will find that the prayers take you round the house, beginning:

AT THE DOORWAY,
then in the LIVING ROOM.
Next you move to the KITCHEN.

There is a blessing to use in each BEDROOM, but special blessings to use as well in a single person's room, a couple's room, or a guest-room, in a child's room, or the room of an older son or daughter.
Read them carefully beforehand and decide which will be appropriate.

Finally you pray a blessing AT THE DOOR or at any place where a cross or Brigid's cross may be.
The householder reads the parts in ordinary type, and everyone reads parts in bold type.

At the Doorway

church

May God give His blessing to the house that is here.
God bless this house from roof to floor,
from wall to wall,
from end to end,
from its foundation and in its covering.

In the strong name of the Triune God
all evil be banished,
all disturbance cease,
captive spirits freed,
God's Spirit alone
dwell within these walls.

**We call upon the Sacred Three
to save, shield and surround
this house, this home,** *church*
**this day, this night
and every night.**

always.

In the Living Room

There is a friend's love
in the gentle heart of the Saviour.
For love of Him we offer friendship
and welcome every guest.

Lord, kindle in my heart
a flame of love to my neighbour,
to my enemies, my friends, my kindred all,
from the lowliest thing that liveth
to the name that is highest of all.

In the Kitchen

I would welcome the poor
and honour them.
I would welcome the sick
in the presence of angels
and ask God to bless and
embrace us all.

Seeing a stranger approach
I would put food in the eating place,
drink in the drinking place,
music in the listening place,
and look with joy for the blessing of God,
who often comes to my home
in the blessing of a stranger.

We call upon the Sacred Three
to save, shield and surround
this house, this home,
this day, this night,
and every night.

Bedrooms

Peace be here in the Name of the King of life,
the peace of Christ above all peace,
the Lord's blessing over you.

For the bedroom of a single person:

Peace be here in the name of the King of life,
the peace of Christ above all peace,
the Lord's blessing over you.

May God the Father be the guardian of this place
and bring His peace,
that fear may find no entry here.
May Christ be a chosen companion and friend.
May loneliness be banished.

May the Spirit bring lightness and laughter,
   and be the comforter of tears.
Courage be at each going out;
rest be present at each return,
each day, each night,
each going out and each returning.

For the bedroom of a married couple:

**Peace be here in the Name of the King of life,
the peace of Christ above all peace,
the Lord's blessing over you.**

Peace between person and person,
Peace between husband and wife.
The peace of Christ above all peace,
Peace between lovers
in love of the King of life.

For a guest room:

**Peace be here in the Name of the King of life,
the peace of Christ above all peace,
the Lord's blessing over you.**

May all be welcomed here
   as the Christ-child at the stable
   in simplicity and joy,
and as Brigid welcomed the poor.
May the smile of the Son of Peace
   be found here
   whenever the door is opened.

**In the room of a young child *(said by Parent if
possible)*:**

**Peace be here in the Name of the King of life,
the peace of Christ above all peace,
the Lord's blessing over you.**

They say nothing is given birth without pain.
I have a secret joy in Thee, my God.
For, if Thou art my Father,
    Thou art my Mother too.
And of Thy tenderness, healing and patience
there is no end at all

I pray for *(Name)*.
(Name), may the joy and peace of heaven
    be with you.
The Lord bless you.

**In the room of an older son or daughter present or
absent *(said by Parent)*:**

**Peace be here in the Name of the King of life,
the peace of Christ above all peace,
the Lord's blessing over you.**

Son of my breast…
or
Daughter of my heart…
the joy of God be in thy face,
    joy to all who see thee.
The circle of God around thee
    Angels of God shielding thee
    Angels of God shielding thee
Joy of night and day be thine
Joy of sun and moon be thine
Joy of men and women be thine.
    Each land and sea thou goest
    Each land and sea thou goest.
Be every season happy for thee
Be every season bright for thee
Be every season glad for thee.
Be thine the compassing of the God of life,
Be thine the compassing of the Christ of love,
Be thine the compassing of the Spirit of Grace,

To befriend thee and to aid thee
(Name),
thou beloved son of my breast.
or
thou beloved daughter of my heart.

At the Door (or At a Cross)

Christ in our coming,
   and in our leaving
the Door and the Keeper,
   for us and our dear ones,
   this day and every day
   blessing for always.

Oswald (605 – 642)

Long ago on the Isle of Iona a young man knelt in prayer, his heart and hands raised in question to the God he loved and served. Oswald was his name, and he had been schooled by the saints of Iona to follow the old paths, in the steps of those who long ago had walked with Christ in His way.

A difficult decision was made. Oswald would return to Northumbria, the land of his heritage, and make it his, reclaiming the throne and crown by battle, and put an end to the years of fighting and division so that his people might live. Oswald planted a wooden cross in the good ground of Heavenfield, setting it up as a waymark. And so Oswald and his companions knelt together at the turn of the road, at the foot of the cross, and prayed.

The battle was decisive, Oswald victorious, and Northumbria united under his kingship. Many of those who fought were intrigued by this new god, the God of the Christians who had won Oswald's allegiance. Oswald sent for missionaries from Iona to teach his people, but everything went wrong and the team withdrew, admitting to failure. The king prayed and trusted and waited and reached out his hands to his God.

Then came Aidan from Iona with a band of helpers. This time the work began in earnest, and Oswald the king, Oswald the Christian, went out into the villages and market places where Aidan would preach and he worked willingly as the interpreter.

Oswald – in practical ways

A Call to Humility

This form of prayer may be used

- on Oswald's day – August 5
- on pilgrimage to Heavenfield or Bamburgh
- as a way of commiting our work to God
- by those who live out their Christianity in ordinary life

(All who wish may read in turn. * Indicates a change of reader. With a large group, split into two halves and read alternately. All say together sections in bold type.)

* This day is Your gift to me;
I take it, Lord, from Your hand
and thank You for the wonder of it.

**God be with me
in this Your day
every day
and every way,
with me and for me
in this Your day
and the love
and affection
of heaven
be toward me.**

* All that I am, Lord,
   I place into Your hands.
All that I do, Lord,
   I place into Your hands.
* Everything I work for
   I place into Your hands.
Everything I hope for
   I place into Your hands.
* The troubles that weary me
   I place into Your hands.
The thoughts that disturb me
   I place into Your hands.
* Each that I pray for
   I place into Your hands.
Each that I care for
   I place into Your hands.

* I place into your hands, Lord,
the choices that I face.
Guard me from choosing
   the way perilous
of which the end is heart-pain
   and the secret tear.

* Rich in counsel,
show us the way
that is plain and safe.

* May I feel Your presence
at the heart of my desire,
and so know it for Your desire for me.
Thus shall I prosper,
thus see that my purpose is from You,
thus have power to do the good which endures.

* Show me what blessing it is that I have work to do.
And sometimes, and most of all
when the day is overcast and my courage faints,
let me hear Your voice, saying,
'you are my beloved one in whom I am well-pleased.'

* Stand at the crossroads and look,
ask for the ancient paths,
ask where the good way is,
and walk in it,
and you will find rest for your souls.

* In the name of Christ we stand, and in His name
move out across the land in fearfulness and blessing.

* To gather the kingdom to the King
and claim this land for God,
a task indeed.

* Give us to see Your will,
and power to walk in its path,
and lo! the night is routed and gone.

* Lord, hasten the day when those who fear You in
        every nation
will come from the east and west, from north and
        south,
and sit at table in Your kingdom.
And, Lord, let Your glory be seen in our land.

* He has shown you, O man, what is right,
and what does the Lord require of you,
but to do justly, and to love mercy
and to walk humbly with your God?

* Keep me close to You, Lord.
Keep me close to You.
I lift my hands to You, Lord,
I lift them up to You.

**Hands, Lord, Your gift to us
we stretch them up to You.
Always You hold them.**

* Help me to find my happiness
in my acceptance of what is Your purpose for me:
in friendly eyes, in work well done,
in quietness born of trust,
and, most of all,
in the awareness of Your presence
in my spirit.

Pause for reflection before resuming activity

Aidan

Aidan came to Lindisfarne in 635 and died in 651.
From here missionaries went out to evangelize most
of England, in the simple Celtic tradition of Columba
and others.

Long ago on the island of Iona a meeting had been
called. An angry brother spoke about his failure,
telling of the hardness of heart in the kingdom of
Northumbria, a land of darkness refusing the life-
giving light, a stubborn, unreachable people. And one
man heard, and his heart was stirred with compassion
for that land and its people. To open his heart to this
could cost him everything: leaving the island he
loved, the companionship of his brothers, their prayer
and work. Were there not others still to reach much
closer to home? If he stayed seated among his
brothers no one would notice him, no one would
know what he had heard in his heart: the cry of the
desert, 'Come over to Northumbria and help us.'

'O Lord', he prayed, 'give me springs and I will
water this land. I will go, Lord. I will hold this people
in my heart.' A moment later it was his own voice, the
voice of Aidan, that broke the awkward silence.

'Perhaps, my brother, if you had spoken with more gentleness, and of the love of Christ, giving them the gospel to nourish them like milk is given to a tiny baby, then you would have won them and remained among them.'

Aidan – in the power of the Spirit

A Call to Mission

This form of prayer may be used

- on Aidan's day, August 31
- on pilgrimage to Holy Island or Bamburgh
- for sending out anyone going away on mission
- by any mission team while they are away

(All who wish may read in turn.* Indicates a change of reader. With a large group, split into two halves and read alternately. All say together sections in bold type.)

* Then I heard a voice in heaven saying,
Whom shall I send?
and who will go for us?
Then said I,
Here am I. Send me.

* I will go, Lord, if You lead me:
I will hold Your people in my heart.

* Deeper in my heart I will hear Your call
I will cry for the desert
until my eyes run with tears because
people do not obey Your laws.

* If I open my eyes to the world around me,
if I open my heart to the people
that surround me,
then I feel pain and brokenness,
I see suffering and injustice.

* Lord, see what evil the prince of this world is
      devising,
Let the wind of Your Spirit blow
and reverse the works of darkness
and Your fire will cover the earth.

**Deliver us, Lord, from every evil
and grant us peace in our day.
In your mercy, Lord, keep us free from sin,
and protect us from all anxiety
as we wait in joyful hope
for the coming of our saviour, Jesus Christ.
Let your Kingdom come, Lord, in me.**

**I pray the protection of Christ to clothe me,
Christ to enfold me,
to surround me and guard me
this day and every day,
surrounding me and my companions,
enfolding me and every friend.**

*We pray for ourselves,
for the gift of friendship
– and of faithfulness,
and that we would be freed
– from selfishness.

**We will journey with the kindhearted Saviour.
If we have fed the hungry from our own table
God will feed us with all good gifts.**

*We will keep before us
the deepening and strengthening
of our companions' faith,
assisting each other in meditation and prayer.

* May we protect each other's times for silence.
Give us the courage to say,

Leave me alone with God as much as may be.

As the tide draws the waters
close in upon the shore
make me an island, set apart,
alone with you, God,
holy to you.

Then with the turning of the tide
prepare me to carry your presence
to the busy world beyond,
the world that rushes in on me
till the waters come again
and fold me back to you.

Pause for reflection

* Lord, give us the desire to love goodness,
to passionately love goodness,
teach us moderation in all things.
Teach us to love wisdom,
and to greatly love Your law.

* So often we hold too lightly to our belief.
May we plant the faith patiently,
calmly and untiringly
in the good ground of hungry hearts.

God and the angels guard us!
May he bring us home rejoicing!

Chad (died 672)

Chad and his brothers were early pupils in Aidan's
school at Lindisfarne. Chad went on to study in
Ireland, but returned and when his brother Cedd died
took his place as Abbot of Lastingham. For a time he
was Bishop of York, then removed over a technicality
which he accepted with no reproach. He was sent
instead to be Bishop of Mercia.

He lived in a small cell even as bishop, and also

travelled barefoot whenever possible. When appointed first bishop to the people of Mercia Chad spoke warily of this honour: 'I never thought myself worthy of it; but though unworthy, I consented to undertake it for obedience sake.'

Bishop Theodore of Canterbury had so little success in persuading Chad to ride on horseback as he journeyed that once he lifted Chad bodily himself and put him on a horse to set him on his way!

When Mercia had had Chad as its bishop for only three years, he died, urging each person in his community always to be well prepared for death, which may call for us at any time.

Chad – in willing service

A Call to Readiness

This may be used
- on Chad's day, March 2
- on pilgrimage to Stowe or Lichfield or Lastingham
- by anyone in a time of transition or great change
- by someone going on a journey

(Sections in bold type are read in unison. All who wish may read other sections in turn, one section each. * Indicates a change of reader. The lines in boxes are said by everybody one at a time, until all have said them; with a large group, they are repeated after a single reader.)

My soul thirsts for God, for the living God.
As the deer pants for streams of water,
So my soul pants for You, O God.

* In the Name of the Father
Amen.

*In the Name of the Son
Amen.

* In the Name of the Spirit
Amen.

Father, Son and Spirit
Amen.
Father, Son and Spirit
Amen.
Father, Son and Spirit
Amen.

*Thanks to you,
O ever-gentle Christ,
for raising me freely
from the black and darkness of last night
into the kindly light of this day.

You pour life into me,
    giving me speech, sense, desire,
    giving me thought and action.
My fame or repute will be
    just as You allow:
You mark the way before me.

As I remember saints who have journeyed
    before me,
Lord, teach me the way of their simplicity,
    Strength with humility,
    At peace in the fear of God.
May I also go wherever I am led.

The keeping of Christ about me,
The guarding of God with me
    To possess me, to protect me
    From drowning and danger and loss,
The gospel of the God of grace
    From brow of head
    To sole of foot.

The gospel of Christ,
   King of salvation,
   Be as a mantle to my body

All I speak, be blessed to me, O God.
All I hear, be blessed to me, O God.
All I see, be blessed to me, O God.
All I sense, be blessed to me, O God.
All I taste, be blessed to me, O God.
Each step I take, be blessed to me, O God.

Peace between me and my God.
Peace between me and my God.

May I tread the path
to the gates of glory,
may I tread the path
to the gates of glory.

On your path, O my God,
   and not my own,
be all my journeying.
Rule this heart of mine
that it be only yours.

*We look for solitude.
In solitude we learn to grow and love,
to grow in love for God,
to grow in love for others.

* Christ's cross would I carry,
my own struggle forget.

* Christ's death would I ponder,
my own death remember.

* Christ's agony would I embrace,
my love to God make warmer.

*The love of Christ would I feel,
my own love waken.

Great God of wisdom,
Great God of mercy,
give me of your fullness
and of your guidance
at the turning
of each pass.

Great God of shielding,
Great God of surrounding,
give me of your holiness
and of your peace
in the fastening of my death
give me your surrounding
and your peace upon my death.

Peace between me and my God.
May I tread the path
to the gates of glory,
rule this heart of mine
that it be only yours.
God's path would I travel,
my own path refuse.
May I tread the path
to the gates of glory.

Hild (614 – 680)

King Edwin of Northumbria was her great uncle.
At age 13 she was baptized by Paulinus. At 33
she became a nun and at Aidan's urging became
abbess at Hartlepool. She founded a double
monastery at Whitby where she governed both
men and women religious, but also was sought

out for her wise counsel by ordinary folk and
rulers alike.

Hild – in the right place

A Call to Obedience

This may be used

- on Hild's day, November 17
- on pilgrimage to Whitby or Hartlepool
- by women who wish to be taken seriously
- by anyone, man or woman, who is wrestling with a
  sense of vocation

All who wish may read in turn.* Indicates a
change of reader. A small group may prefer to read
as individuals in turn. It may be preferable (and, with
a large group, necessary) to split down the centre
to form two groups reading alternately with each *.
All say together sections in bold type. Each in turn
say lines in boxes (or leader reads, then all
repeat together).

*Take me often from the tumult of things
into Thy presence.
There show me what I am
and what Thou hast purposed me to be.
Then hide me from Thy tears.

> O King and Saviour of men,
> what is Thy gift to me?
> and do I use it to Thy pleasing?

* Now we must praise the guardian of Heaven,
the might of the Lord
and His purpose of mind,
the glorious all Father,
for He, God eternal, is kind.

*The will of God be done by us;
The law of God be kept by us.

* Our evil will controlled by us,
Our sharp tongue checked by us,

* Quick forgiveness offered by us,
Speedy repentance made by us,

*Temptation sternly shunned by us,

* Blessed death welcomed by us,
Angels' music heard by us,

* God's highest praises sung by us.

* Christ, You are the Truth;
You are the light.

*You are the Keeper of the treasure
we seek so blindly.

* My soul's desire is to see the face of
God and to rest in His house.
My soul's desire is to study the Scriptures
and to learn the ways of God.
My soul's desire is to be freed from
all fear and sadness, and to share Christ's risen life.
My soul's desire is to imitate my King,
and to sing His purposes always.
My soul's desire is to enter the gates
of heaven and to gaze upon the light
that shines forever.

**Dear Lord, You alone know
what my soul truly desires,
and You alone can
satisfy those desires.**

* I have prepared a place for you, says the Lord. A place that is for you, and only you, to fill. Approach my table, asking first that you might serve. Look even for the lowest tasks. Then, the work of service done, you may look for your own place at table. But do not seek the most important seat which may be reserved for someone else. In the place of my appointing will be your joy.

> Lord, show me the right seat;
> find me the fitting task;
> give me the willing heart.

* May I be equal to Your hope of me. If I am weak, I ask that You send only what I can bear. If I am strong, may I shrink from no testing that shall yield increase of strength or win security for my spirit.

Each say in turn, or sing together.

> I trust in Thee, O Lord.
> I say, Thou art my God.
> My times are in Thy hand,
> My times are in Thy hand.

Cuthbert (635 – 687)

Cuthbert was called by God to follow Him on the very night that Aidan died. He entered the monastery at Melrose where he was welcomed by Boisil. Cuthbert's faithfulness was demonstrated in his years at Melrose, then as guestmaster at Ripon. After Boisil departed to the Lord, Cuthbert was made Prior of the monastery at Melrose, and many were instructed by the authority of his teaching and the example of his life. It was also his custom to travel and preach, particulary in those remote districts and villages which were situated in high and rugged mountains, which others shrank from visiting.

Many miracles followed Cuthbert's preaching, and he was given grace to see into people's hearts. As a result, many were converted from a life of foolish custom to the love of the joys of Heaven.

After the Council of Whitby Abbot Eata transferred Cuthbert from the monastery at Melrose to that on Lindisfarne where he had to teach the revised rule of monastic life and gradually won the love and obedience of the brothers. After many years in the monastery he finally entered with great joy, and with the goodwill of the abbot and monks, into the remoter solitude he had so long sought, thirsted after, and prayed for. To learn the first steps of solitude he retired to a place in the outer precincts of the monastery. (This is believed to be the tiny tidal island adjoining Lindisfarne which is known as St Cuthbert's Island.) Not until he had first gained victory over our invisible enemy by solitary prayer and fasting, did he seek a more remote place, The Farne Island.

The island was inhabited by demons; Cuthbert was the first man brave enough permanently to live there alone. Bede tells us that at the entry of this soldier of Christ, armed with the helmet of salvation, the shield of faith and the sword of the Spirit which is the word of God, the demons fled.

After nine years he was prevailed upon to leave his solitude to become a bishop. Exchanging places with Eata he avoided Hexham and for two years was bishop at Lindisfarne. Then he returned to the Inner Farne to resume his life of prayer. On his death one of the monks watching nearby went without delay and lit two candles and went up, one in each hand, to a piece of high ground to let the Lindisfarne brethren know that Cuthbert's holy soul had gone to the Lord.

Cuthbert – into a desert place

A Call to Prayer

This may be used

- on Cuthbert's day, March 20
- on pilgrimage to Cuthbert's Cave or at Lindisfarne, St Cuthbert's Island, Melrose, Ripon, Durham Cathedral or the Inner Farne
- on solitary retreat anywhere
- by those drawn to the solitary life

On an individual retreat the sections could be used as a focus one day at a time, encouraging the experience of prayer, abandonment, reconciliation, resisting evil, and then prayer of the heart.

I Prayer

Hear my voice when I call, O Lord;
    be merciful to me and answer me.
My heart says of You, 'Seek His face!'
    Your face, Lord, I will seek.
Do not hide Your face from me,
    do not turn Your servant away in anger,
        You have been my helper.

Do not reject me or forsake me,
　O God my Saviour.
Though my father and mother forsake me,
　the Lord will receive me.
Teach me Your way, O Lord,
　lead me in a straight path.
Amen.

Lord, I have heard your voice
calling at a distance
　Guide my steps to you, Lord,
　Guide my steps to you.
Lord, I have heard your voice
calling at a distance
　Guard my way to you, Lord,
　Guard my way to you.

Lord, I have heard your voice
calling at a distance.
　Keep my heart for you, Lord,
　Keep my heart for you.
Lord, I have heard your voice.
Amen.

II Abandonment

Softly as the dew-fall of heaven
may the Holy Spirit come upon me
to aid me and to raise me,
to bind my prayer firmly
at the throne of the King of life.

God's will would I do,
My own will bridle;
God's due would I give,
My own due yield;
God's path would I travel
My own path refuse.

All whom I love,
Into your safe keeping;
All that I am,
Into your tender care;
All that will be,
Into your perfect will.
Amen.

III Reconciliation

O King of Kings,
O King of the universe
King who will be, who is,
may You forgive us and every one.
Accept my prayer, O King of Grace.

Anyone who claims to be in the light
but hates his brother is still in the darkness.
Whoever loves his brother lives in the light,
and there is nothing in him to make him stumble.

Examine your own heart

Lower my vengeance, my anger and my hatred,
and banish my wicked thoughts from me;
send down a drop from heaven of Your Holy Spirit
to vanquish this heart of rock of mine.
Amen.

Lord,
Let our memory
provide no shelter
for grievance against another.

Lord,
Let our heart
provide no harbour
for hatred of another.

Lord,
> Let our tongue
> be no accomplice
> in the judgement of a brother.

IV Resisting Evil

Under the protection of the King of Life,
a protection that will not betray us.
May the Holy Spirit come upon us,
May Christ deliver us, bless us.

Do not put out the Spirit's fire,
> do not treat prophecies with contempt.
Test everything.
> Hold on to the good.
> Resist every kind of evil.

Jesus, great Son of Mary, I call on your name,
And on the name of John the Beloved,
And on the names of all the saints in the wide world
to shield me in the battle to come.
Amen.

Jesus, only Son of the Father, and Lamb,
> who shed your heart's true
> blood, dearly to buy us,
> protect me, accompany me,
> be near me ever.

Jesus, only Son of the Father and High King,
> your name is above every name,
In the Name of Jesus
> let no evil be welcome in our hearts,
> or in this place.

V *Prayer of the Heart*

My eyes, my eyes
have seen the King.
The vision of His beauty
has pierced me deep within.
To whom else can I go?

My heart, my heart
desires Him.
He's touched something inside of me
that's now reaching out for Him
And I know that I must go.

My God is my love,
my guard, my healing one,
my bright love
is my merciful Lord,
my sweet love is Christ,
his heart is my delight,
all my love are You,
O King of Glory.
Amen.

VI *Commitment*

In the true faith may we remain,
in Jesus may we find hope,
against exploitation of the poor may we help,
against our faults may we fight,
our bad habits abandon,
the name of our neighbour may we defend,
in the work of mercy may we advance,
those in misery may we help,
every danger of sin may we avoid,
in holy charity may we grow strong,
in the well of grace in confession may we wash,

may we deserve the help of the saints,
the friendship of our brother Cuthbert win.
Amen.

**In the Name of the Father, the Son
and the Holy Spirit. Amen.**

RITES OF PASSAGE

Coming into the Light: Birth

These are prayers which may be used at the
christening or dedication of a child. Sections in
square brackets should be omitted where parents
are not both believers.

Celebrant or Friend or Godparent:
The blessing of Christ
comes to you in this child.
His blessing is mercy
and kindness and joy.
Blessing comes to home
and to family.

(This section is intended for use only when the child
is a girl.)

Parents:
(Name of child), Lord,
Your gift to us,
we lift her up to You.
Always You hold her.
This life You entrusted to us,
a sign of Your love and Your faith.

[Our names are inscribed upon Your palms.
You pour blessing on the details of our days.]

We are giving her back to You, dear Lord.
We are giving her back to You.

[Your kingdom come
and Your will be done
in everything that we do.
We are giving her back to You.]

Of Your tenderness and healing and patience
there is no end at all.
We know we can trust You, Lord
We know we can trust You.

Celebrant (or godparent or friend):
Welcome, *(Name of child)*,
child of love.
God is here to bless you.
And blessed are you,
beyond telling
to be born to parents
who love you
and love each other
[servants of the
great King Jesus].

Godparent (or celebrant or friend):
Grow gently, *(Name of child)*,
in love of God.
We bless you,
and pray
Christ be near you,
now and each hour
of your life.

All:
**God be with you
in this your day,
every day,
with you and for you
in this your day,
and the love
and affection
of heaven
be toward you.**

(This section is intended for use only when the child
is a boy:)

Celebrant (or friend or godparent):
As a tiny baby your parents cover
and clothe you
in their love
[and with their faith].

As you grow
    may faith grow with you.
May you find the presence
    of Christ your clothing
    and protection.
And year by year may the
    knowledge of His presence
    be greater for you
that daily you may put on Christ
and walk as His own in the world.

Parents:
(Name of child),
May God make clear to you each road,
may He make safe to you each steep,
should you stumble, hold you,
if you fall, lift you up,
when you are hard-pressed with evil,
deliver you,
and bring you at last to His glory.

Celebrant (or friend or godparent):
The blessing of Christ
comes to you in your *(Name of child)*;
this blessing is mercy
and kindness and joy.
Blessing comes to home
and to family.

Coming into the Light: Rebirth

A Confession of Faith

This may be used

- at Baptism of a believer
- at confirmation or its equivalent
- for renewal of baptismal vows

I call all heaven to witness today
that I have put on Christ.

I choose no other Lord
than the Maker of Heaven and earth.

This day I walk with Him
and He will walk with me.

I fasten close to me this day
that same Jesus
who came to us as flesh and blood
and was himself baptized in the Jordan river.

He died upon a cross to rescue me,
broke free from death, its conqueror.
He left us, to return the more certainly.
All these truths and their power
I fasten close to me this day.

Resisting my own selfishness and sin,
refusing to live as a slave to riches,
pleasure or reputation,
rejecting Satan and all his lies,
I call on heaven to witness today
that I have put on Christ.

Marriage – light and shadow

A Marrying Prayer

All we have came only from you,
everything we hope for will
only come from your love;
all that we enjoy you gave us freely,
everything we ask for is only
yours to give.

Give us the light to understand;
put fire behind our will,
be at the beginning of all we begin.
Excite our love,
strengthen our weakness,
encompass our desire.

Shield our thoughts,
and cradle our bodies,
and as we breathe this prayer,
in our hearts may we feel
Your Presence.

Father, Son and Holy Spirit,
Father, Son and Holy Spirit,
Father, Son and Holy Spirit.
Amen.

Peace-prayer for a Wedding

Christ, King of tenderness.
Christ, King of tenderness
Bind *us* with a bond
that cannot be broken.
Bind *us* with a bond of love
that cannot be broken.

(*us* may be changed to *them*)

(See also 'When I do not know what to pray', p. 60.)

Blessings

May God and your marriage
bring you joy.
God give you joy of one another!

Be ever
in the embrace of the Father.
Be ever
in the embrace of the Son.
Be ever
in the embrace of the Spirit.
Be ever
in the embrace of one another.

May the Lord
tie a bond of your love
between you for ever
without loosening.

In Difficulties

O God, make clear to us each road.
O God, make safe to us each steep.
When we stumble, hold us,
When we fall, lift us up.
When we are hard-pressed with evil,
Deliver us,
And bring us at last to Your glory.

Reconciliation

Lord,
let our memory
provide no shelter
for grievance against each other.

Lord,
let our heart
provide no harbour
for hatred of each other.

Lord,
let our tongue
be no accomplice
in the judgement of each other.

Prayer at a Time of Separation from Loved Ones:

Give *them* peace
   to know I am unharmed.
Give *them* hope
   to know I will return.
Give *them* patience to wait
   and courage to endure the waiting.
Give *them* strength
   so that they will not grow weary.

A Prayer in Time of Darkness

All that I love
   into Your keeping.
All that I care for
   into Your care.
Be with us by day,
   be with us by night;
and as dark closes
   the eyelids with sleep
may I waken
   to the peace of a new day.

The Shadow of Death

Some day I must die;
I know not the time nor the place.
Let me not die in sin,
but wrapped in Your loving grace.

Death and Dying

Preparing for what may be just ahead

Tonight, as on other nights,
I'm walking alone
through the valley of fear.
O God, I pray
that You will hear me,
for You alone know
what is in my heart.
Lift me out of the valley of despair
and set my soul free.

Bright King of Friday and Father Almighty,
make a roof for me by night and guard me by day.
If You are to bring me along the path
I have never seen before,
make it a pathway for me to the life of glory.

Prayer on Behalf of the Dying

(*woman* changed to *man*, etc. as appropriate)

God, omit not this *woman* from Your covenant.
The many evils that in this life *she* has committed
she cannot count or list this night.

Gather this soul with Your own arm, O Christ,
great King of the City of Heaven.
It was Your work, O Christ,
the buying of the soul
at the time of the balancing of the beam,
at the time of bringing of judgement.
Be this soul hidden in Your right hand.

May Michael, prince of angels,
come to meet *her* soul,
leading it home
to the heaven of the Son of God.

Watching with One Who Is Dying

Sleep thou, sleep, and away with thy sorrow,
Sleep thou, sleep, and away with thy sorrow,
Sleep thou, sleep, and away with thy sorrow;
Sleep thou, beloved in the Rock of the fold.

Sleep, O sleep in the calm of all calm.
Sleep, O sleep in the guidance of guidance.
Sleep, O sleep in the love of all loves.
Sleep, O beloved in the Lord of life.
Sleep, O beloved in the God of life.

The Darkness of Bereavement

Walking with Grief

Do not hurry
as you walk with grief;
it does not help the journey.

Walk slowly,
pausing often:
do not hurry
as you walk with grief.

Be not disturbed
by memories that come unbidden.
Swiftly forgive;
and let Christ speak for you
unspoken words.
Unfinished conversation
will be resolved in Him.
Be not disturbed.

Be gentle with the one
who walks with grief.
If it is you,
be gentle with yourself.
Swiftly forgive;
walk slowly,
pausing often.

Take time, be gentle
as you walk with grief.

When I Do Not Know What to Pray

David Adam's version of the 'Caim' or encircling
prayer is often a good way of praying when words get
in the way, and it seems impossible to focus:

Circle *(me/us/them/person's name)*, Lord.
keep *(comfort)* near
and *(discouragement)* afar
keep *(peace)* within
and *(turmoil)* out.

Sometimes the prayer can be written down and
returned to when praying through the same
troubledness or praying for the same person.
　　Here is another example (written as night prayer
for someone recently bereaved):

This night and every night
seems infinite with questions
and sleep as elusive
as answers.
Pain and longing are always present,
dulled only a little
by the distractions of day.
I am weary; I am angry.
I am confused.

Circle me, Lord.
Keep despair and disillusion without.
Bring a glimmer of hope within.
Circle me, Lord;
keep nightmare without.
Bring moments of rest within.
Circle me, Lord;
keep bitterness without.
Bring an occasional sense
of Your presence within.

Christmas

Christmas Eve at dusk, to be repeated again before midnight.

(* denotes a change of voice. All say the words in bold type.)

*This night is the long night
when those who listen await His cry.

*This night is the eve of the great nativity
when those who are longing await His appearing.

*Wait, with watchful heart.

* Listen carefully, through the stillness,
listen, hear the telling of the waves upon the shore.

* Listen, hear the song of the angels glorious –
e're long it will be heard
that His foot has reached the earth,
news – that the glory is come!

*Truly His salvation is near
for those who fear Him,
and His glory shall dwell in our land.

*Watch and pray, the Lord shall come.

*Those who are longing await His appearing.

*Those who listen await His cry.

*Watch ...

*Wait ...

* Listen ...

This night is the long night.

After midnight as Christmas Eve turns to the Feast of the Christ Mass, the Nativity of the Christ Child.

This night is born Jesus
son of the King of glory.
This night is born to us
the root of our joy.
This night gleamed sea and shore
together.
This night was born Christ,
the King of greatness.

* (*sung*)
Though laid in a manger,
He came from a throne;
on earth though a stranger,
in heaven He was known.

(*sung*)
How lowly, how gracious
His coming to earth!
His love my love kindles
to joy in his birth.

* Sweet Jesus, King of glory!

* Now You sleep in a manger,
in a stable poor and cold;

* but for us You are the highest King,
making our hearts into Your palace.

Christmas Day (After it has grown light)

*All hail! let there be joy!

Hail to the King, hail to the King.
Blessed is He, blessed is He.

*The peace of earth to Him;

* the joy of heaven to Him.

*The homage of a King be His,
King of all victory;

*The welcome of a Lamb be His,
Lamb of all glory:
The Son of glory down from on high.
All hail, let there be joy.

* Deep in the night
the voice of the waves on the shore
announced to us: Christ is born!
Son of the King of kings
from the land of salvation,
the mountains glowed to Him,
the plains glowed to Him,
then shone the sun on the mountains high to Him.
All hail, let there be joy.

* God the Lord has opened a Door.
Christ of hope, Door of joy!
Son of Mary, hasten thou to help me:

In me, Lord Christ, let there be joy.

New Year

'The Opening Door' is to be used as a first-footing
prayer. In Scotland, and the northern parts of England,
New Year is given much importance. Folk go from
house to house wishing each other a good year ahead,
and celebrate their good wishes with food and plenty
of drink. It is often seen as important who should be
the first to cross the threshold and 'bring in the year'
once midnight has passed.

This song (spoken or sung) asks Christ Himself to
come and first-foot for us. The door is opened to

welcome Him in and invite His blessing, whether He comes in silence or in the company of other guests.

The Opening Door

This day is a new day
that has never been before.
This year is a new year
the opening door.

Enter, Lord Christ
we have joy in Your coming.
You have given us life
and we welcome Your coming.

I turn now to face You
I lift up my eyes
Be blessing my face, Lord,
Be blessing my eyes.
May all my eye looks on
be blessed and be bright.
My neighbours, my loved ones
be blessed in Your sight.

You have given us life
and we welcome Your coming.
Be with us, Lord
we have joy, we have joy.
This year is a new year
the opening door.
Be with us, Lord
we have joy, we have joy.

Covenant Service

This may be used at the first opportunity at the beginning of a year, or at some other appropriate time of new beginnings. This may be for a community, household or a small group of friends. Because the service is long, it is important to take time to pray it reflectively, and go through it slowly.

With each * a change of reader is indicated. Some groups will wish to have each person take a turn in reading. A larger group or congregation will focus more easily if a few people who can read clearly are selected on their behalf.

I bind unto myself this day
   the strong name of the Trinity.
I humbly praise the aweful name
   The Three in One, the One in Three.
Of whom all nature hath creation,
   eternal Father, Spirit, Word.
Praise to the God of my salvation!
   Salvation is of Christ the Lord.
I bind this day to me for ever
   by power of faith Christ's incarnation,
His baptism in the Jordan river,
   His death on cross for my salvation,
His bursting from the spicèd tomb
   His riding up the heavenly way:
His coming on the day of doom
   I bind unto myself today.

Christ be with me, Christ within me,
   Christ behind me, Christ before me,
Christ beside me, Christ to win me,
   Christ to comfort and restore me.
Christ beneath me, Christ above me,
   Christ in quiet, Christ in danger,
Christ in hearts of all that love me
   Christ be with me this day.

* O God, You have been good.
You have been faithful;
You have been good.

* You have shown us Your love,
not just in the year that is past,
but through all the years of our lives.

O God, You have been good.
You have been faithful;
You have been good.

* You have given us life and reason
and set us in a world which is full of Your glory.

* You put family around us
and comfort us with friends.
You touch us through the thoughtfulness
and warmth of other people.

O God, You have been good.
You have been faithful;
You have been good.

* In darkness You have been our light,
in adversity and temptation a rock of strength.

You are the source of our joy,
and all the reward we ever need.

> **Your loving kindness is everlasting.**
> **Your loving kindness is everlasting.**

* You remembered us when we had forgotten You,
followed us when we ran away,
met us with forgiveness
whenever we turned back to You.

> **Your loving kindness is everlasting.**
> **Your loving kindness is everlasting.**

* God our Father,
You have set forth the way of life
for us in Your beloved Son:
we confess with shame
our slowness to learn from Him,
our reluctance to follow Him.

* You have spoken and called,
and we have not given heed.
Your beauty has shone forth,
and we have been blind.

Be tender in Your mercy, Lord,
Be tender in Your mercy.

* Forgive us,
that we have not loved You
with all our heart,
with all our soul,
with all our mind,
with all our strength.

*We have taken much, and returned little thanks;
we have been unworthy of Your unchanging love.

* Forgive us
our coldness and indifference,
our lack of constant love,
our unbelief,
our false pretences,
our refusal to understand Your ways.

Be tender in Your mercy, Lord,
Be tender in Your mercy.

*Teach us Your ways, O Lord
and let us walk in Your truth.
We put behind us
our stubborn independence,
and turn again to You.

* Now let us willingly fasten ourselves
to the God of covenant
that we be Christ's
and Christ be ours.

* Christ has many tasks for us.
Some are easy, others are difficult.
Some bring honour, others bring reproach.
Some are to our liking, and coincide
with our own inclinations, and are
in our immediate best interest;
some are just the opposite.
In some we may please Christ
and please ourselves;
in others we cannot please Christ
except by denying ourselves.
Yet the power to take on all of these
is most definitely given us in Jesus;
for it is He who strengthens us,
and comes to help us when we are weak.

* Let us say Yes to the covenant
that He makes with us.

Each in Turn:

I am no longer my own, but Yours.
Use me as You choose;
rank me alongside whoever You choose;
put me to doing, put me to suffering;
let me be employed for You, or laid aside for You,
raised up for You, or brought down low for You;
let me be full, let me be empty;
let me have all things, let me have nothing;
with my whole heart I freely choose to yield
all things to Your ordering and approval.

So now, God of glory,
Father, Son and Holy Spirit,
You are mine, and I am Your own.

(Holy Communion may now follow, beginning at the peace, or a simple meal of bread and wine. This is to remind us that the new covenant was sealed with the blood of Christ.)

Approaching Easter

Maundy Thursday

The Foot Washing

* Indicates a change of reader; all other sections said by all. A large gathering of people should divide into smaller groups. A towel and basin are needed.

**Jesus said,
'A new commandment I give to you,
that you love one another, as I have loved you.'**

Said or sung:

In an upstairs room a parable
is just about to come alive;
and while they bicker about who's best
with a painful glance He'll silently rise.
Their Saviour-servant must show them how,
through the will of the water
and the tenderness of the towel.

And the call is to community,
the impoverished power that sets the soul free,
in humility to take the vow
that day after day
we must take up the basin and the towel.

In any ordinary place,
on any ordinary day,
the parable can live again
when one will kneel and one will yield.
Our Saviour-servant must show us how,

through the will of the water
and the tenderness of the towel.
And the space between ourselves, sometimes,
is more than the distance between the stars.
By the fragile bridge of the servant's bow,
we take up the basin and the towel.

And the call is to community
the impoverished power that sets the soul free,
in humility to take the vow
that day after day
we must take up the basin
and the call is to community
and day after day
we must take up the basin and the towel.

Michael Card

'I was dreaming that I was treading the streets of
the Holy City, pottering about like a tourist. In my
wandering I came upon the museum of that city of
our dream. I went in, and a courteous attendant
conducted me round. There was some old armour
there, much bruised with battle. Many things were
conspicuous by their absence. I saw nothing of
Alexander's, nor of Napoleon's. There was no
Pope's ring, nor even the ink-bottle that Luther is
said to have thrown at the devil, nor Wesley's seal
and keys. I saw a widow's mite and the feather of a
little bird. I saw some swaddling clothes, a hammer,
and three nails, and a few thorns. I saw a bit of a
fishing-net and the broken oar of a boat. I saw a
sponge that had once been dipped in vinegar, and a
small piece of silver. But I cannot enumerate all I
saw, nor describe all I felt. Whilst I was turning over
a common drinking cup which had a very
honourable place, I whispered to the attendant,
"Have you not got a towel and basin among your
collection?" "No," he said, "not here; you see they are

in constant use." Then I knew I was in Heaven, in the Holy City, and amid the redeemed society.'

Knowing that He came from God and went to God ... Jesus took a towel and basin.

A. E. Whitham

Brother, let me be your servant,
let me be as Christ to you.
Pray that I may have the grace to
let you be my servant, too.

We are pilgrims on a journey.
We are brothers on the road.
We are here to help each other
walk the mile and bear the load.

I will hold the Christ-light for you
in the night time of your fear.
I will hold my hand out to you,
speak the peace you long to hear.

I will weep when you are weeping;
when you laugh I'll laugh with you.
I will share your joy and sorrow,
till we've seen this journey through.

When we sing to God in heaven
we shall find such harmony,
born of all we've known together
of Christ's love and agony.

Brother, let me be your servant,
let me be as Christ to you.
Pray that I may have the grace to
let you be my servant, too.

Footwashing

Each in turn washes another person's feet, until all have participated. This is an informal time; songs may be sung, music played, coffee served!

The Way of the Cross

At each point, or station, on the journey a reading is provided which acts as a narration. Following this is a prayer in which one phrase is repeated by everyone as a response.

1 Jesus is Condemned to Death

His accusers brought many false charges against Jesus, but He spoke not a word in His own defence. 'CRUCIFY HIM' they shouted.

Pilate washed his hands, to show the decision was not his own, but he did not dare to side publicly with Jesus, instead, he was willing to content the people.

So Jesus was condemned to death.

Prayer

Lord, You gave us opportunity to choose Jesus, but for so long we have chosen the rebellion that demanded Your death.
Lord, have mercy.

Lord, have mercy.

2 Jesus Receives the Cross

Jesus was scourged. The whips cut His back until it was shredded and bathed in His blood. A crown of thorns was set upon His head in mockery. Then they returned His robe to Him, and brought Him to the cross on which He was to die.

Jesus embraced the cross, resting it painfully on the smarting wounds on His back.

Prayer

Lord, You were scourged and wounded,
You deserved no punishment,
but were punished in our place.
Thank You, Jesus.

Thank You, Jesus.

3 Jesus Falls for the First Time

Jesus had willingly embraced the cross, but His physical body was weak from lack of sleep, from the pressures of arrest and trial, and from torture and beating.

The spirit is willing, but the flesh is weak. Jesus said yes, but His body hesitated and He fell to His knees, determining to rise again even in His weakness.

Prayer

Jesus, You said YES to the Father's will
and only Your body hesitated.
May we, Your Body, no longer hesitate,
but follow You in Your obedience saying:
Your will be done.

Your will be done.

4 Jesus is Met by His Blessed Mother

As Jesus again shouldered the cross and bore its burden, He glanced ahead and saw His mother. He could not stop to talk, to explain, to gather her in His arms and comfort her. All His energy was being soaked into that cross.

Who are my mother and brothers? Those who do the will of my Father.

Not my will, Father, but Yours.

Prayer

Lord, when we leave all and follow You
and it hurts those we love,
help us to know that You have been there, too,
that no one leaves behind Father, Mother or loved one
but is more than rewarded in the end.
Help us to pray:
My God, I trust in You.

My God, I trust in You.

5 The Cross is Laid on Simon of Cyrene

The soldiers compelled a stranger, Simon, who was black, to carry the cross part of the way for Jesus.

Simon, himself a stranger, an outcast, often misunderstood, perhaps identified with Jesus, and felt the gratitude of this Man above all men, and amid the pity Simon felt for Him he felt a burning compassion flowing back to him from Jesus, a burning, life-changing love. Simon carried the cross of Christ.

Prayer

As Simon took the weight of the cross from Jesus.
You have taught us that we must bear one another's
    burdens,
and so fulfil the law of Christ.
May we carry Your cross.

May we carry Your cross.

6 Veronica Wipes the Face of Jesus

An act of compassion. A woman called Veronica
reaches a cool cloth upon His hot and tired face. He
feels the coolness of the cloth, and the love with
which it is offered. And through His pain He smiles –
a smile never to be lost, never to be extinguished. She
reaches out to touch His face, and He leans His head
into her hands, within her reach.

O blessed day, the Master touched her life, her
heart, her outstretched hand. What faith! What lovely
face! What timeless meeting – O blessed Christ.

Prayer

Legend or living person, Veronica, by example,
teaches us to be Your witness,
that others may gaze into Your loving eyes
and know Your smile.
Show us Your lovely face.

Show us Your lovely face.

7 Jesus Falls the Second Time

The pain, the exhaustion, the love that drives Him on.
But the cross is so heavy, again He falls beneath the
weight, and in bitter resolution – 'Thy will be done' –
and in fatigue, Jesus again drives Himself up against
the cross and carries it on towards the fateful Hill
of Death.

Prayer

Lord, often I fall,
and the temptation is not to rise again
and continue with You.
When I fall and others watch and laugh
or say 'I told you so, you'll never make it'
give me the strength to fulfil my promise:

Lord, I will go on with You.

Lord, I will go on with You.

8 Jesus Meets the Women of Jerusalem

As Jesus continued, painfully stumbling along the road
to Calvary, a group of women joined themselves to the
procession, wailing in the manner normally
considered appropriate for a funeral procession. But
Jesus told them instead to cry out to God for
themselves and their own children.

Prayer

Lord, some of us are never far from tears
and some of us have forced ourselves to not cry.
Bring our tears into Your captivity and direction,
that they respond to Your voice.
You have the words of eternal life.

You have the words of eternal life.

9 Jesus Falls the Third Time

Jesus fell again. Oh God, how many times must I fall
and pick up that cross again? As many as seven times?
Or seventy times seven times? For ever, until this
never-ending road is ended, until the impossible is
completed, the unbearable borne through all eternity.

For the sake of My children, My sons, My loved
ones, My bride, My people, I must go on. I will not,
I must not, give up now. The way of sorrows, the
way of pain, the way of self-renunciation, the way of
My cross.

Prayer

You picked up the weight of Your cross,
the weight of our sins.
We are Your burden, an overwhelming burden,
but that burden is sweet to You
because of the love You also bear to us,
an overwhelming love.
Your love has no limits.

Your love has no limits.

10 Jesus is Stripped of His Garments

At the place of death the King of life is stripped of His
clothes. Naked, He came into the world; naked, He is
taken from the world. Vulnerable, exposed, God
became man. He was a crying, helpless, dependent
baby. Now, vulnerable, exposed, His heart, His life, His
body all bared before the world, He will be hung up to
be mocked. But God is not mocked – His very
nakedness is a parable, a sacrament, a picture of the
Father's hurting heart exposed in love to us.

Prayer

Lord, for our sake You left the riches of heaven
and became poor.
You came within our reach.
The nakedness of God was exposed before the world.
Lord, O lovely Christ,
may we be open to You and to each other.

May we be open to You and to each other.

11 Jesus is Nailed to the Cross

The journey was at an end. Jesus was quickly thrown
backward with His shoulders against the wood. The
soldier felt for the depression at the front of the wrist.

He drove a heavy, square, wrought-iron nail through
the wrist and deep into the wood. Quickly, he moved
to the other side and repeated the action, being
careful not to pull the arms too tightly. The title 'Jesus
of Nazareth, King of the Jews' was nailed into place,
and the cross-bar lifted into position. The left foot was
pressed backward against the right foot. With both
feet extended, toes down, a nail was driven through
the arch of each, leaving the knees moderately flexed.

The victim was now crucified.

'Jesus of Nazareth, King of the Jews'.

He is *our* peace.

Prayer

You were lifted high upon that cross
even as You had prophesied when You promised:
'I, if I be lifted up from the earth,
will draw all people to Me.'
It was love that held You there.

It was love that held You there.

12 Jesus Dies upon the Cross

As Jesus slowly sagged down with more weight on the
nails in the wrists, excruciating, fiery pain shot along
the fingers and up the arms to explode in the brain. As
He pushed Himself upward to avoid this stretching
torment, He placed His full weight on the nail through
His feet. Again there was searing agony as the nail tore
through the nerves. As the arms fatigued, great waves
of cramps swept over the muscles, knotting them in
deep, relentless, throbbing pain. Jesus fought to raise
Himself, in order to get even one short breath. 'Father,
forgive them, for they know not what they do.'

To the thief dying at His side: 'Today thou shalt be
with Me in Paradise.' To His mother and His closest

friend: 'Woman, behold thy son' – 'Behold thy mother.'
In the words of the psalm foretelling the death of
Messiah, He cried 'My God, why hast Thou
forsaken Me?'

Prayer

Father, what love is this of His?
What love is this of Yours
that His dying love reflects?
Your forgiveness for me as we gaze upon His
    sacrificial death, is as truly an undeserved gift
as the pardon He spoke to the dying thief.

It is mine if I will only receive:
He was wounded for my transgressions.

He was wounded for my transgressions.

13 Jesus is Taken from the Cross

Jesus could now feel the chill of death creeping
through His tissues. And with a loud voice He cried:
'It is finished.' His mission of atonement had been
completed. Finally, He could allow His body to die.
With one last surge of strength, He once again pressed
His torn feet against the nail, straightened His legs,
took a deeper breath, and uttered His seventh and last
cry: 'Father, into Thy hands I commit My spirit.' A while
later, the soldier pierced a long spear into the side of
the dead man, to His heart. The watery fluid and blood
that flowed out show us He had literally died of a
broken heart – not the usual crucifixion death of
suffocation. The friends of Jesus were allowed to
remove His holy body, and for a moment his mother
held Him again upon her lap, cradled in her arms.
    Let Him sleep now. It is finished.

Prayer

Forbid it, Lord, that I should boast
save in the death of Christ my God.
All the vain things that charm me most,
I sacrifice them to His blood:
It was for me.

It was for me.

14 Jesus is Laid in the Sepulchre

Laid in a borrowed tomb, awaiting the sign of Jonah
(the only sign that would be given to His generation),
that after three days and nights in the womb of the
earth, the belly of the fish, the grave and hell, He
would come forth to do His Father's will – Jesus the
humble Son of God, the exultant Son of Man, the
eternal contradiction, the Blessed One.

The end is not yet. Weeping endures for a night, but
joy comes in the morning. The good news – 'He is
risen' – will burst upon the Son-rise.

Therefore with joy shall we draw water out of the
wells of salvation.

Prayer

When all is dark,
and Hope is buried,
it is hard to trust His words
that promised before the pain,
He died that I might live.

He died that I might live.

15 Jesus is Risen!

Where is my Lord? They have taken Him away. All I see
is a tomb, a place that is empty. And just when I need
Him, and long for His voice even His body would not
wait for my tears.

Shut away in a box, He has conquered their coffin. Shut away in a book, He fulfils, Living Word. Shut away in our concepts, He shatters such shackles. No prison can hold Him, no tomb can thwart the miracle. His life is our liberty, His love changed my life. No dying can rob me of what He has given. Once blind, now I see. Hallelujah, His promise: In the day when the hearts of men fail them for fear, then look up, little flock, your redemption draws near.

Prayer

Let all creation
give thanks to the Risen Lord.

Give thanks to the Risen Lord!

Filled with His praises,
give thanks to the Risen Lord.

Give thanks to the Risen Lord!

He is our Shepherd and we are His sheep.
Give thanks to the Risen Lord.

Give thanks to the Risen Lord!

Boldly we follow.

Give thanks to the Risen Lord!

Blessings over Food before Eating

1 Hebridean

Lord God, giver of all good things,
may we who share at this table
like pilgrims here on earth
be welcomed with your saints
to the heavenly feast.
Amen.

2 Brigid

God bless our food
God bless our drink
And keep our homes
and ourselves
in Your embrace,
    O God.
Amen.

3 Shabbat

Bless, O Lord,
    this food we are about to eat,
    and we pray you, O God
that it may be good
    for our body and soul,
and if there is any poor creature
    hungry or thirsty walking the road
may God send them in to us
    so that we can share the food with them,
just as Christ shares His gifts
    with all of us.
Amen.

4 *A Short Grace (from the Isle of Lewis)*

Our God, we are Your guests,
and 'tis You who keep the generous table.
We thank You.
Amen.

5 *The Stranger's Blessing*

The Sacred Three be blessing thee,
    thy table and its store
The Sacred Three be blessing
    all thy loved ones evermore.
Amen.

DAILY READINGS

January Readings
Be Thou My Vision

January 1

New Year's Day

(see 'The Opening Door' and 'Covenant Service', p.65)
Psalm 123:2   Exodus 33:18-23   Mark 8:24-5

Be thou my vision,
   O Lord of my heart,

The studies this month are based around the words of the song 'Be Thou my Vision'. It is an old Irish Celtic poem, set to music in the nineteenth century, and still found in many hymn-books.

I ask not to fly from the world but to be involved with the world. I am in the world but also in the presence of Jesus. I listen for His word to a broken world. He sees my brokenness and the brokenness of the world around me. I stand in God's presence looking at Him, listening to Him, bringing to Him the things of the world that have filled my vision. I listen for His word – Be Thou my vision, O Lord.

January 2

Psalm 131:1-3   Ezekiel 36:26
               Matthew 15:11, 15-20

Be Thou my vision,
   O Lord of my heart,

Do you respond first of all with your head? Or with your heart? Or do you just give a gut reaction? It varies from time to time; and we are very different from each other. The mind can be a very heartless thing in its responses. But the heart 'has a mind of its own'. At the end of the day we need a place of rest inside ourselves to return to.

Focus your gaze, and then when the arrow of your attention is released it will hit the mark, and find Him.

The aim: Him
The glory: His

He is my vision, and the Lord of my heart!

January 3

Psalm 103:1–6　　　　　　　　　　*Exodus 3:1–14*
Philippians 3:1–8

naught be all else to me,
　save that Thou art;

Everything else is nothing. Pile it all up, and what does it amount to? Nothing, really. Then, turn around and instead see I AM. I am what? No, just I AM. His very name is a statement of reality. God IS, and everything else is an irrelevance in comparison. I AM is in the here and now, in the present moment, and present at this moment.

In His presence, in His power, live a moment at a time: live that moment fully. To try to live a holy life is to be crushed by the enormity of the task, but a whole life consists of a series of such moments.

…and naught be all else to me.

January 4

Psalm 42:8　　　*Daniel 6:10–11*　　　*Philippians 4:8*

Thou my best thought
　in the day and the night,

All kinds of things fill our thoughts. But when we think of Him, sanity enters the picture. It is as if the conductor takes his place at the rostrum: all the discordant sound, the tuning up and fidgeting, turns to silence; and then a melody, a full-bodied score in many parts, comes to birth in the very place where there had been chaos and confusion.

Lord, I think many things. I have many thoughts. Let me not forget you, nor lose sight of you, even for a moment:

Thou, my best thought.

January 5

Psalm 16:7   2 Samuel 22:7-16   Galatians 6:17

Thou my best thought
  in the day and the night,

The night can be a time that makes us uneasy. It is a time to feel isolated, a time of darkness, of the unknown. And darkness is the covering of God: it is where He lives. He is light; and the light in darkness is a greater light than a light at day. It is in the dark we can see stars, not in the daytime. But, it is at night, in the early hours, when most people are likely to die. But we do not talk about that. Nowadays, man is sanitized from much suffering and death. It happens in the specialized places, hospitals, nursing homes. It is removed from us, and we lose part of our perspective on life.

But we need darkness – for is not God closer to those who suffer? Have you not felt closer to God at the times of suffering than at the other times when everything has been going well for you? Who is it the doctor visits; the one who is well? or the one who is ill?

Do not go looking to have pain happen to you, but do not always hurry out of its path when it comes, remember it is the day *and* the night.

January 6

Psalm 119:105-112   *1 Samuel 3:3-4*
Acts 2:16-18

waking or sleeping,
  thy presence my light.

Joel promised dreams to the people and we are living
in the time of this promise, the time of the dream.
Dream on, and let God speak through your dreams.

  Lord, in the multitude of my thoughts, thy comforts
delight my soul. Waking or sleeping, it is thy presence
which enlightens me.

January 7

Psalm 139:11-12   *Exodus 33:14-15*
1 John 2:3-11

waking or sleeping,
  thy presence my light.

In a book called *It's All Right to Cry* I found this
quotation:'Nobody is wise who does not know the
darkness. I appreciate the dark hours of my existence
in which my senses are sharpened.'

  Lord, in your presence is fullness of joy. You make
sense of the darkness. You understand it. Even my
darkness is no surprise to you, and your presence is
my light.

January 8

Psalm 18:28-9 *Daniel 3:23-5* *John 8:12*

Be Thou my vision
   O Lord of my heart,
Naught be all else to me
   save that Thou art,
Thou my best thought
   in the day and the night,
Waking or sleeping
   thy presence my light.

January 9

Psalm 51:6 *Proverbs 4:5-9* *Ephesians 1:17*

**Be Thou my wisdom,
   be Thou my true word,**

Wisdom cannot be learnt with just the head; to
temper its logic the heart must also be engaged.
Wisdom is not in short supply, but anyone would
think that was the case. We have not, precisely
because we forget to ask.

Wisdom is to be desired more than gold. Solomon
asked for wisdom; and God was very pleased he did
not ask for riches. However, having asked for wisdom
he got riches too.

Lord of my heart, be Thou my wisdom. Be at the
beginning of all I speak, of all that I begin. Be Thou my
true word.

January 10

Psalm 139:7-12   2 Kings 6:16-17   Romans 8:38-9

I ever with Thee,
  and Thou with me, Lord;

I am with you always, He says. He is all around His
people, as strong and reliable as the mountains. He
wants us to be with Him, prepares a place for us to
share, comes to our place, to our ordinariness, shares
bread and wine at table. The commonplace is given
great significance because of His presence.

Jesus often turned up in unexpected places and in
unexpected ways. When we do not see Jesus around
us it is often because we do not look well enough.
Open my eyes to see, I ever with Thee and Thou with
me, Lord.

January 11

Psalm 40:7   Zechariah 4:1   Luke 15:20

Thou my great Father,
  and I Thy true son;

We can never be at peace till we have performed
the highest duty of all, till we have arisen and gone
to our Father. If we come from God, nothing is more
natural, than to want Him; and when we haven't got
Him, to try to find Him.

May the one Father make us all clean at last, and
when the right time comes, wake us out of this
sleep into the new world, which is the old one,
when we shall say as one that wakes from a dream
'Is it then over, and I live?'

G. MacDonald

January 12

Psalm 32:4-9   Jeremiah 1:5   Galatians 4:5

Thou my great Father,
  and I Thy true son,

> God is nearer to you than any thought or feeling of
> yours ... Do not be afraid. If all the evil things in the
> universe were around us, they could not come
> inside the ring that He makes about us. He always
> keeps a place for Himself and His child, into which
> no other being can enter.
>
> G. MacDonald

God prepares good works for us to walk in, and will
not give His child any gift that is less than the best.

God has plans for us, plans for good – good not evil
– but when we walk outside His will He is still there
pulling us back to Himself. We are His son if we do His
will.

We do, because we know it will please Him, not to
win His love. The love is freely given and quite
undeservedly. And it is only fitting that such a great
Father should have in me a true son.

January 13

Psalm 131:2   Jeremiah 17:7-8   Luke 2:25-38

Thou in me dwelling,
  and I with Thee one.

In 1 Thessalonians 4:11 we are told to study to be
quiet or study to be still. This stillness must begin in
the heart. It is a decision, an active choice, to become
still, to still my soul. Sometimes, it is as if there is a
bunch of monkeys in the tree which is your mind and
you will not still them by shouting. If you speak

quietly and gently – just as you would to a petulant
child – peace will result. The mind is like a child,
always wanting more, something new; each thing it
sees it wants.

It is stillness I need, Lord, and Thou in me dwelling.

January 14

Psalm 4:4   *Isaiah 32:17*   *Galatians 2:20*

Thou with me dwelling,
  and I with Thee one.

Stillness is not simply silence, but an attitude of
listening to God and of openness towards him.
Philokalia

Thou in me dwelling, and I with Thee one.

January 15

Psalm 24:8   *Jeremiah 38:1–6*
            1 Corinthians 13:12

We become drowned in the detail of our despair and
it is precisely then that we must turn our focus away
to the larger picture, which is hidden from us. We
trust, and we believe now that we will see then. We
believe now that God is still working and we will
understand one day.

Be Thou my breastplate,
  my sword for the fight;
Be Thou my armour
  and be Thou my might;
Thou my soul's shelter,
  and Thou my high tower;
raise Thou me heavenwards,
  O Power of my power.

January 16

Psalm 119:11   *1 Samuel 17:38-9*
Ephesians 6:14,17

Be Thou my breastplate,
   my sword for the fight;

The breastplate protects the heart, all the ways to the
heart are covered, righteousness is the breastplate.
This is being right, or made right, able to stand in
confidence. Unlike David, we will find that the armour
our King provides fits us perfectly.
   Great God, be Thou my breastplate.

January 17

Antony of Egypt (c. 251-356) was a hermit who was
one of the earliest of the 'Desert Fathers'. Much of
monasticism was inspired by his example of prayer
and spiritual warfare, as described by Athanasius. His
wisdom and integrity are also evident in the various
sayings attributed to him. (See also September 27.)

Psalm 51:6   *Jeremiah 31:33*
2 Corinthians 10:4-5

Be Thou my breastplate,
   my sword for the fight;

The fight in which we find ourselves is the fight
against the powers in the heavenlies. The tools for the
fight are the ones provided for us by God, our job
being to use them. We need to know our weapons. We
also have a fight in our own lives in the realm of our
thoughts and our wilfulness. The revelation of God
must be drawn from its scabbard at our side and its
point directed even at our own breast, keenly cutting

even between soul and spirit, between our own
thoughts and the quiet wisdom of God.

Be Thou my sword for the fight!

January 18

Psalm 34:7   *2 Chronicles 20:15-22*
                2 Corinthians 10:3

Be Thou my armour,
   and be Thou my might;

Whether we sit, walk or stand we fight for God. The
battle belongs to the Lord. Let him fight for you – do
not put your hand outside His protection.

   Amma Sarah turned to the ascetic life, living in the
desert, but was for 13 years tempted by lust. It was
said that she never prayed that this warfare should
cease, but instead she said, 'O God, give me strength.'

   When tempted, do not try to fight on your own;
surrender to the temptation, letting God fight for you.
We admit our weakness, allowing God to be our
strength.

   Be Thou my armour and be Thou my might.

January 19

Psalm 131:1   Zechariah 4:6   2 Corinthians 4:7-8

Be Thou my armour
   and be Thou my might;

   God made the world out of nothing, and it is only
   when we become nothing that God can make
   anything of us.

                                             M. Luther

Thou my true might.

January 20

Psalm 144:1-2   Deuteronomy 29:5   John 10:29

Thou my soul's shelter,
  and Thou my high tower;

The Lord is a refuge that is strong, and a very present
help. In a shelter you are passive and the shelter does
the 'work' of sheltering. You have to stay in the shelter
and not venture out. In the shelter you can rest and be
quiet, you are looked after and are safe. Even though
the Israelites walked through the wilderness for
40 years, their clothes did not wear out nor did their
shoes need mending. The Lord was their protection
and defender.

Thou my soul's shelter, and Thou my high tower.

January 21

Psalm 137:4   2 Kings 2:1   Colossians 1:11

raise Thou me heavenwards,
  O Power of my power.

His power is at work in us, and if only we set our mind
on the things which concern Him we will see this
power in operation. The power of God makes great
works possible, but is just as operative in the small,
perhaps unnoticed, things of life.

The power of God is great, yet He gives of it freely
for His purposes. We have to wait for the power, not as
a time delay, for the Spirit has already come, but to
prevent us dashing ahead reliant on our own ability
instead of His enabling. Even when works of power or
'miracles' occur these only confirm the message: Look
heavenward!

The works of power are a signpost which says, 'Go,

this direction, to God.' It was never intended that we
worship the signpost.

Raise my gaze heavenward, Great Power of my
power.

January 22

Psalm 23:4   *Exodus 20:3*   *Galatians 2:20*

Riches I heed not,
  nor man's empty praise,
Thou mine inheritance
  through all of my days.
Thou and Thou only
  the first in my heart;
High King of Heaven,
  my treasure Thou art.

Death is implicit in this verse. There is so much of us
to die; but it needs to die completely if we are to live
in the newness of life which comes with a definite
break between the old and the new. It is not
superficial dying that is called for, but the utter death
of every aspect of our life. God is jealous, and wants us
to shut Him out of nothing.

Do you love the Lord with all your heart? He
accepts us as we are now, and slowly moulds us
towards His image of what we can be. He knows us as
we will be and works to conform us to that image.

January 23

Psalm 73:26   *2 Kings 5:20–27*   *Philippians 2:3*

**Riches I heed not,
  nor man's empty praise;**

Outward esteem, praises of those round about us,

their flattery, compliments, soon prove hollow if they are all we have to feed upon. Looking good, looking clever, looking busy can consume much of our energy as we compete for medals in people-pleasing.

We judge strangers by the clothes they wear. In some circles cleverness and intellectual ability are regarded highly.

Being busy attracts praise, but are we doing what God wants us to be doing? Whose approval do we really want?

The answer to this question will determine the values we live by. Listen to this comment from a devout Hebridean soul: 'Though we prospered little, yet we were rich in faith and unfearingness.' (*Hebridean Altars*)

January 24

Psalm 16:5-6   2 Kings 2:9-16   Ephesians 1:14

Thou mine inheritance
through all of my days;

In *Hebridean Altars* there is recounted the concern of a mother for her daughter who was about to leave and make her life in a far away city, 'where gold weighs more than love, and folk are too busy to think of the sun or sea'. The mother prayed a blessing upon her, and sought in this way to impress upon her the richness of her true heritage, before other values could cloud her mind.

Jesus, draw Thou nearer and shield my soul.
Thou mine inheritance now and always.

January 25

Psalm 51:6   *Jeremiah 17:5–10*
Luke 10:30, 33, 34

Thou and Thou only,
   the first in my heart,

We live in a world where mental ability is rewarded. But the heart is not trained, it just muddles along. Soon we know more and more, and understand less and less. Sophisticated media reports bring information about wars and disasters right into our living room, but we are less affected than previous generations would have been by reports of a mishap in a neighbouring village. But compassion reaches out across barriers of status, class or ability, and reaches out to the person who is hurting. Compassion does not depend upon knowledge or learning; the 'Samaritan' only needs to know where the sore is so he can anoint it with oil. If something in us is still able to respond a little, then all is not lost. The heart is alive and kicking, able to be coaxed into generosity, able to prioritize its focus. Love of God should be the first priority, for true love of self and of neighbour both flow from this.

    Do I love Thee, the living God, with all my heart? Amen. Lord, have mercy. Thou, and Thou only.

January 26

Psalm 45:1   *Hosea 2:23*   *Revelation 19:11–16*

High King of heaven,
   my treasure Thou art!

The Lord is high King. We need to be careful not to forget this, not to treat Him with contempt, just because He does not lash out at us when we fail to respond as He wishes. In their day the Israelites did not value what God was doing for them. We should not disappoint Him, as they did in their day. God is love, but that love is no stranger to anger and pain because of our weakness and foolishness and unresponsiveness.

My heart runs to you, my Lord, my high King, high King of heaven.

January 27

Psalm 45:10-15   *Song of Solomon 4:16*
Matthew 6:19-21

High King of heaven,
    my treasure Thou art!

Do I count all things as loss for the sake of knowing Him? Is He what I treasure the most, so that my heart and heaven are already one? What do I value most in my life? What is it that I spend most time thinking about? Am I careless in my relationship with God? Do I neglect to spend time cultivating this relationship? Do I treasure it? Do I set as much value on it as He has on me?

Pelagius in the company of his fellow bishops looked at a beautiful woman who passed by them while the others looked away discreetly. Pelagius apparently profited from a long hard look for he launched into the following outburst:

What do you think, beloved brothers, how many hours does this woman spend in her chamber giving all her mind and attention to adorning herself for the play, in order to lack nothing in beauty and adornment of the body: she wants to please all those who see her, lest those who are her lovers today find her ugly and do not come tomorrow. Here we are, who have an almighty Father in heaven offering us heavenly gifts and rewards, our immortal Bridegroom who promises good things to His watchmen, things that cannot be valued, which eye has not seen, nor ear heard, nor has it entered into the heart of man to know the things that God has prepared for them that love him. What else can I say? When we have such promises, when we are going to see the great and glorious face of our Bridegroom which has a beauty beyond compare, upon which the cherubim do not dare to gaze, why do we not adorn ourselves and wash the dirt from our unhappy souls, why do we let ourselves lie so neglected?

My treasure Thou art, O High King of heaven.

January 28

Psalm 22:4   *Isaiah 25:8*   *Revelation 2:10-11*

when battle is done,
  Grant heaven's joy to me,

The picture is one of a team game where each competitor must complete the obstacle course for themselves, but on reaching the finish line is greeted excitedly by other team members, and then turns to cheer on those who are still to complete the race. In heaven the angels rejoice whenever a single competitor sets out. The rewards are great, but so are the difficulties. Each trophy of victory is at cost beyond our imagination.

  The loud cry: It is finished!

  When all is accomplished, Lord, grant heaven's joy to me!

January 29

Psalm 119:105   *Genesis 1:2-3*
                Revelation 21:1-3, 22, 23

Grant Heaven's joy to me,
  bright heaven's Sun;

We are reaching the end of the song, and the end
refers back to the beginning and rounds off the story
...as it was in the beginning is now and ever shall be.

In the beginning was darkness and God spoke to
dispel the darkness, as His first act of creation. At the
end, the darkness is gone for He Himself is the light in
the new Jerusalem, bright heaven's Sun.

January 30

Psalm 46:1-4   *Ezekiel 36:26-7*   *Romans 8:28*

Christ of my own heart,
  whatever befall,

Love goes into God's presence,
while at the gate
Reason and Knowledge
must remain
and for an audience wait.
                Angelus Silesius

What can separate us from God's love? Wherever
we go, we find it there; and if we do not see it, we
need to trust in its presence.

Only with your heart can you see clearly. The
most important things are invisible to the eye.
                Antoine de Saint-Exupéry

The love between God and you is very intimate and
private. It is personal and secret. It is like the

relationship of a couple who are truly intimate. Your bedroom is a place of closeness, honesty, openness and remaining vulnerable. You don't always need to talk. You can, occasionally, just be there, touching each other, holding hands. Christ of my own heart, look not on the outer courts, but on the inner – then you will see. The king's bride is all beautiful within.

January 31

Psalm 17:15   *Job 19:25*   *Hebrews 12:2*

**still be Thou my vision,
    Thou Ruler of all.**

In his poem 'Little Gidding', T. S. Eliot says that we shall not cease our exploring until we 'arrive where we started, and ... know the place for the first time'.

Be Thou my vision ... and so it was that we came back to the beginning of our looking – 'Sir, we would see Jesus' – conquered by love, and a love that overcomes each of us.

Every time one of them looked at Jesus, or Jesus looked at them, they saw more.

Still be Thou my vision, O Ruler of all.

February 1

Brigid's Day (See Brigid liturgy p. 22; May 9, 20, 31;
November 16)

Psalm 138:3   *Leviticus 9:24*   *Matthew 22:8-10*

Doorkeepers

Brigid was famous not only for the perpetual fire that
burned at her monastery in Kildare, but for her
hospitality and welcome.

Brigid's feast

I should like a great lake of finest ale
    for the King of kings.
I should like a table of the choicest food
    for the family of heaven.
Let the ale be made from the fruits of faith
    and the food be forgiving love.

I should welcome the poor to my feast,
    for they are God's children.
I should welcome the sick to my feast,
    for they are God's joy.
Let the poor sit with Jesus at the highest place,
    and the sick dance with the angels.

God bless the poor,
God bless the sick,
    and bless our human race.
God bless our food,
God bless our drink;
    all homes, O God, embrace.

February 2

Psalm 146:7-8   Jeremiah 9:2a   Isaiah 58:6-7
Mark 11:1-2, 7-11

'He was a friend to man, and lived in a
house by the side of the road.'

> *Homer*

One Celtic brother called Cronan moved his whole
establishment to Roscrea after a royal visitor had been
unable to find him in Sean Ross. 'I shall not remain in
a desert place' he said, 'where strangers and poor folk
are unable to find me readily. But here, by the public
highway I shall live, where they are able to reach me
easily.'

This urge to dispense hospitality to the wayfarer
and the indigent led to the founding of Christian
settlements along the main roads of Ireland.

February 3

Psalm 84:5   2 Kings 4:8-10
Matthew 21:12, 14, 17

There are hermit souls that live withdrawn
in the peace of their self content;
There are souls like stars that dwell apart,
in a fellowless firmament,
There are pioneer souls that blaze their paths
where highways never ran;
But let me live by the side of the road
and be a friend to man.

> *Sam Walter Foss*

February 4

Psalm 143:2   2 Kings 4:11-17   John 11:1-53

Let me live in a house by the side of the road,
Where the race of men go by –
The men who are good and the men who are bad,
As good and bad as I.
I would not sit in a scorner's seat,
Or hurl the cynic's ban; –
Let me live in a house by the side of the road
And be a friend to man.

Sam Walter Foss

February 5

Psalm 143:8   2 Kings 4:18-24   John 12:1-3

I see from my house by the side of the road
By the side of the highway of life,
The men who press with the ardour of hope,
The men who faint with the strife.
But I turn not away from their smiles nor their tears –
Both parts of a infinite plan;
Let me live in a house by the side of the road
And be a friend to man.

Sam Walter Foss

February 6

Psalm 143:10   2 Kings 4:25-37   Romans 12:15

I know there are brook-gladdened meadows ahead
And mountains of wearsome height;
That road passes on through the long afternoon
And stretches away to the night,
But still I rejoice when the travellers rejoice,
And weep with the strangers that moan,
Nor live in my house by the side of the road
Like a man who dwells alone.

Sam Walter Foss

February 7

Psalm 142:5   Jeremiah 9:23-4   Luke 2:3-7

Let me live in my house by the side of the road,
Where the race of men go by.
They are good, they are bad, they are weak, they are
     strong
Wise, foolish – so am I.
Then why should I sit in the scorner's seat
Or hurl the cynic's ban?
Let me live in my house by the side of the road
And be a friend to man.

Sam Walter Foss

February 8

Psalm 50:12; 141:4   Daniel 1:3-4   Acts 17:23-5

It is a sin against the Holy Spirit stubbornly to refuse
to learn from other people who know about life in
today's world. We can ask them for a drink. Jesus did
not hesitate to listen to the Samaritan woman

(when His own people would have nothing to do with Samaritans).

We have a message for the world, but we need the world too. Without understanding the world we have no relevant language in which to share that message. Also the world helps us understand ourselves better, especially our need to be open to the newness of the Gospel.

Adapted from Jean Francois Six.

February 9

Psalm 82:3-5　　　　　　　　　*Esther 4:14b*
1 Corinthians 14:8-10

We are alive today, not in Paul's time. The men and women we meet have different ideas from those of the jews and pagans he met. It is the ideas of today's people, and what is important to them that must be confronted with the good news. These values will not be destroyed, but set on fire by the life of the Risen Jesus. Paul VI has said:'It is not a good thing to be promised to the world or unite ourselves with its thoughts, customs and tastes, but instead we should study it, love it and serve it.'

Yes, it is important to understand the world, to love it so much, and to serve it, in its unique culture as to become bilingual.

Adapted from Jean Francois Six

February 10

Psalm 144:3-5, 7   Micah 4:4   Isaiah 53:3
Galatians 3:26-9   Philippians 2:5-10

I heard about a King who owned a castle in the sky
where serfs and kings were all the same and nobody
    ever had to die.
I heard all wealth and power was shared with the
    common man;
and, as a serf, it seemed to me like a dream in a
    wonderland.

And as the years went by I still had doubts about it all,
but something burned down deep inside so I
    searched for the castle wall.
I said 'Hey, King, can you see me from your castle in
    the sky?
There's just no way to look inside 'cause the walls are
    much too high!

Won't you come down from your castle into my
    wishing well?
Tell all the sunken memories they've each got a dream
    to tell.'
And though you may not understand, it's just my way
    to say:
castle kings and poor man's dreams fill your life only
    with toil and pain.

And finally I met a serf who seemed a lot like me.
He said, 'I am the castle King, won't you come and I'll
    set you free?'
He took me to the castle moat, and the bridge was
    quickly drawn.
I fell in shame to hide my face as the serf turned to
    take the throne.

And he came down from his castle into my wishing
    well,
picked up the sunken memories with each their
    dream to tell.
And though no one else could, he understood the
    words I had to say.

The castle King changed everything and now I walk
    with him every day,
In all my dreams I'd never seen the serf with a smiling
    face,
but now it's true, I'm telling you, for the serf and the
    king did embrace.

Tim Sheppard

February 11

Caedmon – 7th century (see May 24; November 24)
Psalm 143:7　　　*Ecclesiastes 9:3*　　　*John 1:29*

The capacity and tendency to *not* believe is truly
'the sin of the world'. This is more crucial than a
narrow and childish idea of sin where the
individual does something they are told they
should not, then feels guilt and blame, creating a
prison of self-centred delay in having it put right.
That is not the sin of the world although it gives it
power and strength. Being prince of your own
illusion, deluding yourself about yourself, about
others and about God – that is the sin of the world.

(It is important that I do more than confess my
sins – I must confess that I am a sinner. I must not
just receive forgiveness, but live as a forgiven
person.)

To believe in the Risen Christ is to believe that
through the 'yes' of Jesus, God breaks through and
gives birth to new humanity. Up to the moment of

this 'yes' men were primarily locked in incredulity.
Jesus comes to break this circle and this propensity
of man to 'non-believing'. He opens hearts to trust
in God who then responded and who does not
cease to respond now to man through the
Risen Christ.

Jean Francois Six

February 12

Psalm 14:1a, 85:13   1 Kings 18:21   Mark 9:23–4

The believer can only perfect his faith on the ocean
of nihilism, temptation and doubt; he has been
assigned the ocean of uncertainty as the only
possible site for his faith. On the other hand the
believer is not to be understood undialectically as a
mere man without faith.

Just as we have already recognized that the
believer does not live immune to doubt but is
always threatened by the plunge into the void, so
now we can discern the entangled nature of human
destinies and say that even the non-believer does
not represent a rounded and closed existence.
However vigorously he may assert that he has long
left behind him supernatural temptations and
weaknesses, and now accepts only what is
immediately certain, he will never be free of
secret uncertainty.

Just as the believer is choked by the salt water of
doubt constantly washed into his mouth by the
ocean of uncertainty, so the non-believer is troubled
by doubts about his unbelief, about the real totality
of the world which he has made up his mind to
explain as a self-contained whole. He can never be
absolutely certain of the autonomy of what he has
seen and interpreted as a whole; he remains

threatened by the question whether the belief is not after all reality which it claims to be.

Just as the believer knows himself to be constantly threatened by unbelief which he must experience as a continual temptation, so for the unbeliever faith remains a temptation, and so a threat to his apparently permanently closed world.

Joseph Ratzinger, Introduction to Christianity

February 13

Psalm 85:7   Jeremiah 29:13   John 14:6

Two men please God: one who serves him with all his heart because he knows Him, one who seeks Him with all his heart because he knows Him not.

Panin

February 14

Psalm 144:11   Isaiah 40:28-31   Luke 15:20

Speaking of younger people today, some really are unbelieving, that is they have recognized that the God of Jesus, this God of tenderness actually exists – and they refuse Him.

Others are not really unbelievers as such since they have rejected only the picture of God they have seen portrayed through certain Christians now or in history.

Adapted from Jean Francois Six

If you are running away from a wrong picture of God, does that take you further away or closer to Him?

February 15

Psalm 22   Isaiah 53:6   Luke 22:40-5

Jesus experienced the extreme of dereliction.
Pronouncing on the cross the first words of the
psalm,'My God, my God, why have you deserted
me?' Jesus wants to express the meaning of the
whole psalm.

But how can we fail to see that this psalmody of
Jesus on the cross is the expression, once more, of a
temptation overcome, of a despair outrun? Faith,
trust, hope are not natural to humanity: religion,
law, sentence, are. But to reveal, in the very heart of
failure and at the hour of death, amid human
clamour and the silence of God, that God is Love, is
that not the true, intense and free acknowledging of
God? And is it not a turning of the back, in manner
more victorious than any other, on the temptation
of unbelief? Evil, wretchedness and failure are, in
effect, the first grounds of unbelief and this is
understandable: how can one not curse God and
despair when evil is there – period – and heaven
seems empty? Jesus overcame this temptation.

The cry that Jesus uttered on the cross – 'a loud
voice' says the Scripture – must not be
romanticized but, rather, taken in its precise texture.

Jean Francois Six

February 16

Psalm 139:12   Isaiah 45:15   Exodus 32:32
                       Galatians 6:2

Thérèse of Lisieux underwent profound changes in
her experience of faith during the Easter of 1896:
Before that time she thought that atheism was a

flaunted position, a sham. 'I could not believe that there really were godless people who had no faith at all: it was only by being false to his own inner convictions that a man could deny the existence of heaven.'

Finally, her eyes were opened to realize that unbelievers really exist. She experiences the sense of the darkness, such impenetrable darkness, a darkness which cannot recognize the King of Light. 'But here I am, Lord, to whom your divine light has made itself known.' She finds herself in a situation which seems absurdly contradictory. She does not cease to participate in the light of the faith and at the same time she participates in the darkness in which unbelievers live. She is immersed in suffering never experienced previously and in joy greater than she ever felt before. She thinks that if Jesus has made her see the reality of unbelief and has made her participate in the night of unbelief, it is only so that she may turn the tables: so that she may live this state of darkness for the sake of unbelievers themselves. And, consequently, for her it is a new joy that she had never experienced until then – the joy of not living the joy of faith so that precisely these 'others', these unbelievers who do not know this joy, might finally attain to it: 'What does it matter, that I should catch no glimpse of heaven's beauties, here on earth, if that will help poor sinners to see them in heaven.'

Jean Francois Six (abridged)

February 17

Psalm 84:6, 78:19   Job 22:2-4, 7   Luke 4:1-3

The night Thérèse experiences is a sharing of life with Jesus and unbelievers at one and the same time. From the moment she recognizes the existence of genuine unbelievers she reckons herself as their companion.

'Lord, one of your own children, to whom your divine light has made itself known ... by way of asking pardon for these brothers of mine, I am ready to live on a starvation diet as long as you will have it so.' Her concern is to remain with those who eat the bread of unbelief: she does not want to 'rise from this appetising meal'. She is prepared, she says, to remain there as the last one until 'all those who have no torch of faith to guide them catch sight, at least, of its rays.'

This manner of sharing the bread of unbelief is at the same time a manner of breaking bread with Jesus, of sharing the Eucharistic table: for it is Jesus who has led her to this table of unbelievers. Of this she is certain. For Thérèse, the perfect joy is to find herself among unbelievers and, eating at their table, to be shaken by their questions while remaining in the faith.

'I find it difficult to believe in the existence of anything except the clouds which limit my horizon. It is only then that I realize the possibilities of my weakness; find consolation in staying at my post, and directing my gaze towards one invisible light which communicates itself, now, only in the eye of faith.'

Jean Francois Six

February 18

Colman – died 676 (see May 8, 17, 22; November 28)
Psalm 84:7   *Genesis 32:24-8*   *Job 23:10*
Philippians 4:11-12

The more a human being advances in the Christian
faith, the more he lives the presence of God as an
absence, the more he accepts to die to the idea of
becoming aware of God, of fathoming Him. For he
has learned, while advancing, that God is
unfathomable. And from then on the presence of
God assumes value in his eyes only against the
backdrop of absence. The mystic, in his long and
complicated pilgrimage, experiences alternately
the presence and absence of God. But, by degrees,
the absence of God is felt more and more and the
mystic understands that this absence is now the
norm. Thus the mystic is someone who has had a
long-term confrontation with God, like Jacob in the
struggle that he waged all through the night,
someone who does not cease to confront God. God
always precedes us, we see Him only from behind,
He walks ahead, He is ahead of us. What the mystic
experiences – and every Christian is a mystic
because it is not the great illuminations that are the
mark of the mystic but the night, an everyday night
– is a kind of distancing from God in proportion to
advances in the deepening of his faith.

Jean Francois Six

February 19

Psalm 84:1-4   *1 Chronicles 15:23-4*
Mark 14:32-7, 50-52

Almighty Father, Son and Holy Ghost,
to me, the least of saints,
to me allow that I may keep a door in Paradise,
that I may keep even the smallest door,
the farthest door, the darkest, coldest door,
the door that is least used, the stiffest door,
if so it be but in Thy house, O God;
if so it be that I may see Thy glory,
even afar, and hear Thy voice, O God
and know that I am with Thee, Thee, O God.

F. Mcleod, Prayer of Columba

February 20

Psalm 145:3,14   *Isaiah 12:3-4*
John 10:9, 13:14-15,   Revelation 4:1a

God the Lord has opened a door
Christ of hope, Door of joy!
Son of Mary, hasten Thou to help me:
in me, Lord Christ, let there be joy.

The one who was no less than God
took on the flesh of lowly man,
and came to wash the feet of clay
because it was Your holy plan.
And I, no greater than my King,
would ever seek a place
of humble service in Your house
to gaze into the light that is Your face.

February 21

Psalm 142:2   *Isaiah 26:2-3*   *Luke 2:29-30*

He had been recently converted to Christ, and thrilled
with the wonder of the truths he so newly had
grasped, that one day all his trials would be over, that
in heaven everything would be different. But then one
Sunday in the meeting he heard them sing a song he
had not heard before, 'Sweeping through the gates of
the New Jerusalem'.

'Aw, no!' he said, 'I thought I'd be done with all that!'
His work-a-day occupation?

He was a road sweeper.

Some years ago my sister remarked, 'When I was
younger and I heard older folk in a church say that
they'd been church-treasurer or organist or a Sunday-
school teacher for thirty or more years in the same
place I used to think, how boring! How
unimaginative! Now I realize how much faithfulness
it takes to not get offended, not get fed up, but
continue in the task God had allotted.'

February 22

Psalm 85:11; 141:2   *1 Chronicles 17:16*
Matthew 24:45-7; 25:1-4

I dreamed I saw my name in lights
    And spoke Your word for all to hear.
I dreamed my name was recognized
    By people far and people near.
But I have come to understand
    Like David long ago,
That humble service in Your house
Is still the greatest dream a heart can hold.

Oh let me be a servant
A keeper of the door.
My heart is only longing
To see for evermore
The glory of Your presence,
The dwelling of the Lord.
Oh let me be a servant
A keeper of the door.

Ye servants of the Lord
Each in his office wait,
Observant of His heavenly word
And watchful at His gate.

Let all your lamps be bright,
And trim the golden flame;
Gird up your loins, as in His sight,
For awful is His name.

Watch: 'tis your Lord's command;
And, while we speak, He's near;
Mark the first signal of His hand,
And ready all appear.

O happy servant he,
In such employment found!
He shall His Lord with rapture see,
And be with honour crowned.

Christ shall the banquet spread
With His own royal hand,
And raise that faithful servant's head
Amid the angelic band.

Twila Paris/Philip Doddridge

February 23

Psalm 84:4　　　*Isaiah 40:9*　　　*John 1:35-9*

I stand by the door
I neither go too far in, nor stay too far out,
The door is the most important door in the world –
It is the door through which men walk when they
　　find God.
There's no use my going way inside and staying there,
When so many are still outside and they, as much as I,
Crave to know where the door is.

Samuel Moor Shoemaker

February 24

Psalm 143:6　　　*Isaiah 59:9-10*　　　*Acts 9:10-20*

And all that many ever find
Is only the wall where a door ought to be,
They creep along the wall like blind men,
With outstretched, groping hands.
Feeling for a door, knowing there must be a door,

Yet they never find it ...
So I stand by the door.

Samuel Moor Shoemaker

February 25

Psalm 84:12　　　*1 Chronicles 23:2-5*　　　*Acts 12:5-16*

The most tremendous thing in the world
Is for men to find that door – the door to God.
The most important thing any man can do
Is to take hold of one of those blind, groping hands,
And put it on the latch – the latch that only clicks
And opens to the man's own touch.

Men die outside that door, as starving beggars die
On cold nights in cruel cities in the dead of winter –
Die for want of what is within their grasp.
Others *live*, on the other side of it – live
    because they *have* found it,
And open it, and walk in, and find him ...
So I stand by the door.
          Samuel Moor Shoemaker (altered for emphasis)

February 26

Psalm 84:3   *Isaiah 65:17-19*   *John 14:2*

Go in, great saints, go all the way in –
Go way down into the cavernous cellars,
Away up into the spacious attics –
It is a vast, roomy house, this house where God is.
Go into the deepest of hidden casements,
Of withdrawal, of silence, of sainthood.
Some must inhabit those inner rooms,
And know the depth and heights of God,
And call outside to the rest of us how wonderful it is.
Sometimes I take a deeper look in,
Sometimes venture in a little farther;
But my place seems closer to the opening ...
So I stand by the door.
          Samuel Moor Shoemaker

February 27

Psalm 84:10, 85:8   *Joel 3:14*   *John 21:2-5*

There is another reason why I stand there.
Some people get part way in and become afraid
Lest God and the zeal of his house devour them;
For God is so very great, and asks all of us.
And these people way inside only terrify them more.

Somebody must be by the door to tell them that they
    are spoiled
For the old life, they have seen too much:
Once taste God, and nothing but God will do any
    more.
Somebody must be watching for the frightened
Who seek to sneak out just where they came in,
To tell them how much better it is inside.

The people too far in do not see how near these are
To leaving – preoccupied with the wonder of it all.
Somebody must watch for those who have entered
    the door,
But would like to run away.
So for them, too, I stand by the door.

Samuel Moor Shoemaker

February 28

Psalm 143:5   Nehemiah 8:10   John 4:28-30, 34-8

I admire the people who go way in.
But I wish they would not forget how it was
Before they got in. Then they would be able to help
The people who have not yet even found the door,
Or the people who want to run away again from God.
You can go in too deeply, and stay in too long,
And forget the people outside the door.

Samuel Moor Shoemaker

February 29

Psalm 84:10, 12   2 Kings 23:4   Luke 14:10a

As for me, I shall take my old accustomed place,
Near enough to God to hear him, and know he is
    there,
But not so far from men as not to hear them,
And remember they are there, too.

Where? Outside the door –
Thousands of them, millions of them.
But – more important for me –
One of them, two of them, ten of them,
Whose hands I am intended to put on the latch.
So I shall stand by the door and wait
For those who seek it.
'I had rather be a door-keeper ...'
So I stand by the door.

Samuel Moor Shoemaker

March Readings
Small Beginnings

March 1

David, sixth-century founder of many monasteries in Wales, imitated the ascetic ways of the desert fathers.

Psalm 119:25-6   Ecclesiastes 7:8   Matthew 13:44

This month's notes are largely quotations which reflect the direction in which the Northumbria Community has been built and is in the process of moving.

The title 'Small Beginnings' is drawn from 'Simple Joys' which is the quotation for March 18.

> The desert fathers' creative subversion, their simple and radical renunciation, cut powerfully through the subtleties of religion and reminded ordinary people that behind all the argumentation was the simple gospel challenge: 'If anyone wants to be a follower of Mine; let him renounce himself, take up his cross and follow Me' (Matthew 16:24).
>
> *William McNamara*

March 2

Chad (see Chad liturgy, p. 35)
Psalm 17:15   1 Kings 19:11-12   Luke 7:40-43

> The monk is not defined by his task, his usefulness; in a certain sense he is supposed to be useless, because his mission is not to do this or that job but to be a man of God.
>
> *Thomas Merton*

March 3

Psalm 71:2-3   Isaiah 58:8   Luke 15:11-32

For this is the wonder of God, that when we walk in
the light of His countenance, the very shadows of
our life are charged with healing power.

Hugh Redwood, 'God in the Shadows'

March 4

Psalm 119:27-8   Proverbs 15:16   Luke 12:16-21

Christianity has to be disappointing, precisely
because it is not a mechanism for accomplishing all
our human ambitions and aspirations; it is a
mechanism for subjecting all things to the will of God.

Simon Tugwell OP

March 5

Psalm 144:1, 9, 14   Song of Songs 2:15
Luke 16:19-31

Community is a terrible place, a place where our
limitations and egoisms are revealed to us. When we
begin to live full time with others we discover our
poverty and our weakness, our inability to get on
with others ...

our mental and emotional blocks; our affective
and sexual disturbances, our frustrations and
jealousies ...

and our hatred and desire to destroy.

Jean Vanier

March 6

Psalm 63:1-2, 5-6   Ruth 3:10   Matthew 13:45-6

To worship God *means* to serve him. There are two
ways to do it. One way is to do things for him that
he needs to have done – run errands for him, carry
messages for him, fight on his side, feed his lambs,
and so on. The other way is to do things for him
that you need to do – sing songs for him, create
beautiful things for him, give things up for him, tell
him what is on your mind and in your heart, in
general rejoice in him and make a fool of yourself
for him the way lovers have always made fools of
themselves for the one they love.

   ...Unless there is an element of joy and
foolishness in the proceedings, the time would be
better spent doing something useful.

Frederick Buechner

March 7

Psalm 71:2-3   Isaiah 1:26   Luke 18:9-14

If the Catholicism that I was raised in had a fault,
and it did, it was precisely that it did not allow for
mistakes. It demanded that you get it right the first
time.

   There was supposed to be no need for a second
chance. If you made a mistake, you lived with it and,
like the rich young man, were doomed to be sad, at
least for the rest of your life. A serious mistake was
a permanent stigmatization, a mark that you wore
like Cain.

   I have seen that mark on all kinds of people:
divorcees, ex-priests, ex-religious, people who have
had abortions, married people who have had

affairs, people who have made serious mistakes
with their children, and countless others who have
made serious mistakes. There is too little around to
help them.

We need a theology of brokeness. We need a
theology which teaches us that even though we
cannot unscramble an egg, God's grace lets us live
happily and with renewed innocence far beyond
any egg we may have scrambled.

We need a theology that teaches us that God
does not just give us one chance, but that
every time we close a door He opens another
one for us.

Ronald Rolheiser, 'Forgotten among the Lilies'

March 8

Psalm 126:6; 65:13   *Isaiah 60:22*
Mark 4:2-9, 13-20

A sense of direction was fixed in my soul. Before
me lay the road of life: much of it hidden, obscure,
but my destination was clear, a full view of certainty.
Heaven was ahead. Its gates were open, Jesus was
there. Stretched between me and that glorious
goal was a lifetime of service in the Lord's
harvest fields.

Heaven would have to wait. I knew now what I
wanted more than anything else, even more than
heaven itself. I looked up, kneeling by my bed, tears
streaming down my face.

Oh Jesus, here's my life. Add to it or take from it
what you will, only there is just one thing I would
ask, dear Lord. Please, when I have finished my life's
work in Your fields, let me meet You with my arms
laden down with golden sheaves. Oh, don't let me

meet You empty handed. Give me, dear Lord,
precious souls for my hire. When I reach heaven,
however long that may take, give me the joy of
bringing many others with me.

Jean Darnall, 'Heaven here I come'

March 9

Psalm 85:13   *Isaiah 61:1–4*   *Luke 14:15–24*

What is both Good and New about the Good News
is the wild claim that Jesus did not simply tell us
that God loves us even in our wickedness and folly
and wants us to love each other the same way and
to love Him too, but that if we let Him, God will
actually bring about this unprecedented
transformation of our hearts himself.

What is both Good and New about the Good
News is that mad insistence that Jesus lives on
among us not just as another haunting memory but
as the outlandish, holy, and invisible power of God
working not just through the sacraments but in
countless hidden ways to make even slobs like us
loving and whole beyond anything we could
conceivably pull off by ourselves.

Thus the Gospel is not only Good and New but, if
you take it seriously, a Holy Terror. Jesus never
claimed that the process of being changed from a
slob into a human being was going to be a Sunday-
School picnic. On the contrary. Child-birth may
occasionally be painless, but rebirth never. Part of
what it means to be a slob is to hang on for dear life
to our slobbery.

Frederick Buechner

March 10

Psalm 34:18, 33:20-21   Isaiah 30:17   Luke 14:7-11

True discretion is impossible without true humility.
Self-deception is unlikely when a person is humble
enough to submit to the judgement of another.

John Cassian

March 11

*Psalm 142:1-3, 6   Song of Songs 8:8-9
                    Matthew 7:24-7*

The man who fashions a visionary ideal of
community demands that it be realized by God, by
others and by himself. He enters the community of
Christians with his demands, his own law, and
judges the brethren and himself accordingly. He
acts as if he is the creator of community, as if it is his
dream which holds the community together. When
things do not go his way, he calls the effort a failure.
When his ideal picture is destroyed, he sees the
community going to smash. So he becomes first an
accuser of his brethren, then God, and finally the
despairing accuser of himself.

Dietrich Bonhoeffer

March 12

*Psalm 144:5, 11-12, 15   Isaiah 28:10
                    Matthew 13:52*

The renewal of the church will come from a new
type of monasticism, which has only in common
with the old an uncompromising allegiance to the
Sermon on the Mount. It is high time men and
women banded together to do this.

Dietrich Bonhoeffer

March 13

Psalm 144:3, 12-13   *Ezekiel 17:22-4*
          Matthew 13:31-2

Dynamic and erratic, spontaneous and radical,
audacious and immature, committed if not
altogether coherent, ecumenically open and often
experimental, visible here and there, now and then,
but unsettled institutionally. Almost monastic in
nature but most of all ... enacting a fearful hope for
human life in society.

                                        William Stringfellow

March 14

Psalm 85:1, 6-7   *1 Kings 18:44-5*
          Matthew 25:1-13

Looking down I saw Scotland, England, Wales and to
the Northwest, Ireland. The treetops upon the hills
and the clustered clouds hid the people. Suddenly
small, flickering lights appeared. They were
scattered all over the isles. I came closer to the land.
The light was firelight. There were fires burning
from the top of Scotland to Land's End on the tip of
Cornwall. Lightning streaked downward from the
sky above me. I saw it touch down with flashing
swiftness, exploding each of the fires into streams
of light. Like lava, they burned their fiery path
downward from the top of Scotland to Land's End.
The waters did not stop them, but the fire spread
across the seas to Ireland and to Europe.
    Then the Lord said:
    I will penetrate the darkness with a visitation of
my power. With lightning swiftness I will release
the power of my Spirit through a renewed people

who have learned how to be led by the Spirit. They will explode with a witness that will touch every part of society in Britain. I'm strategically placing them in touch with the farms, villages, towns and cities. No one will be without a witness whether they be children in the schools, farmers in the fields, workers in the factories and docks, students in the universities and colleges, the media, the press, the arts or government.

I seemed to see an army of all types of people moving into the continent with a compassionate ministry – participating, caring communities involved with each other at a grass-roots level, sharing the love of God everywhere. I saw the empty cradles of Europe, her churches, holding a new generation of Christian leaders

Jean Darnall, from 'Heaven, here I come'

March 15

*Psalm 85:2-9; 86:10-11   Joshua 14:6-14, 15:13-16
Zechariah 4:10   Matthew 5:19, 20:1-16*

A student is not above his teacher, nor a servant above his master. It is enough for the student to be like his teacher, and the servant like his master.

Matthew 10:24-5a

O Lord, I pray that in You
I'll break ground both fresh and new.
As a student let me stand,
break the hardness of the land
with Your forgiving Father-hand.

Paul Stamper 'Student Song'

March 16

Psalm 85:8-12   *Isaiah 58:11-12*   *Luke 17:7-10*

Lindisfarne

A point on earth – where land and sea
    God and man, meet
    in total, timeless harmony

A church – where the sanctuary
    lamp has flickered throughout the ages –
    telling the presence of Christ,
    to sunshine and storm, saint and sinner.

A house – where love draws the traveller in;
    a haven created by loving people that
    renews the spirit of love
    in world-weary souls.
                          Sheila M. Whittle, October 1982

March 17

Patrick (c. 385–461) (see November 13)
Psalm 137:4   *Genesis 12:1-2*   *Matthew 9:16*

Jacques Ellul quotes a second-century Christian
apologist describing the believers of his day:

> Though they are residents at home in their own
> countries, their behaviour there is more like aliens;
> they take full part as citizens, but they also submit
> to everything as if they were foreigners. For them,
> any foreign country is a motherland and any
> motherland is a foreign country.

March 18

Psalm 122:7-8   *1 Samuel 2:18-19*
Matthew 25:14-30

Simple Joys
If you want your dream to be,
build it slow and surely.
Small beginnings,
greater ends.
Heartfelt work grows purely.

If you want to live life free,
take your time, go slowly.
Do few things,
but do them well:
simple joys are holy.

Day by day
stone by stone,
build your secret slowly.
Day by day,
you'll grow too;
you'll know heaven's glory!
Donovan, music for the film
Brother Sun, Sister Moon

March 19

Psalm 145:3-4, 7   1 Chronicles 22:19   Mark 4:26-9

Years ago a small seed
was planted deep into the
heart of hopeful souls.

Over the years that seed grew
and spread itself to other souls
during Easter Workshops
and companionships.

Now that plant flourishes
in many hopeful souls
all working together as one.

Last Easter, buds
could be seen on every bough
of that widely spread plant.

The people of the Nether Springs
prepared themselves to flower
in their base founded by God.

This base was God's aim
for the Northumbria Community,
even though
they never knew it until now.

Anne Louise Haggerstone, 1992

March 20

Cuthbert (see Cuthbert liturgy p. 43; November 27,
29; May 26, 28; see also Herebert, May 28)
Psalm 63:1-2, 7   *Proverbs 1:7*   *Mark 13:33-7*

The world gives itself
up to incessant activity
   merely because
   it knows of nothing
     better.
The inspired man
   works among
   its whirring wheels
   also, but he knows
   whither the wheels
     are going.
For he has found
   the centre
   where all is
     stillness ...

Paul Brunton

March 21

Psalm 27:13   Nehemiah 2:17-18
Matthew 21:28-32

Observe, admire and obey may be given as the
novice's watchwords. The ideal must not remain an
ideal, but has to be realized at whatever the cost.
The cost is heroism.

John Cassian

March 22

Psalm 63:1-3, 8 Proverbs 9:10 Matthew 18:10-14

Those who lean on Jesus' breast hear God's
heartbeat.

Monk of Patmos

March 23

Psalm 27:3-5, 121:3-4   Ecclesiastes 3:1-3
Matthew 9:17

PERPETUAL CHANGE
is here to stay!

March 24

Psalm 118:17-21 Malachi 4:2 Matthew 22:1-14

To confess your sins to God is not to tell him
anything he does not already know. Until you
confess them, however, they are the abyss
between you. When you confess them, they
become the bridge.

Frederick Buechner

March 25

Psalm 145:10-12   *Song of Songs 5:10, 16*
Luke 10:29-37

A Christian is one who points at Christ and says,
'I can't prove a thing, but there's something about
his eyes and his voice. There's something about the
way he carries his head, his hands, the way he
carries his cross – the way he carries me.'

Frederick Buechner

March 26

Psalm 149:5   *1 Kings 17:10-16*
Matthew 13:47-50

Who knows how the awareness of God's love
first hits people. Every person has his own tale
to tell, including the person who would not
believe in God if you paid him. Some moment
happens in your life that you say Yes right up to
the roots of your hair, that makes it worth having
been born just to have happen. Laughing with
somebody till the tears run down your cheeks.
Waking up to the first snow. Being in bed with
somebody you love.

Whether you thank God for such a moment or
thank your lucky stars, it is a moment that is trying
to open up your whole life. If you turn your back on
such a moment and hurry along to Business as
Usual, it may lose you the ball game. If you throw
your arms around such a moment and hug it like
crazy, it may save your soul.

How about the person you know who as far as
you can possibly tell has never had such a moment
– the soreheads and slobs of the world, the ones the

world has hopelessly crippled? Maybe for that person the moment that has to happen is you. Salvation is a process, not an event.

Frederick Buechner

March 27

Psalm 71:2-3   Proverbs 16:8   Matthew 25:31-46

'Your sins are forgiven,' Jesus said to the paralytic, then 'Rise' whereupon the man picked up his bed and went home (Matthew 9:2-7).

It is as hard to absolve yourself of your own guilt as it is to sit in your own lap. Wrongdoing sparks guilt sparks wrongdoing *ad nauseam*, and we all try to disguise the grim process from both ourselves and everybody else. In order to break the circuit we need somebody before whom we can put aside the disguise, trusting that when he sees us for what we fully are, he will not run away screaming with, if nothing worse, laughter. Our trust in him leads us to trust his trust in us. In his presence the fact of our guilt no longer makes us feel and act out our guiltiness. For a moment at least the vicious circle stops circling and we can step down onto the firm ground of his acceptance, where maybe we'll be able to walk a straight line again.

Frederick Buechner

March 28

Psalm 145:1-3   2 Samuel 6:5, 14-15   Luke 18:1-8

Dynamos of Praise

O my child, lean upon Me; for I am your helper;
I am your shield and your buckler. Yes, I am your
strong tower and support. No evil shall befall you,
for you are surrounded and protected by My
presence, and no evil can touch Me. Yes, let your
heart rejoice in Me, and occupy your heart with
praise. There is no need that I will not fulfil as you
praise and worship – both your needs and the
needs of others.

Man has contemplated the power of faith and of
prayer, but only rarely have I revealed to men this
far greater power of praise. For by prayer and faith
doors are opened, but by praise and worship great
dynamos of power are set in motion, as when a
switch is thrown and an electric power plant such
as Niagara is thrown into operation. Praying for
specifics is like requesting light for individual
houses in various scattered places, while
worshipping and praise flood the whole area with
available current.

I do not discount prayer (petitions). I only show
you a more marvellous way – a faster means of
bringing more help to more people with less elapse
of time. So many need Me. So little time is available.
Turn loose your praises, and in proportion to your
liberality, you shall see My generosity expressed,
and in infinite magnitude.

Labour not to analyse each need. Leave the
diagnosis and the mechanics of it in My hands.
Complexities are nothing to Me. They exist only in
your mind, sown by the enemy, to dull your faith.

Ignore all this. Weigh nothing, unless you inquire of your own heart how much love for Me is there. Hold Me closely, nor let Me go. I will surely bless you, and I will make you a blessing.

I will make you a blessing. Think not to take a blessing to someone, or hope that I will send a blessing. Lo, I will make you as My ambassador, to be yourself a sweet savour of life and grace. Through your saltiness shall others be made thirsty. Through your joy shall others be made to long after reality.

Frances Roberts, 'Come away, My beloved'

March 29

Psalm 140:12   *Genesis 50:21*   *Luke 11:5-13*

In the early days of our time at Hetton Hall, John Skinner was walking near the stable block where Chris was knocking holes in the walls. John was talking to the Lord, saying,

> How are we going to pay for all this? And what about all the mission work? It's all too much – You know what a worrier I am! What can You do?

The Lord seemed to stand before him, wearing only a simple, seamless homespun garment. He said, simply, 'I am poor, too.' He paused, then added, 'But I will go to the Father for you.'

March 30

Psalm 121:8   *Job 42:12-13*   *Matthew 21:33-46*

The Covenant of Community, profound as it is, can never guarantee that a certain person will always stay physically close to another. It guarantees only that there will always be someone there, inspired by the same Spirit.

Jean Vanier, 'Man and Woman He made them'

March 31

Psalm 133:1; 121:8   *Exodus 34:21-2*
Matthew 13:24-30, 36-43

A Time to Gather

A time to gather, a time to reap
the fruits we've planted, hoping to bear peace.
The seeds have fallen so many months ago:
the harvest of our life will come.

In tenderness is life's beauty known;
and as we listen the morning star will shine.
The days go by; why not let them be filled
with new and surprising joys?

A time for kneading love's leaven well,
to open up and go beyond ourselves;
And as we reach for this moment, we know
that love is a gift born in care.

A time for hoping and being still,
to go on turning away from brittle fear.
A time to come back with all of one's heart
and bending to another's call.

This is our journey through forests tall;
our paths may differ and yet among them all
life's dreams and visions sustain us on our way
as loving gives birth to joy, gives birth to joy

Gregory Norbet, Weston Priory

April Readings
Abandonment

April 1

Psalm 9:2　　　*Isaiah 40:9*　　　*Romans 1:15-16*

This month's notes are taken from the letters, prayers and meditations of Charles de Foucauld.

You are powerful over your creatures, you can do all things in me. Give me a right mind, give me the wisdom that you promise to all who ask for it. Convert my heart and let me glorify you to the utmost till my last breath and through all eternity.

I ask this in the name of Our Saviour Jesus Christ. Amen. Amen. Amen.

Je veux crier l'Evangile
　　toute ma vie.
(I would shout the Gospel all my life.)
Charles de Foucauld

April 2

Mary of Egypt (see November 6)
Psalm 6:1-4　　　*Isaiah 40:2*　　　*Romans 7:19*

What shall I tell you about my soul? It is still more or less as you knew it, I still have a lot to do about humility, obedience, charity, meditation too, and many other things; it seems to me that where my soul is concerned I lose rather than gain; I ought to admit this as a tragic certainty; the only thing, basically, that prevents me from doing so, that prevents me from admitting this sad fact, is my huge desire for it not to be true.

I have no humility, no simplicity. What a huge sheet

of paper I would need to enumerate all that I have too little of and all that I have too much of!

April 3

Psalm 42:7　　　*Isaiah 40:1*　　　*Romans 12:15*

When we love, what is sweeter than to give something to the loved one, especially to give him something we hold dear, to suffer for love of him, to give him our very heart's blood. And then not only have we offered something to our Lord Jesus – our tears – but it is so marvellous that he lets us offer him these on behalf of each other.

April 4

Psalm 1:2　　　*Ruth 3:7*　　　*John 12:3*

When one loves one longs to be for ever in converse with him one loves, or at least to be always in his sight. Prayer is nothing else. This is what prayer is. Intimate intercourse with the Beloved. You look at him, you tell him of your love, you are happy at his feet, you tell him you will live and die there.

April 5

Psalm 91:1-2, 7　　　*Ruth 3:14a*　　　*Luke 10:39,*
　　　　　　　　Matthew 14:23

O my God, thank you for letting me be at your feet! How divinely good you are! You love me. It seems madness to think it. You, perfect God, love me, a poor evil, cowardly creature, falling a thousand times a day. No, it is not madness, it is truth, the truth of your Divine Heart, and your love is far beyond our love and your heart far beyond our hearts.

Whilst everything sleeps, drowned in silence and darkness, I live at the feet of God, unfolding my soul to His love, telling Him that I love Him, and He replying that I will never love Him, however great may be my love, as much as He cherishes me. What happiness to be allowed to spend these nights with God.

Teach me to prolong these hours in which I watch alone at your feet. Everything sleeps, no one knows of my happiness nor shares it. I rejoice through the solitude of the night in your presence, O my God.

April 6

Psalm 27:3-4 *Isaiah 40:4* *John 10:10*

Let us try with all our strength to occupy our minds with only God. Even whilst doing our tasks we must keep our eyes fixed constantly on him, never detaching our heart from him, only keeping our attention on our tasks as much as is right and necessary, never our hearts. God must be the King of our minds, the Lord of our minds, so that the thought of him never leaves us, and we speak, think and act always either for him or guided by the love of him. Let our souls be thus a house of prayer and not a den of thieves. Let no stranger enter in, no profanity even in passing. Let it always be occupied with its Beloved. When one loves one never loses sight of that which one loves.

April 7

Psalm 5:1-3 *Lamentations 2:19a* *Mark 1:35*

Let us do what Our Lord did and rise early in the morning, whilst everything is at rest in silence and darkness, when sleep envelops everything in torpor, in profound quiet. Let us rise and watch with God, lifting our hearts to him, laying our souls at his feet, and at this early hour when intercourse is so secret and so sweet let us fall at his feet and enjoy converse with our Creator. How good He is to let us come to His feet whilst all is sleeping. Whilst all is sleeping in silence and shadow, let us begin both our day and our prayers. Before our working day begins let us pass long hours praying at the feet of Our Lord.

April 8

Psalm 31:1-2   Isaiah 40:28-9   Mark 1:38

During the many occupations that fill the day our minds must be constantly fixed on God, and our eyes always turned towards Him either by using ejaculatory prayer or simply by turning our thoughts to Him. It matters little what means we use, so long as the soul gazes on her Beloved.

The hours given up entirely to prayer will give us the strength, with God's grace, to keep ourselves in His presence through the rest of the day and give up all our time to what is called 'perpetual prayer'.

April 9

Psalm 6:9   Isaiah 40:27   Mark 15:34

We must speak to God with perfect simplicity, telling Him all our thoughts, even our complaints. Since our sufferings are allowed by Him we may make our plaint to God as Our Lord did, but we should complain with all reverence, love, submission, unbounded and loving conformity to His will.

April 10

Psalm 30:10-12   *Isaiah 40:25-6*   *Luke 22:43*

The more you suffer the more you are tempted, the
more you need to pray; prayer now alone can
strengthen you with help and consolation. Let not
pain and fierce temptation paralyse your prayer. The
devil does all he can to prevent you praying at these
times. But rather than give in to weak human nature
which absorbs the soul in its pain so that it sees
nothing else for the time, turn you eyes to Our Lord
and speak to Him standing so near. He is with you,
looking on you lovingly, listening for your words. He
tells you to speak, that He is there to hear you, that He
loves you and you have not a word to say to Him, no
look to give Him. What ingratitude! Look at Him, speak
to Him without ceasing. The deeper your agony, the
deeper you must bury yourself in the Heart of your
Beloved, and cling to His side with ceaseless prayer.

April 11

Psalm 4:7-8   *2 Chronicles 30:8a*   *Luke 23:46*

'Father, into thy hands I commend my spirit' (Luke
23:46.)
   This is the last prayer of our Master, our Beloved.
May it be ours. And not only ours at our last moments,
but at all times.

   My Father, I commend myself to you, I give myself
   to you, I leave myself in your hands. My Father, do
   with me as you wish. Whatever you do with me,
   I thank you, I accept everything. I am ready for
   anything. I thank you always. So long as your will is
   done in me and in all creatures, I have no other
   wish, my God. I put my soul into your hands, giving

it to you, my God, with all my heart's love, which
makes me crave to abandon myself to you without
reserve, with utter confidence. For are you not my
Father?

April 12

Psalm 16:1   *Habakkuk 2:4*   *Matthew 9:22*

It is the rarest virtue of all to have real faith, faith that
inspires all one's actions, and faith in the supernatural
which tears the mask from the world and sees God in
everything, which makes all things possible, which
takes all meaning out of such words as worry, peril,
fear, which makes us pass through life calmly,
peacefully, happily, like a child holding its mother's
hand, which gives the soul perfect detachment from
all material things, showing it their emptiness and
puerility; which gives to prayer the confidence of a
child asking something he deserves from his father;
a faith to which all is falsehood except to do the Will
of God.

It will help us to regard all other living things as aids
to the winning of Heaven, for we can always give God
praise for them, or use them, or renounce them.

Faith will show us the greatness of God and our
littleness. It will make us undertake whatever is
pleasing to God without hesitation or false shame or
fear and without looking back. Ah! such faith is rare
indeed. My God, give me this faith; my God, I believe,
help thou my unbelief; my God, let me believe
and love.

I ask it in the name of Our Lord Jesus Christ.

April 13

Psalm 23:3-4   Proverbs 3:11-12   Luke 11:11-12

You are a Father, all powerful and infinitely wise and good and tender. You say to us as your children, so frail we are and hardly able to walk except with our hands in yours, 'all that you ask I will give you if only you ask with confidence.'

If we ask you for dangerous playthings you refuse them in goodness for us, and you console us by giving us other things for our good. If we ask you to put us where it would be dangerous for us to be, you do not give us what is not for our good, but you give us something really for our welfare, something that we would ask for ourselves if our eyes were open.

You take us by the hand and lead us, not there where we would wish to go, but there where it is best for us to be.

April 14

Psalm 8:3-4   Isaiah 40:6-8   Romans 11:33-4

All created beauty, all beauty of Nature, the beauty of the sunset, of the sea lying like a mirror beneath the blue sky, of the dark forest, of the garden of flowers, of the mountains and the great spaces of the desert, of the snow and the ice, the beauty of a rare soul reflected in a beautiful face, all these beauties are but the palest reflection of yours, my God. All that has ever charmed my eyes in this world is but the poorest, the humblest reflection of your infinite Beauty.

April 15

Psalm 139:7-10   *Isaiah 40:5*   *Romans 11:36*

Those creatures in whom I admire a reflection of his
perfections, on whom there falls a little ray of the
infinite sunshine, are outside me, far removed from
me, distant and separate, whilst you, who are
Perfection, Beauty, Truth, Infinite and Essential Love,
you are in me and around me. You fill me altogether ...
there is no particle of my body that you do not fill,
and around me you are nearer than the air in which
I move. How am I blessed! What happiness to be
united so completely to Perfection itself; to live
in it, to possess it living in myself! My God, you
who are in me, in whom I am, let me know
my happiness.

Give me a perpetual sense of your Presence, of your
Presence all around me, and at the same time that
loving fear one feels in the presence of him one loves
passionately, and which makes one, in the presence of
one's Beloved, keep one's eyes on him with great
desire and firm purpose to do all that may please him
and be good, and gently fear to do or think anything
that may displease or harm him.

In you, by you, and for you.

Amen.

April 16

Psalm 7:17   *Isaiah 40:18-20*   *1 Corinthians 13:12*

I know you enough to show me that I should love you
without measure.

I rejoice that I shall know you better in Heaven;
and, seeing your Beauty, I shall love you more
and more.

April 17

Psalm 139:23a   Ezekiel 36:26, 33-6   Mark 1:40-1

Compassion to weep for your sorrows: truly this
would be a great grace. Of myself I am incapable of
drawing tears from this heart of stone at the thought
of your cross, so horribly hard is it. But I ask from you
the gift of compassion, so that I may give it to you.
Turn my stony heart to a compassionate one and give
me grace to kiss your footprints with the tears you
would have me shed from my soul and from my heart.
I must have zeal for souls, a burning love of souls
which have all been bought at the same price.

April 18

*Psalm 22:31   Zechariah 9:9   Luke 14:8-10
Philippians 2:7-9,   Matthew 11:29*

Charles de Foucauld here quotes the words of Abbé
Huvelin who was instrumental in bringing him to
God. These words, from a sermon, are addressed to
Christ:

You took always the lowest place
and did it so completely that no one
ever since has been able to wrest it
from you.

April 19

*Psalm 16:11   Isaiah 40:13-14   Matthew 5:11-12
Acts 5:41-2*

Faith is that which makes us believe
from the depths of our souls
all the truths that the Gospel holds.

The just man lives truly by his Faith, for it replaces for him the greater part of his natural senses; it so transforms all things that the senses are of little use to the soul, which through them is only deceived, whilst Faith shows it realities. Where the eye sees but a poor man, the Faith sees Jesus. Where the ear hears curses and persecution, the Faith sings: 'Rejoice and be joyful.'

The touch feels only blows and stonings, but Faith says 'be glad that you are deemed worthy to suffer for the name of Christ.' Our taste perceives only a wafer of unleavened bread, Faith shows us our Saviour Jesus, God and man, soul and body.

April 20

Psalm 18:28-9   *Isaiah 40:21-4*
2 Corinthians 11:26-7, 30

The senses hold suffering in horror. Faith blesses it as a gift from the hand of Jesus, a bit of his cross which he lets us carry. The senses take fright at that which they call danger, at all that might mean pain or death; but Faith is afraid of nothing; she knows nothing can happen to her but what is the will of God. Thus in everything that may happen, sorrow or joy, health or sickness, life or death, she is content and fears nothing. The senses are anxious about the future and ask how shall we live tomorrow, but Faith feels no anxiety. He who lives by Faith has his soul full of new horizons open before him, marvellous horizons lit with a new light, and with a divine beauty surrounded with new truths of which the world is not aware. Thus he who believes begins a new life opposed to that of the world, to whom his acts seem like madness. The world is in the darkness of night, the man of Faith is in full light.

April 21

Psalm 3:3-5   Isaiah 40:3   2 Corinthians 12:9-10

I was lowly and disdained. Seek, ask for and love those occupations which degrade you, such as sweeping dung or digging the ground, whatever is most lowly and common; the more you make yourself lowly in these ways, the more you will be like me. Even if you are thought mad, all the better. Thank me infinitely. I was thought mad, that is a point of resemblance between us. If you should be stoned and reviled and cursed in the streets, all the better. Thank me, for it is a great grace. Did they not do the same to me? You should rejoice that I make you like myself in this. But you must not bring this treatment upon yourself by eccentricity or strange behaviour; I did nothing to be so treated, I did not deserve it in any way, and yet I was so treated; so do nothing to deserve ill-treatment, but if I give you the grace to undergo it, thank me for it. Do nothing to prevent it or stop it. Act as I should have done. Do only good, but give yourself to the lowest, humblest task; show yourself to others, by your dress, your lodging, your friendliness with the humble, equal of the humblest.

April 22

Psalm 18:35   Isaiah 40:11   1 John 4:16

He who loves has his Beloved always in his mind; that time to him is well spent that is spent in contemplating him, and the time to him is wasted in which he is out of his sight. He counts as profitable only those hours in which he contemplates the only thing that to him has any reality. All else is for him emptiness and nothingness. Let your soul melt into mine, immerse yourself in me, lose yourself in me.

Think how often I have told you to hope for the day
when you will lean for ever on my breast. And since I
allow it I tell you now to begin to live this life, in
silence, lay your head upon my breast and so
accomplish your pilgrimage.

April 23

Psalm 4:1-4   *Isaiah 40:15-17*   *1 John 4:19*

O my God, you are there before me. What will you that
I think or that I say to you out of the depths of my
heart?

'I do not ask you to think a great deal, but to love a
great deal,' the Holy Spirit answers. 'Adore me, love me,
contemplate me; tell me and repeat over and over
again that you love me, that you give yourself to me,
that you long for all my children to give themselves to
me and love me.'

All is sleeping, all is at rest. Thank you, my God, for
calling me to adore you and love you. Hold my eyes
open and set wide the gates of my soul. Let me lose
and sink myself in the contemplation and love of you.

April 24

Psalm 31:7   *Isaiah 40:12*   *Matthew 14:22-3*

Trust nothing, yourself least of all; but in me have that
perfect confidence that banishes fear.

Remember how many storms I have quieted by a
word, making a great calm to follow. Remember how I
held up Peter walking on the waters. I am always as
near to all men as I was then to him, and as ready to
help and succour in all that is for the good of the soul.
Be confident, faithful, courageous; have no fear for your
body and soul, for I am there, loving and all-powerful.

Never forget that I am there. In this life the tempest
never ceases, and your boat is ever ready to sink. But I
am there, and with me it will never be wrecked.

April 25

Psalm 40:8   Song of Songs 8:7   Matthew 22:36-8

The greatest commandment is to love God with all
your heart and all your soul and all your strength. It
means to love me as your King, above everything, as
much as you can, as much as the grace I give you
makes it possible to love me.

What does loving mean? To one soul God may give
this feeling, to another that feeling. First and foremost
is the longing to see, to know, to possess the Beloved;
the longing to be loved by him, the longing to please
him, to do him some good; the desire to praise him,
admire him, imitate him; the desire to be approved by
him, to obey him in everything, to see him pleased, to
see him possessed of all that is good and to his glory;
the longing, in a word, for all that is for his good; the
wish to suffer for him, to share his labours, his life, his
conditions; to conform one's soul entirely to him; the
wish to give oneself to him, to live only for him; the
longing to labour for his service, to share the pain of
his sufferings, the joy of his joy, the pain of those
things that grieve him, and in union with him to
rejoice in those things that please him.

All these sentiments are the effect, result, outcome
of love. They belong to love and are part of love, but
they are not all love itself. A single one of them is
really the essence of love – that is to desire
passionately and above all things the well-being of the
Beloved, to that degree that all else means nothing to
one, that one lives only for the accomplishment of this
desire.

April 26

Psalm 18:1-2   2 Samuel 7:20   Luke 11:13

Prayer is the cry of our hearts to God. So that it must
be something perfectly natural, perfectly genuine, the
expression of the deepest things in our heart. It is not
your lips that should speak, nor your mind, but your
will. Your will manifested, spread out before your
Father, true, naked, sincere, simple, and presented
before him by you. This is what prayer should be. This
needs neither a long space of time nor many words,
nor many thoughts. It varies: sometimes it will be
longer, sometimes quite short, according as your
heart's desire prompts you.

   Prayer, in the widest sense of the word, may be
either a silent contemplation or one accompanied by
words. *The best prayer is the most loving prayer.* The
more it is laden with love, the more the soul holds
itself tenderly and lovingly before its God, the more
acceptable is that prayer.

April 27

Psalm 123:1   1 Kings 8:60-1   1 Thessalonians 5:17

My children, what I ask for you in your prayer is love,
love, love. Besides the time that you should consecrate
entirely to prayer every day, you should lift up your
hearts to me as often as possible. When at work, you
can, whilst giving yourself up to it, either keep me
constantly in your thoughts as is possible in purely
manual labour, or perhaps you will only be able to lift
your eyes to me from time to time, whenever you can.
It would be sweet and right to contemplate me
always, never to lose sight of me - but this is not
possible in this world, for ordinary men; it is only

possible in Heaven. What you can and should do is to lift your hearts to me as often as you can during the time that is not taken up solely with prayer; lift the eyes of your soul up to me as often and as lovingly as you can, and whilst you are at work keep the thought of me as much present to your mind as is compatible with your work.

April 28

Psalm 52:8   Isaiah 40:30-1   1 Thessalonians 5:18

We must not trouble about health
or life any more than a tree
troubles about a leaf falling.

April 29

Psalm 7:8, 10   Job 42:2, 5   1 Thessalonians 5:21

Six months before his death Charles de Foucauld wrote to Louis Massignon on July 15:

As for Jesus' love for us, he has proved it clearly enough for us to believe in it without being able to feel it.

To feel we loved him and he loves us would be heaven.

But heaven is not, except at rare moments and in rare cases, for us here below.

April 30

Psalm 34:13   Isaiah 49:15   1 Thessalonians 5:23-4

The day of his murder Charles de Foucauld was writing a letter to his cousin:

It seems we do not love enough. How true it is we shall never love enough. But the good Lord Who knows from what mud He has fashioned us and Who loves us more than any mother can ever love her child, He Who never lies, has told us that none who come to Him shall ever be rejected.

May Readings
To a Young Disciple

May 1

Psalm 138:6   Isaiah 28:11   Matthew 20:25-7

This month's readings are a development of
Columbanus's 'Letter to a Young Disciple'.

BE HELPFUL WHEN YOU ARE AT THE BOTTOM
OF THE LADDER AND BE THE LOWEST WHEN
YOU ARE IN AUTHORITY.

Too many of our models for authority are ones of
hierarchy or domination. We think of rulers and
leaders as those who are over other people and
supported by them. Instead of a pyramid model
where the few dominate the many, in God's Kingdom
it is more helpful to picture a huge saucer into which
is thrown all the people of God in all their giftedness,
from the least to the greatest. Those more strongly
gifted for ministry will not rise to the top, but sink to
the bottom where they may under-gird and provoke
the rest of the people of God.

One true example of Christian humility was King
Oswald of Northumbria who himself willingly
worked as interpreter for Aidan so that his people
might receive the gospel.

May 2

Psalm 2:10-12   Daniel 1:3-9   Matthew 17:24-7

BE SIMPLE IN FAITH BUT WELL TRAINED IN
MANNERS.

When Augustine came to Kent he summoned bishops and teachers from the Celtic church in Wales to a conference at which they would discuss working together in the process of evangelization. He remonstrated with them to change their traditions for Roman ones, but also prayed over a blind man who was duly healed.

To the second such conference the Welsh sent seven British bishops and many learned men, mostly from Bangor (where three thousand were amongst Comgall's disciples). Before the second meeting they consulted a hermit for direction. He answered, 'If he is a man of God, follow him.' They asked how they could tell. The hermit reminded them that Jesus said He was meek and lowly of heart. If Augustine were the same it would be obvious that he himself bore the yoke of Christ and was offering it to them, but if he were harsh and proud this was not God's doing and they should disregard him. The test should be this, that the British party arrive later than Augustine and his party then observe whether he stood to greet them or insolently remained seated.

Not only did he remain sitting down, but began to lay conditions upon their fellowship, that they should change the manner of their calculation of the date of Easter, their monastic tonsure, and their way of baptizing. They recognized that under such circumstances he despised already what they stood for and would do so even more if they gave in to his demands. For want of manners much healthy co-operation in the gospel was thus forfeited.

May 3

Psalm 16:5-6, 8   *Proverbs 26:17, 20-22*
         John 21:15-22

**BE DEMANDING IN YOUR OWN AFFAIRS BUT
UNCONCERNED IN THOSE OF OTHERS.**

Isaiah 58 speaks of the possibility of being guided
continually by the Lord, of being a watered garden – a
spring with waters that never fail – but insists that the
condition for this happening is the taking away from
in our midst the pointing finger that accuses our
brother, saying 'It's all YOUR fault!' or 'Look what you
have done' or 'You are a disgrace to us all.'

If we attend to ourselves, are demanding of
obedience from ourselves, if we remove the plank
from our eye, then should we notice the splinter in
our brother's eye at all we will willingly help him
remove it – at his request – and without needing to
see it through a magnifying glass.

May 4

Psalm 19:12-13   *1 Samuel 20:8-17*   *John 15:15*

**BE GUILELESS IN FRIENDSHIP, ASTUTE IN THE
FACE OF DECEIT.**

A friend is someone you can be yourself with. Trying
to be someone we are not will not win us friendship.
Our need to impress is the enemy of any true
beginning. But when we know ourselves to be
accepted it is a true friend who can help us uncover
any areas of self-deceit, and love us into deeper reality.

When we are aware that another person has lied to
us, deceived us, betrayed our trust or deliberately

misled us, if we are wise we will not easily trust them again. We are required to show them love, to meet them with forgiveness – but trust should be earned. To close our heart to that person would be contrary to forgiveness, but to allow their behaviour to go unchecked may not be in their best interest. Here our response should be discerned carefully.

May 5

Psalm 132:1–4   *Proverbs 17:17*   *1 Peter 5:8*

BE TOUGH IN TIMES OF EASE, TENDER IN HARD TIMES.

When things are hard, often we are more reliant on God, leaning on Him in our hardship. When things become easier we tend to be more self-assured, blasé and independent. It is important then to keep our promises, and not forget the lessons we have learnt – or soon we may find ourselves having to learn them a second time. When outward circumstances are not checking us it is important to find appropriate disciplines to stop us becoming lazy or unfit. We never know how suddenly we may be called upon, or how we may regret wasted days of opportunity.

But when we are weary, heavy-laden, and circumstances press upon us, Jesus counsels us to allow Him to be yoked beside us, shouldering much of the weight. When times are hard it is the wrong time for recriminations – gently we should ease one another's burdens.

May 6

Psalm 139:12   Isaiah 30:20-21   Titus 1:15-16

KEEP YOUR OPTIONS OPEN WHEN THERE IS
NO PROBLEM, BUT DIG IN WHEN YOU MUST
CHOOSE.

Too often the Christians are hiding out in their
mission citadels peering out, cautiously preparing
to run out quickly and lasso some poor passer-by,
claim them for God and haul them back into the
safety of the citadel. This is called making a difference
in the world ...? What happened to the promise that
'greater is He who is in you than he that is in the
world'?

We are not asked to live a blinkered or protected
existence in a safe ivory-towered environment. We are
sent to walk confidently with a pure heart into the
world of people and culture and pain and pressure. It
need not contaminate us, if only we live the life that
has taken root deep inside of us. God wants to plant
us in places we can make a difference, be His
presence and that act not in any self-conscious way.

There may be times when we need to speak out,
opt out, explain our beliefs are different from
those around us – but we should not provoke
confrontations or become defensive. These times
when they happen may lead to miracles or to
persecution – or both.

May 7

Psalm 119:71, 113-114, 116-117   Isaiah 50:4-5
Romans 5:3-5

BE PLEASANT WHEN THINGS ARE UNPLEASANT,
AND SORROWFUL WHEN THEY ARE PLEASANT.

A container that is brim-full of sweet waters cannot spill bitterness no matter how sharply it is jostled. Unpleasant situations can drive us closer to God, and to each other if we let Him into them. We learn so much in these times that some mature souls are sad to see a pressure-cooker situation come to an end. They have learnt that it is a mistake to be at ease with ease. It is important to be kind to someone when we know they are under pressure, and when things are difficult for us it is equally important that we do not become difficult for other people!

Jim Wallis of the Sojourners Fellowship says that his favourite theologians are always under six years of age. One such child heard their parent's apology; 'I'm sorry I shouted at you, honey, it's just that I am really under pressure just now.' The child responded; 'So being under pressure makes you yell at small children? I think you really have a problem ...'

May 8

Psalm 119:165–8   *Genesis 13:5–9*
       Acts 15:36–41,   1 Corinthians 12:3

DISAGREE WHERE NECESSARY, BUT BE IN AGREEMENT ABOUT TRUTH.

Jesus said, 'He who is not against us is for us.' There is no excuse for division and antagonism between believers or groups of believers. It is possible to disagree strongly or deeply and still affirm that we hold fundamental truths in common, and that we are still family. Barnabas and Paul could not agree as to the wisdom of taking John Mark on mission again. In consequence they worked separately then, but still extending the Kingdom through different geographic areas. Who knows if this diminished or increased their

overall effectiveness? Similarly, after the Council
of Whitby in 664 Bishop Colman returned to Iona
with all the Irish monks and about 30 native to
Northumbria who chose to go to Scotland rather than
remain and implement the council's decision. Even
Bede refers to Colman as 'a man of innate prudence
and good sense'. After a short stay on Iona, Colman
and his brothers went to Ireland and he founded two
monasteries there.

The first of these monasteries was at Inis-bo-finde
off the west coast of Ireland. The Northumbrians
settled well, but complained that each summer the
Irish monks travelled the countryside, and were not
around to bring in the harvest but were content not
to travel during the winter! Colman then built a
second monastery on the Irish mainland for these
Northumbrians, which in time grew but later
conformed more to Roman practice than Celtic. Bede
does not tell us the nature or purpose of the
journeyings of these Irish monks who had come
from Lindisfarne.

May 9

Psalm 104:13–15, 33–4   *Nehemiah 8:9–11*
Colossians 3:20

BE SERIOUS IN PLEASURES, BUT KINDLY WHEN
THINGS ARE BITTER.

Our God is One who turned gallons of water into
wine at a wedding, the extravagant Creator who
plants flowers in places no one but Him is likely to
find. No wonder He tells us that whatever we do we
should do with all our hearts, and show consideration
for those in trouble of all kinds. Jewish culture reflects
this celebration of life, and so do the stories of the

Celtic saints. As an example I include this story from a 'Life of Brigid'.

There was a certain man biding in Lassair's church, and his wife was leaving him and would neither eat nor sleep with him. Brigid blessed water for him and said 'Put that water over the house, and over the food, and over the drink of yourselves, and over the bed in your wife's absence.' When he had done thus, the wife gave exceeding great love to him, so that she could not keep apart from him, even on one side of the house; but she was always at one of his hands. He went one day on a journey and left the wife asleep. When the woman awoke she rose up lightly and went after the husband and saw him far from her, with an arm of the sea between them. She cried out to her husband and said that she would go into the sea unless he came to her.

May 10

Psalm 119:165-6   *Proverbs 18:19-21*
1 Corinthians 6:1-8

BE STRONG IN TRIALS, WEAK IN DISSENTIONS.

Too often we are weak in trials, but very strong in dissent. Often it takes two parties to make a quarrel, and if I am determined not to take offence easily, the quarrel can be averted. Why is the other person picking a fight, anyway? What has upset them? Was it me? Was it my lack of thoughtfulness or lack of love on my part? Or has someone else upset them?

If we tried more often to be weak, vulnerable and forgiving, unpleasantness would be more readily averted and we would win our brother. Sometimes we would even win our cause. Sadly, we too often care more about being right than acting rightly. Trials may not be enjoyable, but the joy of the Lord may sustain us and hold us together through all kinds of trying circumstances.

May 11

Psalm 37:8   *Proverbs 10:17–19*   *James 1:19–20*

BE SLOW TO ANGER, QUICK TO LEARN, ALSO TO SPEAK, AS SAINT JAMES SAYS, EQUALLY QUICK TO LISTEN.

Be quick to hear the hard words that people bring to you. Then be slow to react. Don't rush into denial, retaliation, and rationalisation. Our challenge is to convert the energy once used by our self-defence machines into listening power, vulnerability power and contemplation power. We need to say to ourselves, Before I flare up, I'm going to quiet myself and listen. I'm going to be quick to hear, slow to speak, and slow to anger. I'm going to search for the truth in what this person is saying, and learn from it.

Bill Hybels

We were given two ears and one mouth to use in that proportion. Jesus never commanded us to engage in theological debates with strangers, flaunt four-inch crosses and Jesus stickers or throw out Christian catch-phrases. But he did tell us to work and live in such a way that when the Holy Spirit orchestrates opportunities to speak about God we will have earned the right.

Bill Hybels

May 12

Psalm 17:2   *Deuteronomy 32:34-6*
Colossians 3:13-14, 17

BE UP AND DOING TO MAKE PROGRESS, SLACK
TO TAKE REVENGE, CAREFUL IN WORD, EAGER
IN WORK.

It should never be said of Christians that as workers
they are half-hearted, careless, tardy, irresponsible,
whiny, or negligent. Behaviour like that embarrasses
God. It brings reproach on Him. At work Christians
should epitomize character qualities like self-
discipline, perseverance, and initiative. They should
be self-motivated, prompt, organized, and
industrious. Their efforts should result in work of
the very highest quality. Why? Because they're not
just laying bricks; they're building a wall for God's
glory ... They're not just driving a tractor; they're
ploughing a straight furrow for God's glory ...
Christians must strive every day to be beyond
reproach in all their marketplace dealings and
practices.

Bill Hybels, 'Honest to God?'

May 13

Psalm 15:4a   *Proverbs 8:13*   *Matthew 5:6*

BE FRIENDLY WITH MEN OF HONOUR, STIFF
WITH RASCALS.

C. S. Lewis in his *Reflections on the Psalms* says that
providing someone is rich and powerful it seems
people will treat them as a celebrity – far from
disapproving of their misdeeds, the notoriety adds to
their charm, and instead of shunning them even

Christians can be drawn into admiring such people.

What is OUR behaviour? Whose approval matters to us? What is the standard against which we measure people and their behaviour? Do we think as citizens of another kingdom? Or just use Christian jargon on the outside?

May 14

Psalm 41:1   *Ezekiel 3:8-9*
Matthew 11:2-5, 12:17-21

BE GENTLE TO THE WEAK, FIRM TO THE STUBBORN, STEADFAST TO THE PROUD, HUMBLE TO THE LOWLY.

Columbanus in his letter instructs the young disciple how to behave towards different sorts of people or how to behave towards the same people when they are in a different stage or have a particular attitude.

With the weak it is appropriate to be gentle, encouraging and strengthening them, following the example of Christ who would not crush the bruised reed. When someone is stubborn it is important not to give way to them, but remain firm and immovable. They will not then overpower you and get their own way; instead they recognize you will not be intimidated by their attitude. Your face will be strong enough to meet their gaze fair and square without becoming angry and obstinate in turn. When they back down or become reasonable you will have won their respect. A proud person is one who sets a wrong value on themselves, who thinks too much or too little of themselves, constructing a fearfully exaggerated self-image as out-and-out success or hardened failure. They project a belief, but you ARE.

Their self-image fluctuates: you remain constant, yet

are growing slowly. Their attitude changes to show their 'best side': your focus remains steady. Circumstances may help to humble us, but can equally make us resentful, bitter and proud: it is all our choice how we respond, whether we choose to humble ourselves under the mighty hand of God or are resistant.

May 15

Psalm 131:1   *Judges 7:4-7*   *Philippians 4:5*

BE EVER SOBER, EVER CHASTE, EVER MODEST.

The words of the letter here remind us of Jesus' remarks about the happy servant who is found sober and diligently about the Master's business when his Master returns unexpectedly. It is not exam technique that is required here, but preparation for continuous assessment.

May 16

Brendan (c. 486-578), a Celtic saint remembered with affection for his great sea voyages which captured the imagination of the people of his own time and many in every age since. The accounts seem to read partly as travelogue and partly as a spiritual journal or allegory. Ita had fostered him as a boy, and he founded large monasteries including that of Clonfert in Galway where he was eventually buried.

Psalm 69:9a   *Isaiah 59:12-19*   *Titus 2:14*

BE PATIENT AS FAR AS IS COMPATIBLE WITH ZEAL.

Zeal is defined as ardour, energy, fervour. Patience is well and good, but not if it swamps zeal and extinguishes its direction and energy. Where it is not possible to direct that zeal into action it can be channelled into urgency of prayer, grasping the right arm of God by the elbow to reach and open doors of opportunity fastened tight shut because of our prayerlessness.

When zeal abates or evaporates we need to discern whether we were wrongly counselled to 'have patience' or whether the original fervour was misplaced and immature and would have energized some misdirected scheme embraced in rash enthusiasm.

It still remains true that it is easier to alter the course of an already moving vehicle than to push-start one that has forgotten how to even let its engine tick over.

We need hearts consumed with passion to activate the coming of the Kingdom, that will not rest till its brightness appears as the noon-day sun.

May 17

Psalm 116:12 *2 Chronicles 31:20-21*
2 Corinthians 9:6-7

NEVER BE GREEDY, BUT ALWAYS GENEROUS, IF NOT IN MONEY, THEN IN SPIRIT.

Bede describes the lifestyle of Colman and his community on Lindisfarne:

They owned no wealth apart from their livestock, since any money they received from the rich was at once given to the poor. They had no need to save money or provide accommodation in order to receive the rulers of the world, who only came to the church for the purpose of prayer and to hear the word of God. King Oswy himself, whenever the opportunity allowed it, came with only five or six thanes, and went away after completing his prayers in the church. Even if it chanced that they had a meal there they were content with the simple daily fare of the brothers, and asked for nothing more.

Bless, O Lord, my kitchen with thy right hand!
My kitchen, the kitchen of the white God.
Mary's Son, my Friend, cometh to bless my kitchen.
My Prince, may we have abundance with Him!

St. Brigid

May 18

Psalm 119:164   Daniel 6:10   Matthew 25:1-13

BE TIMELY IN FASTING, TIMELY IN THE NIGHT-OFFICES, DISCREET IN DUTY.

Dave Cape in his book *On the Road with Jesus* tells of how he walked across South Africa with a towel and basin and a cross, washing the feet of people he would meet and witnessing to the love of God. Often the journey seemed pointless, and only obedience kept him there.

We were faithfully to do the things that we told people we did. For example, we would have a regular daily schedule, and on the days designated for my being out on the road, I would ensure that I was out there on time and for a particular time-span. Some days would be extremely hot, making walking a test of endurance; other days would be cold, or windy, and people who accompanied me or met with me would often express surprise at my being out in those extreme conditions.

May 19

Psalm 119:54   *Isaiah 42:4*   *Acts 17:11*

BE PERSISTENT IN STUDY, UNSHAKEN IN
TURMOIL, JOYFUL IN SUFFERING.

Bede says of Aidan:

> He cultivated peace and love, self-discipline and
> humility. His heart had the mastery over anger and
> avarice, and was contemptuous of pride and
> vainglory. He spared no effort in carrying out and
> teaching the commands of Heaven, and was diligent
> in his reading and keeping of vigils.

May 20

Psalm 91:4b-5   *Proverbs 15:1*
1 Thessalonians 5:21-2

BE VIGILANT IN THE CAUSE OF TRUTH,
CAUTIOUS IN TIME OF STRIFE.

In the event of a dispute it is especially important to
establish what is the truth, but great discretion and
wisdom is needed. Not all of us are anointed with
wisdom as obviously Solomon was when he
threatened to slice a baby in two in order to identify
the child's mother (1 Kings 3:16–28).

Brigid was presented with a case of similar
difficulty, but God intervened to assist her.

At an assembly of Irishmen held in Teltown a
woman brought with her a child who she claimed had
been fathered by Bishop Bron. Bron, one of Patrick's
community, denied the child was his. Brigid asked the
woman how she had conceived, and charged her not

to speak falsehoods. The woman accused Bron yet
again. Then tumour and swelling filled her tongue so
she was unable to speak. Brigid made the sign of the
cross over the child's mouth, and asked: 'Who is your
father?' The infant answered: 'A wretched, miserable
man in the outskirts of this assembly, that is my father.'
So Bishop Bron's good name was saved.

May 21

Psalm 1:1   Jeremiah 4:22   John 10:1-10

BE SUBMISSIVE TO GOOD, UNBENDING TO
EVIL.

Our society teaches us to be suspicious of what is
good, and to listen passively to whatever is evil. It is
imperative that we learn to be teachable and
submissive if God is to use us. But even the
suggestions of the Thief must be given no
opportunity to remain. The difficulty may come in
deciding which voice is whose. And time spent with
the Shepherd is the surest way of recognizing His
voice, and of knowing when an impostor is seeking to
pursuade us. The true Shepherd would not say that,
He does not come to steal, kill or destroy.

May 22

Psalm 145:3-4, 7   Genesis 22:14-18
Romans 12:16a, 17b-18

BE GENTLE IN GENEROSITY, UNTIRING IN
LOVE, JUST IN ALL THINGS.

Bede speaks of Bishop Colman and his predecessors
Aidan and Finan:

The sole concern of the teachers of those days was to serve God, not the world, and to feed the soul, not the belly. The religious habit, therefore, was held in great respect at that time, so that whenever a cleric or monk appeared he was welcomed gladly by everyone as a servant of God. Even if one was discovered passing on the roads they would run up to him and bow their heads, and were glad to be signed with the cross by his hand or blessed by his lips; and they paid close heed to such men's exhortations. On the Lord's Day they gathered eagerly in the church or monasteries, not to get food for their bodies but to listen to the word of God; and if a priest came by chance to their village the people at once came together, eager to receive from him the word of life. The priests and clerics themselves visited the villages for no other reason than to preach, baptize, visit the sick and, in sum, to care for their souls; and so free were they from any taint or avarice that none accepted grants of land and estates for building monasteries unless compelled by the secular rulers!

Lord, daily order my steps that I might be transformed into your likeness; imperfect as I am, make me a mirror that reflects your uncompromising love. Covenant-keeper, make me like you.

Dave Cape

May 23

Psalm 145:14-17   Job 29:11-13a   Matthew 26:11a

BE RESPECTFUL TO THE WORTHY, MERCIFUL TO THE POOR.

It is no sin to have wealth, but it is sinful to be

attracted to wealth. It is the love of money, not money itself, which is the root of all evil.

Aidan, dining one Easter with King Oswald, was himself ill at ease with the feast set before them. Just then a servant arrived to say that many poor people had arrived at the castle asking for alms. Oswald with a wave of his arm ordered their own meal to be taken away and fed to the people outside, and the silver plate broken and distributed between them. Aidan was so overcome that he exclaimed, 'May the hand that did this never perish.'

Any society or 'civilization' may best be judged by the way it treats its weakest members.

May 24

Psalm 107:43   Joshua 6:25   Ephesians 4:26b

BE MINDFUL OF FAVOURS, UNMINDFUL OF WRONGS.

Caedmon of Whitby seemed to know he was about to die for he asked to be taken to the sick-house, and there he and his attendant talked and joked in good spirits with each of the other occupants until after midnight. Then Caedmon asked for the Eucharist. Taking it in his hand he asked if their hearts were all at peace with him, and they had no complaint, quarrel or ill-feeling towards him? They all replied that their hearts were entirely at peace with him and quite without anger, and they asked him in turn to be at peace with them in his heart. He quickly replied: 'My heart is at peace, little children, with all God's servants.' Then he received communion, and then enquired how long it was till the brothers had to awake to sing their nightly praises to the Lord. They replied, 'It will not be

long.' 'Good,' he said, 'then let us wait for that hour.'
He signed himself with the cross, laid his head on
the pillow, slept for a while, and so ended his life
happily, peaceably, in silence.

Bede

May 25

Psalm 119:19   Proverbs 22:29   Philippians 2:4

BE A LOVER OF THE ORDINARY MAN, AND DO
NOT WISH FOR RICHES.

Bede says of Aidan, 'He showed the authority befitting
a bishop in rebuking the proud and mighty, and was
merciful in bringing comfort to the weak and relief
and protection to the poor.'

Bill Hybels remarks that in the market-place 'profits,
quotas, sales reports, balance sheets, budgets and
competition' are what matter, not people: they have
become the lowest priority.

In the market-place we need to *make* time to
express interest in others – in their spouse, kids,
health, problems, goals, frustrations, hobbies,
holidays, and dreams. Competitors don't care about
these things, but brothers and sisters do.

We also need to be helpers in the market-place.
That may mean offering to take up slack in
another's work-load. It may mean staying late to
help a partner finish a report, or occasionally
working through lunch to help someone meet
a deadline.

May 26

Psalm 116:10-11   *Proverbs 22:11, 24-5*
Matthew 10:16

INSTEAD, COOL DOWN EXCITEMENT AND SPEAK YOUR MIND.

When people submerge their true feelings in order
to preserve harmony, they undermine the integrity
of a relationship. They buy peace on the surface,
but underneath there are hurt feelings, troubling
questions, and hidden hostilities just waiting to
erupt. It's a costly price to pay for a cheap peace,
and it inevitably leads to inauthentic relationships
...No one says anything 'unsafe'. They never
discuss misunderstandings, reveal hurt feelings, air
frustrations or ask difficult questions ...Offences
occur, but nobody talks about them. Doubts about
the other's integrity creep in, but they're never
dealt with. In time such relationships deteriorate.'

Bill Hybels

Denying our true feelings is not advisable, but
calmness can achieve reconciliation more easily than
raised voices or recriminations.

Cuthbert had difficulty in teaching the Rule to
some of the monastics of Lindisfarne. At chapter
meetings he was often worn down by bitter insults,
but would put an end to the arguments simply by
rising and walking out, calm and unruffled.

Next day he would give the same admonitions, as
though there had been no unpleasantness the
previous day. In this way he gradually won the love
and obedience of the brothers.

How do you respond when someone says
something uncomfortable to you? Do you overcome
your natural human instinct to reject it? Do you listen

and seek the truth in the other person's concerns? Or do you get angry? Do you slip into denial, retaliation or rationalization?

Well, do you?

May 27

Psalm 16:3   *Proverbs 27:17*   *James 3:1*

OBEY YOUR SENIORS, KEEP UP WITH YOUR JUNIORS, EQUAL YOUR EQUALS, EMULATE THE PERFECT.

In other words, do not lag behind or become competitive. Show respect to everybody, especially those who have been on the road longer than you. Look especially to those who do not seem to have become embittered or suspicious or sarcastic. Take note of those who seem to carry around the presence of Jesus, learn the secret of their relationship with Him.

May 28

Psalm 19:13   *Proverbs 25:6*   *Hebrews 12:12*

DO NOT ENVY YOUR BETTERS, OR GRIEVE AT THOSE WHO SURPASS YOU, OR CENSURE THOSE WHO FALL BEHIND, BUT AGREE WITH THOSE WHO URGE YOU ON.

Herebert the anchorite of Derwentwater was long a spiritual friend of Cuthbert and would visit him once a year 'with a desire to be ever more enflamed, by the help of his teaching, with longing for the things of Heaven'.

On one such occasion Cuthbert said to Herebert,

'whatever need you have, ask me now, for I am certain that the time is at hand for me to leave aside this earthly tabernacle.'

Herebert begged him that they pray God that in His mercy as they had served Him together on earth, they might pass together to Heaven and behold His grace.

They never saw each other again on earth, but both died the following March 20, companions again.

May 29

Psalm 53:1-4   *Ecclesiastes 4:10*
1 Thessalonians 3:13

THOUGH WEARY DO NOT GIVE UP.

I continued to press on, limping, my feet aching, slipping, sliding, desperately wanting to sit down, chilled to the marrow. Even in this sopping wet state I could feel the hot tears welling in my eyes. Eventually I cried out to God and said, 'God, what is this all about? Why am I out here? What am I doing here? Am I crazy?' Then came the still, small voice of the Spirit as I sensed the Lord saying, 'No, David, I am just teaching you to endure; I am just checking you out.'

Finally after some six hours Carol arrived to collect me and I could hardly bend down to get into the car. I looked at her and said, 'If I were a quitter, today would be the day I quit,' but as Carol turned the car, I knew once again the Lord was saying, 'No-one, after putting his hand to the plough and looking back, is fit for the Kingdom of God.' (*Dave Cape*, On The Road With Jesus.)

All good soldiers keep on fighting. Don't grow weary in well-doing. Just keep looking unto Jesus, 'cause when this age comes to an end I've read the book, and we win!'

Reba Rambo/Dony McGuire

May 30

Psalm 56:8   Ezra 3:11-13   Philippians 4:4,6

WEEP AND REJOICE AT THE ONE TIME OUT OF
ZEAL AND HOPE.

At Hackness a nun called Begu was resting when she
heard the chapel bell tolling summoning the sisters to
pray for a departing soul. She saw the roof gone and
all flooded with light and the soul of abbess Hild being
escorted to Heaven by many angels. She opened her
eyes to realize she was sat amongst the other sisters,
and it was a dream. Running to her own abbess,
Frigyth, she announced that Hild had been taken from
them. The sisters hurried to chapel where they sang
psalms until a messenger arrived to bring news of the
death of Abbess Hild which to the messenger's
surprise was no surprise to them at all. The reality of
the joy of her passing mingled with all their sadness
at her loss.

May 31

Psalm 119:31-2   Isaiah 40:28-31
Philippians 2:12,   Hebrews 10:38

ADVANCE WITH DETERMINATION, BUT
ALWAYS FEAR FOR THE END.

When Brigid was out with her sheep she saw
Nindid the scholar running past. 'What are you
running like that for? and what are you seeking?'
she said. 'I am going to heaven' he replied. Brigid
begged him to pause and pray with her that her
passage there might be easy. 'I can't stop now', he
said, 'you see, the gates of Heaven are open now and
who knows how long it may be before they shut.'

But he stayed and together they prayed an 'Our Father' for he and Brigid and the many thousands she would drag through the gates behind her.

Life of Brigid

As Christians we need to be reliable in both word and deed and not to compromise on that which we promise the Father and others we will do. Being out on the road far from familiar surroundings, we find ourselves continually tempted by the enemy's weapons of mediocrity and compromise. Some days would be extremely hot, making walking a test of endurance, other days would be cold or windy, and people who accompanied me or met with me would often express surprise at my being out in those extreme conditions. My reply would simply be: The weather might have changed, but God hasn't changed his mind. He didn't tell me to walk if the sun was shining or if it wasn't raining, or if it was a beautiful calm day without any wind; he simply said, 'Go'.

Dave Cape, On the Road with Jesus

June Readings
Jesus of the Scars

June 1

Psalm 22:16, 30–31   Isaiah 52:15   Luke 24:30–40

Question: What are the only man-made things
in Heaven?

Answer: The wounds in the hands, feet and side
of Jesus.

'If we have never sought, we seek thee now;
Thine eyes burn throughout the dark,
     our only stars;
We must have sight of thorn pricks on thy brow,
We must have thee, O Jesus of the scars.'

Edward Shillito,
written towards the end of the First World War

June 2

Psalm 129:3–4   Isaiah 50:6–9   1 Peter 2:22–4

Jesus' hands and feet were not just anyone's hands
and feet, but the signs of his real bodily presence.
They were the hands and feet of Jesus marked with
the wounds of his crucifixion. It is of great spiritual
importance that Jesus made himself known to his
disciples by showing them his wounded body. The
resurrection had not taken his wounds away but,
rather, they had become part of his glory. They had
become glorified wounds.

Jesus is the Lord who came to save us by dying
for us on the Cross. The wounds in Jesus' glorified
body remind us of the way in which we are saved.
But they also remind us that our own wounds are

much more than roadblocks on our way to God. They show us our own unique way to follow the suffering Christ, and they are destined to become glorified in our resurrected life. Just as Jesus was identified by his wounds, so are we.

Henri Nouwen

June 3

Kevin - died in 618 at Glendalough, Ireland, where a monastery and school grew up after he came there as a hermit.

Psalm 109:30-31   *Lamentations 1:12*
Revelation 1:7

In the Cross of Christ God says to man, 'That iswhere you ought to be. Jesus my Son hangs there in your stead. His tragedy is the tragedy of your life. You are the rebel who should be hanged on the gallows. But Lo, I suffered instead of you, and because of you, because I love you in spite of what you are. My love for you is so great that I meet you there, there on the Cross. I cannot meet you anywhere else. You must meet me there by identifying yourself with the One on the Cross. It is by this identification that I, God, can meet you in Him, saying to you as I say to Him, My Beloved Son.'

Emil Brunner

June 4

Psalm 22:7-9   *Jeremiah 29:13-14*   *Luke 22:61-2*

Hast thou no scar?
No hidden scar on foot, or side, or hand?
I hear thee sung as mighty in the land,
I hear them hail thy bright ascendant star:
Hast thou no scar?

Hast thou no wound?
Yet, I was wounded by the archers, spent
Leaned Me against the tree to die, and rent
By ravening beasts that compassed Me, I swooned:
Hast thou no wound?

No wound? No scar?
Yet, as the Master shall the servant be,
And piercèd are the feet that follow me:
But thine are whole. Can he have followed far
Who has no wound? No scar?

Amy Carmichael

June 5

Psalm 116:1-2   1 Chronicles 4:9-10   John 12:24

From prayer that asks that I may be
Sheltered from winds that beat on Thee
From fearing when I should aspire,
From faltering when I should climb higher
From silken self, O Captain free,
Thy soldier who would follow Thee.

From subtle love of softening things,
From easy choices, weakenings.
Not thus are spirits fortified,
Not this way went the Crucified.
From all that dims Thy Calvary
O Lamb of God deliver me.

Give me the love that leads the way,
The faith that nothing can dismay
The hope no disappointment tire,
The passion that will burn like fire.
Let me not sink to be a clod,
Make me Thy fuel, flame of God.

Amy Carmichael

June 6

Psalm 69:13   *Zephaniah 3:14-17*
                    2 Corinthians 5:14-15

Love's as hard as nails,
Love is nails:
Blunt, thick, hammered through
The medial nerves of One
Who, having made us, knew
The thing he had done:
Seeing (with all that is)
Our cross, and his.

                                        C. S. Lewis

June 7

Psalm 32:5   *Micah 7:8-9*   *Galatians 6:14*

Knowing God without knowing our own
wretchedness makes for pride. Knowing our own
wretchedness without knowing God makes for
despair.

Knowing Jesus Christ strikes the balance
because he shows us both God and our own
wretchedness. Jesus is a God whom we can
approach without pride and before whom we can
humble ourselves without despair.

                                        Blaise Pascal

June 8

Psalm 37:23-4   Job 42:7-9   Matthew 16:21-6

Deny Yourself

Peter did not understand. Jesus did not come to be
a great healer and miracle worker; nor did He come
to be King. He came to show God's character,
which is mercy and compassion. He healed people;
but His purpose in coming to earth was to go to the
cross. We all accept that now, because it is history.
We know about the resurrection. We have the
benefit of hindsight. The disciples did not, and they
were shocked.

But what about the Messiah's followers? Their
expectations of Him had just been radically altered,
and Jesus was about to do the same to their
expectations of themselves. The followers of a king
are in for a good time – power, prestige, influence –
that is what everyone wants. But if the king is going
to die, what of his followers? Before they had time
to think it through, Jesus let them know. **'If any
man will come after me, let him deny himself
and take up his cross, and follow me.'**

Maurice Barratt

June 9

Columba (521-597) (see November 18; September 5,
26; February 19)
Psalm 71:1-4   Hosea 6:1-3   Philippians 3:7-11

When we say 'Christ has died', we express the truth
that all human suffering in time and place has been
suffered by the Son of God who also is the Son of all
humanity and thus has been lifted up into the inner
life of God Himself. There is no suffering – no guilt,

shame, loneliness, hunger, oppression, or
exploitation, no torture, imprisonment, or murder,
no violence – that has not been suffered by God.
There can be no human beings who are completely
alone in their sufferings, since God, in and through
Jesus, has become Emmanuel, God with us. The
Good News of the gospel, therefore, is not that God
came to take our suffering away, but that God
wanted to become part of it.

Henri Nouwen

June 10

Psalm 27:1   Isaiah 9:2, 6   John 1:4-5; 18:25

A Light came out of darkness;
    No light, no hope had we,
Till Jesus came from Heaven
    Our light and hope to be.
Oh, as I read the story
    From birth to dying cry,
A longing fills my bosom
    To meet Him by and by.

Yet deeper do I ponder,
    His Cross and sorrow see,
And ever gaze and wonder
    Why Jesus died for me.
And shall I fear to own Him?
    Can I my Lord deny?
No! let me love Him, serve Him,
    And meet Him by and by.

William A. Hawley

June 11

Psalm 28:1   Isaiah 64:1   Jeremiah 8:22
Hebrews 11:13-15

The heavens frighten us; they are too calm;
In all the universe we seem to have no place.
Our wounds are hurting us, where is thy balm?
Lord Jesus, by thy scars, we claim thy grace.

Edward Shillito

June 12

Psalm 39:7   Genesis 18:23-6, 31-2   Luke 19:40-41

One of the Just Men came to Sodom, determined to
save its inhabitants from sin and punishment. Night
and day he walked the streets and markets
protesting against greed and theft, falsehood and
indifference. In the beginning, people listened and
smiled ironically. Then they stopped listening: he
no longer even amused them. The killers went on
killing, the wise kept silent, as if there were no Just
Man in their midst.

One June a child, moved by compassion for the
unfortunate teacher, approached him with these
words:

'Poor stranger, you shout, you scream, don't you
see that it is hopeless?'

'Yes, I see,' answered the Just Man.

'Then why do you go on?'

'I'll tell you why. In the beginning, I thought I
could change man. Today, I know I cannot. If I still
shout today, if I still scream, it is to prevent man
from ultimately changing me.'

Elie Wiesel

June 13

Psalm 147:3   Zechariah 13:6   John 20:19-20, 26-7

If when the doors are shut, thou drawest near,
Only reveal those hands, that side of thine;
We know today what wounds are, have no fear,
Show us thy scars, for we know the countersign.

The other gods were strong, but thou wast weak;
They rode, and thou with Cross didst stumble to a
    throne;
But, to our wounds, only God's wounds can speak,
And no god has wounds, but, Thou alone!

                           Edward Shillito

June 14

Psalm 86:8,11   Isaiah 53:4-5   1 Corinthians 1:23

I see your hands,
not white and manicured,
but scarred and scratched and competent,
reach out –
not always to remove the weight I carry,
but to shift its balance, ease it,
make it bearable.
Lord, if this is where you want me,
I'm content.
No, not quite true. I wish it were.
All I can say, in honesty, is this:
If this is where I'm meant to be,
I'll stay. And try.
Just let me feel your hands.
And, Lord, for all who hurt today –
hurt more than me –
I ask for strength and that flicker of light,
the warmth, that says you're there.

        Eddie Askew, Many Voices, One Voice

June 15

Psalm 22:1-2   Song of Solomon 3:2   John 20:13

The nursery poem ends with the exclamation:
'God's in His heaven,
all's right with the world.'

Our experience tells us, that whether God's in His
heaven or not, all is certainly not all right with the
world. Perhaps He is not there after all – that is how it
seems.

In Buechner's novel *The Final Beast* a young
minister whose wife has recently died listens
ironically to one of his little daughters praying
seriously to 'Our Father who aren't in heaven.'
He feels he cannot correct her very easily.

June 16

Psalm 42:3   Lamentations 1:16   Matthew 24:8, 19

Fear

Today the ghetto knows a different fear,
Close in its grip, Death wields an icy scythe.
An evil sickness spreads a terror in its wake,
The victims of its shadow weep and writhe.

Today a father's heartbeat tells his fright
And mothers bend their heads into their hands.
Now children choke and die with typhus here,
A bitter tax is taken from their bands.

My heart still beats inside my breast
While friends depart for other worlds.
Perhaps, it's better – who can say? –
Than watching this, to die today?

No, no, my God, we want to live!
Not watch our numbers melt away.
We want to have a better world.
We want to work - we must not die!
                        Eva Picková, aged 12
                        b. 1929 - d. 1943, Auschwitz

June 17

Psalm 10:1   *Isaiah 45:3-6*   *John 20:27-9*

Strike the thick cloud of unknowing with the sharp
dart of longing love, and on no account think of
giving up.

                        Cloud of Unknowing c. 1370

After the Second World War the following words were
found written on the wall of a Nazi concentration
camp.

I believe in the sun, even when it isn't shining,
I believe in love, even when I feel it not,
I believe in God, even when He is silent.

June 18

Psalm 103:10-12   *Micah 7:18-19*
                 Ephesians 3:14-19

The remarkable Dutch lady, Corrie Ten Boom, you
may recall, lost her beloved sister, Betsy, in a Nazi
concentration camp during the last war. The Ten
Boom family had harboured Jews at their home in
Holland, and the Gestapo exacted a terrible price.
   Corrie was spared and survived the horrors of
the awful camp at Ravensbruck. Afterwards she
dedicated her life to witnessing for Christ by
conducting meetings and writing several books

about her experiences. Eventually, a motion picture of her life story was made. It was called *The Hiding Place*. Corrie tells a very moving incident which happened during one of her testimony meetings in Germany, after the war. She had just finished speaking to the German congregation about the love of God and how He can forgive even our worst sins. 'In fact', she declared, 'God takes our sins and casts them into the deepest ocean.' After the service, as people were leaving the church, she noticed a balding, heavy set man, in a grey overcoat making his way towards her as she stepped off the platform. As he drew closer, her blood ran cold, for she instantly recognized him as one of the cruel, wicked guards from Ravensbruck where both she and Betsy had been so inhumanely treated. Now this guard stood before her with an outstretched hand.

June 19

Psalm 130:7b   *2 Kings 10:15*   *Romans 5:5*

The man began to speak. 'A fine message, Fraulein! How good it is to know that, as you say, all our sins are at the bottom of the sea. You mentioned Ravensbruck in your talk. Well, I was a guard there.' It was obvious to Corrie that he had not recognized her. But she had never forgotten his face. The man continued: 'You know, since that time I have found Christ as my Saviour and I know that he has forgiven me for all the terrible things I did. However, I would like to hear you say it too, Fraulein.' Again he reached out his hand. 'Will you forgive me too?' Corrie stood, looking into the face of her former tormentor, a man responsible for the death of her sister. She recoiled in anger and contempt as the terrible memories came flooding back. Hatred welled up within her. How could she forgive this man? She held her own hand behind her back as she wrestled with the awful contradictions raging inside her. Love and forgiveness had been her message to others. But right now it seemed impossible to practice it herself. One of her favourite sayings was: Forgiveness is not an emotion; it is an act of the will. Poor Corrie, her emotions had failed her. All that remained now was her will. Silently, she lifted up a prayer to heaven.'Jesus, please help me. I can stretch out my hand. I can do that much. You supply the feeling.'Awkwardly, hesitatingly, she reached out her hand. Suddenly her prayer was answered, for immediately her heart was filled with the love of God for this man.'I forgive you, my brother!' she cried.'With all my heart I forgive you too.'

June 20

Psalm 86:5   *Micah 6:8*   *Matthew 18:23-5*

Forgiveness is very easy to talk or even write about, but we need the power of the Holy Spirit to actually forgive. For the Christian, forgiveness is not optional. It is mandatory.

Henry Ward Beecher said 'We are most like beasts when we kill. We are most like men when we judge. We are most like God when we forgive.' Go ahead – stretch out that hand of forgiveness to someone today. Write that letter, make that call, as God for Christ's sake has forgiven you. And always remember the words of Corrie Ten Boom: 'Forgiveness is not an emotion. It's an act of your will.'

D. Goudy

June 21

Psalm 116:10-11   Jeremiah 6:14   Colossians 2:4

Easy answers that come glibly off the tongue are insulting, hurtful and insensitive – especially in times of deep suffering. 'It will be all right in the end', someone says. Will it? Maybe. But often that is not the case. 'There is a purpose in all this', says another. This implies that God intended this awful situation, that he approves of suffering. (Even if, as sometimes happens, we bring trouble on to ourselves we would be insulting God to suggest that the wreckage was his idea in the first place.)

What we can say truthfully in a bad and trying situation is this: 'This is not without significance.'

All that we deeply experience is significant (even if it was not what we or God intended to happen!)

June 22

Psalm 130:4   1 Kings 1:49-53   Matthew 6:14-15

Jesus' prayer was, 'Father, forgive them;
   they know not what they do.'
A prayer born in death, writhing with pain.
A prayer risking faith, facing the sorrow.
A prayer living in hope, seeing the future.
My prayer was, 'God, how can I forgive them?
   They do know what they did.'
A prayer saying, 'It still hurts.'
A prayer wanting vengeance.
A prayer seeking direction.
My prayer became, 'God, help me forgive them;
   they know what they did.'
A prayer saying, 'They were wrong.'
A prayer wanting reconciliation.

A prayer seeking courage.
My prayer became,'God, forgive them;
    they know what they did.'
A prayer that wrestled with injustice.
A prayer that acknowledges weakness.
A prayer that found hope in God's love.
My prayer remains,'God, forgive them;
    they know what they did.'
Because forgiving recreates life from death.
Because forgiving cleanses the healing wound.
Because forgiving builds the bridge of freedom.

A client, in Jared P. Pingleton, The Role
and Function of Forgiveness

June 23

Psalm 143:3-4   *Lamentations 3:27-31*
Mark 14:33-4, 37

To be human is to be lonely. To be human, however,
is also to respond. The human person has always
responded to this pain.

Sometimes it has moved us to greater depth of
openness towards God and others, to fuller life, and
sometimes it has led us to jump off bridges, to end
life; sometimes it has given us a glimpse of heaven,
sometimes it has given us a glimpse of hell;
sometimes it has made the human spirit, sometimes
it has broken it; always it has affected it. For
loneliness is one of the deepest, most universal, and
most profound experiences that we have.

Even if you are a relatively happy person who
relates easily to others and who has many close
friends, you are probably still lonely at times. If you
are a very sensitive person, the type who feels
things deeply, you are probably, to some degree,
lonely all the time.

Ronald Rolheiser, The Restless Heart

June 24

Psalm 84:4-6   *Ecclesiastes 2:22-3*
1 Corinthians 10:13

Carl Rogers once said:

> I have most invariably found that the very feeling
> which has seemed to me most private, most
> personal and hence, most incomprehensible by
> others, has turned out to be an expression for
> which there is a resonance in many people. It has
> led me to believe that what is most personal and
> unique in each of us is probably the very element
> which would, if it were shared and expressed,
> speak most deeply to others.

June 25

Psalm 18:29   *Isaiah 59:1-2*
Ephesians 2:14, 16-18

> We knock fists against the walls that wall us off
> from brothers. Give them to hear us. Give us to hear
> the terrible needs that beat like hearts behind
> brothers' walls.
> We knock fists against the walls that wall us off
> from You. Hear us and know the loneliness of lives
> walled up in flesh and rib.
>
> *Frederick Buechner,* The Final Beast

June 26

Psalm 143:10   *Jeremiah 29:11*   *Ephesians 5:15-19*

Lead me, Lord, lead me by Your Spirit,
Make Your will clear for my future.

For it is You, Lord,
You, the Wounded Healer
who makes my heart sing
and my feet dance for joy

Fill me, Lord, fill me with Your Spirit,
Spirit of love, Spirit of joy and peace.
Be my Rock, be my rock of refuge,
of courage and strength for my journey.
Heal me, Lord, heal me by Your Spirit,
my every wound, my every need and want.

For it is You, Lord,
You, the Wounded Healer
Who makes my heart sing
and my feet dance for joy.

June 27

Psalm 27:1-6   Isaiah 42:5-7   Luke 22:47-8

Why did it have to be a friend
who chose to betray the Lord?
And why did he use a kiss to show them
That's not what a kiss is for?
Only a friend can betray a friend,
A stranger has nothing to gain,
And only a friend comes close enough
To ever cause so much pain.

And why did there have to be a
Thorny crown pressed upon His head?
It should have been a royal one,
Made of jewels and gold instead.
It had to be a crown of thorns
Because, in this life that we live,
For all who would seek to love
A thorn is all this world has to give.

And why did it have to be,
A heavy cross He was made to bear?
And why did they nail His feet and hands?
His love would have held Him there.
It was a cross, for on a cross
A thief was supposed to pay,
And Jesus had come into this world
To steal every heart away.
Yes, Jesus had come into this world
To steal every heart away.

Michael Card

June 28

Psalm 119:80   Isaiah 1:6   Philippians 2:5-8

It is because of the refusal to be vulnerable that, far
too often, instead of enjoying friendship and
intimacy with those around us, we find ourselves
fencing with each other, using our talents,
achievements, and strengths as weapons.

To be vulnerable in the true sense does not mean
that someone must become a doormat, a weakling,
devoid of all pride, going out of his way to let others
know all of his faults and weaknesses. Nor is
vulnerability to be confused with the idea of
'letting-it-all-hang-out', or any other form of
psychological strip-tease. To be vulnerable is to be
strong enough to be able to present ourselves
without false props, without an artificial display of
our credentials. In brief, to be vulnerable is to be
strong enough to be honest and tender. Like Jesus,
the person who is vulnerable is a person who cares
enough to let himself be weak, precisely because he
does care.

Ronald Rolheiser, The Restless Heart

June 29

Psalm 38:4-5, 22   *Isaiah 53:4*   *Luke 10:34*

A debtor to mercy alone,
Of covenant mercy I sing;
Nor fear with thy righteousness on,
My person and off'rings to bring,
The terrors of law, and of God,
With me can have nothing to do;
My saviour's obedience and blood,
Hide all my transgressions from view.

The work which his goodness began,
The arm of his strength will complete;
His promise is Yea, and Amen,
And never was forfeited yet;
Things future, nor things that are now,
Not all things below nor above,
Can make him his purpose forgo,
Or sever my soul from his love.

My name from the palms of his hands,
Eternity will not erase;
Impress'd on his heart it remains,
In marks of indelible grace;
Yes, I to the end shall endure,
As sure as the earnest is giv'n;
More happy but not more secure,
The glorified spirits in heav'n.

Augustus M. Toplady (1771)

June 30

Psalm 31:1   *Isaiah 54:4-5*   *Hebrews 2:9-10*

O Tree of Calvary,
Send thy roots deep down
into my heart.
Gather together the soil of my heart,
the sands of my fickleness,
the stones of my stubbornness,
the mud of my desires,
bind them all together,
O Tree of Calvary,
interlace them with thy strong roots,
entwine them with the network
of thy love.

Chandran Devanesen

July Readings
Tapestry

This month the notes have been prepared as responses by thirty one different individuals. We call it a Tapestry.

Our lives are touched by each others', and the strands of our own experience are also interwoven and offered back to God.

July 1

Psalm 8:3   *Genesis 1:1*   *John 1:38-9*

Send down a Drop From Heaven of Your Holy Spirit.

Fingers roving across strings
Same tunes, accurate, precise, well rehearsed.
Solid and dependable is the accompaniment.
Always reliable. Always in control. Always
     predictable.
Moving with the rhythm, we're alive.

Send down a drop from Heaven of your Holy Spirit.

And the sound is changing.
Clumsily at first, but the tune is new.
A thirst for the new song, struggle to catch the
     chorus, make the melody.
Vulnerable, the guard is down, pushing the
     boundaries.
Moving with this rhythm, we're alive.

Send down a drop from Heaven of your Holy Spirit.

Close your eyes. Bend the note. Pour out your heart
     through these strings
Beyond understanding.

A new solidity, a new dependance.
Always reliable. Always in control. Never predictable.
And moving in this rhythm, he's alive.

Send down a drop from Heaven of your Holy Spirit.

Jeff Sutheran

July 2

Psalm 27:4–5   Proverbs 8:22–6   Matthew 4:21–2

To
behold
the
beauty
of the
Lord

The eyes of the child are wide.
His hand is empty.
The fingernails are gnarled and useless.
All I see is ugliness.
Where are You now, Lord?

His face is expanding with effort, willing a smile.
They say. 'Smile for the cameras, child,
and all will be well.'
The world waits with bulging pockets.
All I feel is ugliness.

So often we meet situations which we are unable to
understand, which disturb us, and we ask, Where is
God now? And yet, God's pain was beautiful,
burning and beautiful. The body on the Cross. The
hope to which we cling. Help us to respond in the
right way.

Sarah Hay

July 3

Psalm 127:3   *Proverbs 8:27-8*   *Luke 8:51-5*

'My dear ones, Lord, bless Thou and keep.'

Our Daniel was a very planned arrival. Yes, he was born out of our love. But we already had Rachel; and she should not be lonely. As we viewed it a brother or sister should not be too far removed in age, so exactly one year to the day after Rachel was born, Daniel Andrew Kirby arrived, bringing all the explosive change that a new baby brings. Totally precious and unique.

Now, eight years on, Daniel has placed himself, like his namesake, in the proverbial 'lion's den' many times (stocking up many grey hairs that I am sure will all descend on me at once and overnight). He is accident prone where Rachel is careful, explodes on the scene where Rachel is quiet, and now speaks fluent Shilbottle, a dialect all on its own. However underneath all that boisterousness God has given us a great charge to look after. Behind his 'Boy' exterior is a sensitive child of God. Yes, he still misses the boat and I sometimes wonder whether there is a motivational gift of 'chaos bringer'!

God has given me a very junior teacher. The fruit of the Spirit is love, peace, patience, kindness, goodness, faithfulness, gentleness, self control. I have constantly required them, and Daniel relentlessly points out where I lack them. I think that both Daniel and Rachel are, as any child to a parent, a most precious gift.

Graham Kirby

July 4

Psalm 148:1-2   Ezekiel 28:13-17   Isaiah 14:12-15
Luke 6:12-16; 9:1-2, 10:1-2, 17-20

**'Do with me what you will. Whatever you do,
I will thank you.'**

Sometimes I find God trying to direct my path
in one way, but I want to go another. For example,
the job I'm in at the moment I don't enjoy. I find
it really hard to do sometimes, but I know that
it is part of God's plan for my life that I do it. So if I
just left, as I often feel like doing, that would be
going against God's will. By trying to allow God to
take 100 per cent control of my life I quite often
find myself having to make difficult decisions
because I want to go one way and I know
God wants me to go another. I have to have a
broken will!

I know that only through this, will God be able to
mould me to be the person He wants me to be. But
the most difficult thing of all, sometimes, is
thanking God for sending me down a path, one that
perhaps I didn't want to take, but that deep down I
know is the best way to live my life, the best way to
be close to God.

Jonathan Campbell

July 5

Psalm 116:6   Genesis 1:2   Matthew 16:24-17:9

**'Deliver us, Lord, from every evil, and grant us
peace in our day.'**

In 1989 we were involved in a serious road

accident. Two admitted to hospital, two patched up in casualty, and then the trauma of it happening to us.

Why us? Why not!

At the time there was a sense of unreality, the initial moment you realize 'it', whatever it is, is going to happen. My cry of 'Oh God, he's not stopping' was involuntary and verbal; my reaction – in releasing the brake – an attempt to minimize damage by some action, also involuntary.

The unreality again; we hadn't hit anything. Then why in a heartstopping moment do you think you are the only one left alive? Blood and silence. No movement in the back of the vehicle.

Panic – no glasses, I can't see.

Panic – we must all get out of the vehicle – leaking petrol.

Panic in the hospital – the monitor stopped bleeping, I could see no breathing.

Panic – he's broken his neck. She's forgotten who we are, forgotten her own name.

Panic – a strange country. (Foreign now, in a way never noticed before.)

Thank you, Lord, for the friends that came running, picking us up when we were down, praying around hospital beds.

'Broken his neck? No, must have been a speck on the scan' and 'Of course I remember who I am.'

Finally, it's all over: time moves on; you are all changed for ever – but God was with you through it all, creating miracles of provision, minimizing bad circumstances, bringing people closer.

Brenda Grace

July 6

Psalm 148:3   *Genesis 1:3-4*   *Luke 22:8-12*

'Lord, You have always lightened this darkness of mine.'

I suppose I had always realized my life was a mess, but, it hadn't seemed too bad at the beginning. Then things went from bad to worse until finally I had to admit I had reached the end of the road. I was beaten and I had nowhere to turn. So in my desperation and despair I cried out to You.

And You, Lord, answered my call. If only I had known that all I had to do was ask. All that misery and pain could have been avoided. Because You were always there, weren't You? I just didn't trust what I really knew to be the truth. I trusted in me and not in You.

And so with infinite patience and love, not like a judge, but like a father reaching for his erring son, You began to change me. Now when I look back at even the darkest times I see You there lighting that darkness and creating something beautiful out of misery and pain. Praise to you, Lord Jesus Christ, King of endless glory.

Sean Williams

July 7

Boisil – Prior at Melrose who first welcomed Cuthbert and recognized how greatly God's hand would be upon him.

Whilst dying of the plague he asked to spend a week with Cuthbert in reading John's gospel and prophesied that one day God wanted Cuthbert to be a bishop.

Psalm 148:4   *Genesis 1:5-7*   *John 18:15-16*

**'This day be within and without me,
Lowly and meek, yet all powerful'**

The greatest joy of the Christian life is the eternal
Presence of Christ within. When I ask Him to be
within and without I am handing over to Him every
situation of the day, allowing Him to act. He then
enables me to be less fearful, less aggressive, more
patient, more caring – in short, to become more
like Him.

Jean Patterson

July 8

Psalm 148:5-6   *Genesis 1:8*   *Mark 14:33-4, 37-9*

**'Whoever has chosen to make the shelter of the
Most High their dwelling place will stay in His
over-shadowing.'**

As we entered the beautiful chapel we were each
given a small lit candle. The atmosphere was
hushed and subdued. We watched as a mime and
then a dance were presented. Then we commenced
what we had gathered for – Compline. This has
long been my favourite office of the day. Sleep has
always come easy after Compline. Going to bed
rested and secure in the 'over-shadowing' of the
Most High. But tonight is different. Tonight the
Compline is convicting, making me realize that I, by
my sin, have put myself outside of His 'shelter'. As I
walk back to my room the cold night reflects how I
feel inside: out in the cold. Back in my room I read
again. 'I will not lie down tonight with sin, nor shall
sin, nor sin's shadow, lie down with me.' As I make

my peace with God, I become aware that, once
again, I have 'chosen to make the shelter of the
Most High my dwelling place' and I lay down to
sleep secure 'in His over-shadowing'.

Derrick Thompson

July 9

Psalm 148:7-13   *Genesis 1:9*   *John 19:25-7*

**'Let thy face, O Lord, shine forth upon us,
and be Thou merciful to us.'**

This is me speaking as a mother who has been in
the 'nappy trap', unable to get out because of
children being sick and children who do not sleep
and want to be fed all of the time (and when you
are breast-feeding every two hours it can be quite
tiring). Even now, being a mum, just the thought
makes me tired ... but apart from that my 'brats' are
my little rays of sunshine ...

Changing from having a job to being a housewife
and mother can alter your view on life and bring
about problems from all directions, making you
feel trapped, and unable to focus on what needs
to be done.

It's at this time this has been my prayer, that
God's face would shine upon me so I can see clearly
how good life is, and for Him to deal kindly with
me, during these busy times.

Susan McGuinness

July 10

Psalm 18:4-5   *Genesis 1:10*   *John 11:33-6*
2 Corinthians 1:3-5

'Let the beauty of the Lord our God be upon us.'

To work with the newly bereaved, within hours of the death is a challenge and a privilege. So many say to me 'How ever do you manage to cope with your work?' Yet rarely is it actually possible to speak of vocation; a call to love and serve this group of people. The call came first and only later did I learn of the Rule of Availability and Vulnerability that made so much sense of what I believed. An availability to God, not in some 'super-spiritualized' conscious way, but in faith and intent that then allows me to be available to the families and friends and their needs. That leads to the vulnerability; and so often the need is for someone to share for just a few moments the intense burden of pain, and to be with them in it to try and show a way forward. And because my role is to be strength for them, only later to share the tears, knowing they are also the tears, and even anger, of the Father who never desired that his special creation should suffer death.

Father, those hours of terrible pain of Christ on the Cross gave away to beautiful moments of intimacy with Mary in the garden. Transform my bereavements and hidden hurts so that I can reach out a hand to those submerged in loss and enable You to be present in each encounter with Your love.

Anne Wadey

July 11

Psalm 65:9-10   *Genesis 1:11*   *John 20:6-10*

'Follow the example of good men of old.'

Where young and old with gladness dance with Me
I'll give My house of hospitality.
Don't store false treasure.
Follow their example, these good men of old;
and buy My field – with mothstrewn gold
True men and women who responded,
these were empty vessels, filled with treasure
hidden deep within them by My hand.
Freely you have received,
so freely you must give your plans to Me,
right from the start, then you will truly live.
Good men of old learned not to say,
'I'm sorry I believe'.
I look not for wary, reluctant
followers on the fringe.
Instead I shall allow, in full community
My Waymarks to proclaim My truth, My name,
empty vessels standing low awaiting
the ebb or flow from My deciding, guiding hand,
of waters hidden deep within the land.
'Son, they have little wine at this feast.'
And at her request the jars are filled,
even the best.
The water now offered is made choicest wine.
And the Father surely smiles.
Oh, to respond, empty vessels,
as good men of times past
and carry this vintage refreshment
to those coming last!

Ken Lydon

July 12

Psalm 137:4   *Genesis 1:12*   *John 21:20-24*

'How can I sing the Lord's song in a strange and weary land?'

How many years I have tried to be as I thought I should be. A lot of the time it was not doing this, not doing that. One personal battle I had for years was smoking, for me it was wrong, and yet I could not deal with it.

Putting pride aside one night at a gathering of believers I went forward and asked especially for prayer. Down I went, and out eventually went the need. Since then I have come to realize, it's not what we do that counts but what we are! Child of God, be yourself: the Father, Jesus and the Spirit made you – you! There is no one in all creation like you. So be yourself and let God make you real in His special way.

Colin Johnson

July 13

Psalm 65:8   *Genesis 1:13*   *John 21:25*

'He is able to bring the people to a place ...'

One of the hardest things to cope with in life is deep disappointment after heightened expectancy and so it was with mixed feelings that I set out from The Grange along with the other Trustees to 'view' yet another possible 'home' for the Nether Springs. We had already known disappointment, the need was great and yet again our hopes were high. After travelling for what seemed miles and miles of twisting lanes and narrow country roads we arrived at Hetton Hall, which seemed to be in the middle of nowhere.

As we walked around it, looked at its setting, the lovely garden and the magnificent Peel Tower, I wondered if the other Trustees felt as I did. Love at first sight! An overwhelming assurance that 'this is it', this is the place! This is home! It didn't take long to find out as tear-filled eyes and nodding heads confirmed what I was feeling in my own heart. We felt like the pilgrims in Psalm 126: 'Our mouths were filled with laughter, our tongues with songs of joy' as we echoed their understanding that 'The Lord has done great things for us and we are filled with joy'.

We returned to The Grange that Saturday afternoon with heightened expectancy knowing that there would be no deep disappointment to follow. Hetton Hall was to be the home of a Northumbria Community, Nether Springs was to take a giant step forward! We sat there in our meeting with no human resources of fabric or finance, but with a strong faith born of God. He would meet all our needs as we went forward in His Name. The unanimous decision was taken. Let's go for it!

'In His time, He makes all things beautiful, in His time. Lord, please show me every day, as you are teaching me your way, that you do just what you say, in your time.'

Trevor Miller

July 14

Psalm 56:8   *Genesis 1:14*   *Acts 1:12-14*

'My eyes run with tears because people do not obey your laws.'

I have experienced this before, the privilege of crying not only my tears, but those of the Father heart of God. But never more so than at Glastonbury.

Looking out from the big white wooden cross to the valley below, full of people, my whole body felt broken, weighted to the earth somehow. I knew my Lord was calling me to stay and pray. Yet how? Despite hesitations, I knew I had to stand His ground that night, and put down all of self, so His Spirit could lead. I had to only listen 'in the cell of my heart' and act on His words. For the next hour and twenty five minutes I moved from this alone.

I know that as I danced 'Cry for the Desert' God's heart poured out for pain-filled lives. I actually felt, and bore, for a little while, the pain of isolation, of destitution and addiction, of life abused and degraded, of loss of integrity and identity.

This night there were so many tears. My heart told me when to stop, that my friends would walk back into the house twenty minutes later – if I'd heard right. I didn't believe I'd got it right, but exactly on time they did – I was refreshed, and my spirit soared at the knowledge that I had simply heard and obeyed. What stops me doing that all the time?

Anita Callow

July 15

Psalm 136:7–9   *Genesis 1:15*   *Acts 4:1–4*

'His love that burns inside me impels me on the road.'

> The experience I had on Lindisfarne was at the feet of Aidan's statue while I was praying with friends. At that moment God entered my life in a strangely new and commanding way. I have since read with great admiration about Aidan and have seen God shining through in his attitudes and works. I especially admire his firmness when talking to Christians, telling them to have more faith, also his gentleness and love when evangelizing, either by words or actions.

Neil Arnold

July 16

Psalm 46:10   *Genesis 1:16*   *Mark 1:35*
                    Revelation 8:1

There is a contemplative
   in all of us,
almost strangled
   but still alive,
who craves quiet
   enjoyment of the Now,
and longs to touch
   the seamless garment
   of silence
   which makes whole.

> This is what I read hanging on the wall in a cottage on Lindisfarne. A call to stop and fulfil all that God had ever required of me. I tried not to look at it for

it was far too much, too real. Overwhelming and yet a complete answer to all the unasked questions within me. We prayed morning prayer and then the same words were spoken as prophecy over me. How could they have known my call and the deep desire of my heart? But God knew.

We went and stood, in the priory grounds, by the tall sculpted figure of Aidan. The sky grew black and the heavens opened. A heavenly baptism! As I left the island the sun reappeared as if to light me into a new way of life. It would take time to acknowledge my call and to find fulfilment in it. But in the end, peace, hope and reality.

Ervin Dörschler

July 17

Psalm 147:4-5   *Genesis 1:17-19*   *Acts 4:13-20*

'If so it be that I may see thy glory, even afar, and hear thy voice O God, and know that I am with thee.'

In 1716 Yamamoto Tsunetomo, a Buddhist priest, wrote *The Way of the Samurai*, a book describing the philosophical and spiritual disciplines of the Japanese warrior caste. In it he writes:

Every morning one should first do reverence to his master and parents and then to his patron deities. If he will only make his master first in importance, his parents will rejoice and the gods will give their assent. For a warrior there is nothing other than thinking of his master. If one creates this resolution within himself, he will always be mindful of his master's person and will not depart from him even for a moment.

Our most perfect service, to our Lord, ourselves and our Church, is never to depart from Him even for a moment. Our relationship with Jesus is the nether spring from which compassion, love and a wider responsibility arise to prompt us to serve those who are strangers to us and to Him.

'For a warrior there is nothing other than thinking of his master.'

Jackie Johnson

July 18

Psalm 18:6   Genesis 1:20   Acts 8:14–17

'He is my God, and I am trusting Him.'

In Your presence there is an absence
silencing my greatest fear.
It is with You that I know the essence
of what is life, now that You're near.

It is in the absence of Your presence
that I rekindle my desire;
and it is when I am without You
that I burn, an inextinguishable fire.

In Your presence there is an absence
of all that preys upon my mind;
for my heart's desire's before me,
and I leave all else behind.

It is in the absence of Your presence
that I have learned to be apart.
It is without You that I am with You;
for You are Joy within my heart.

Janet Rimmer
(21 April 1995, Lindisfarne)

July 19

Psalm 144:13-14   Genesis 1:21   Acts 8:18-20, 25

'For love of Him we offer friendship and welcome every guest.'

Hospitality.
To extend the hand of
Friendship.
To share your home.
To show Christ's love

Give help to the helpless,
Hope to the hopeless
And love to the loveless
Within the love of
A Christian home.

Mike Barfield

July 20

Psalm 40:3-5   Isaiah 43:20-1   1 John 1:1-5

'. . . a song keeps singing in my heart.'

I am learning the importance of seeking God's
heart. Not for the sake of others (although that may
be part of God's call to me) and not for myself
(although God has planted desires in my heart
which He is beginning to fulfil). No, I am learning to
seek God's heart for the sake of it, for that deep
communion with Him. And when we are in that
communion, we find our own heart-strings
vibrating in unison with those of God. Our
desires and decisions are one, and so our power
becomes one.

Allison Davies

July 21

Psalm 115:14   Genesis 1:22   1 John 5:5-10, 13

'in quietness born of trust'

I am blessed; I have God. I am secure; God has me.
I am lucky; I have a job too!

Each day I say my prayers on the half hour train
journey from Southport to Liverpool into work. For
months I struggled to grasp God's mission for me.
Mistakenly I thought I should be like other
Christians and ought to be involved in more
evangelistic or churchy type activities, but daily
prayer changed that. I now have a prayer list formed
of names of work colleagues, friends and family.
Most days I pray for their intentions, anxieties and
doubts; on other days I give each of them a mental
hug. This keeps me close to those who I miss of my
family in the North-East and creates more space for
all in the list in my small heart. This then is my
mission, to evangelize through love and by
example. Some of us must accept that our lives may
be routine or boring; but God is always there.
Through prayer I can be Christ to others. I have no
knowledge of how my actions influence other
people, but He knows. A smile, a word, a touch or
patient ear can mean so much, God will pass
opportunities to 'faith share' when He is ready.

He will give you the strength; strength to speak;
strength for silence. His Spirit is always there to join
with yours. Call on the strength of His Spirit today,
and together you will cross the valley of
uncertainty on a bridge of the wood of the Cross.

Michael Connaughton

July 22

Psalm 143:8   *Genesis 1:23-5*   *2 John 1-4, 12*

'This day is Your gift to me. I take it, Lord, from Your hand, and thank You for the wonder of it.'

I was brought up with the idea that God was the Creator. God had made everything; Jesus had redeemed us; the Holy Ghost was our Advocate. Everything was in the past, nothing was a now thing, even the term 'holy ghost' belonged to the dead.

Somehow all that has changed, for what I believe now is that God the Father did create everything and is still creating everything. God's presence in my life is on a day to day, minute to minute, microsecond to micro-second basis. I am still being formed into the likeness of my God. Over the past few years, it has come to my knowledge that I have Klinefelter's Syndrome. I was born with it, but only in the last few years is there an awareness of what it really means. Many women nowadays, finding out they have a foetus with such a chromosome formation have been told to have an abortion. Yet God, who is my Creator, is still forming me. He has given the strength to find out and then continue to live with that knowledge. Even through that knowledge God still continues to create.

I enjoy walking long distances, for it is here that I devote time to talking with my God. It is here I can be alone, away from the distractions of the bustle of daily life. The walk can be a distraction at first, with a shopping list of things to talk about. Then silence, in which to listen, and God talking in words which I can understand.

I work with people who are labelled as having 'profound or severe learning disabilities'. They allow me to see the child-like trust we must have in God the Father, Son and Holy Spirit. The people who are entrusted to me on a daily basis follow me like sheep. Even if I go round in circles, they follow. Thus it is with Christ in us (or at least it should be). To follow no matter where, or even how stupid it might feel at the time.

I never know what God has in store for me in any day. (It would be easy for me to plan my day round my image of God's desires; and maybe in this way I could cancel God out of my life.) Having a plan for the day which is flexible may be the better way.

The walk to work, which I prefer to do, for it is only a few miles, allows me that time to be with God, and to talk to Him. To remind myself each morning, not just as a prayer which I think should be said, but as a reminder to me that without God, I am nothing; I have nothing; I can do nothing: with God within me there are no limits to my abilities, for now I have everything.

Francis Leonard

July 23

Psalm 43:5   1 Kings 19:4   Luke 15:17-24

'Out of the depths, I have cried to You.'

In the depths I cried to myself, but that only caused my soul to drown more deeply in misery and my mind to become even more confused with no coherent thought. The depths seemed like a pit, a dark prison in which thoughts and feelings pulled each other further down into despair.

When, at last, I cried out of the depths to God, my soul was able to receive His grace and compassion which He had longed to give me. The well of desolation became the well-spring of His love. Love which flows through and around me, bringing forgiveness and restoration; so that with my whole heart I can praise Him.

Louise Whitfield

July 24

Psalm 88:11   *Isaiah 45:3*   *Revelation 1:9–18*

'Though the night is here, today I believe.'

(...I am glad and grateful to do this. Today, as I write, is very poignant for me and my family as it was on this date last year that we scattered Wyn's ashes on the out-going tide on Holy Island opposite St Cuthbert's Isle.)

This is written and drawn from the threshold of young grief; the death of my wife, a beautiful gift from God, given back to Him with love that frees.

The day, daytime, is full of life, full of happiness, of children, of plans and ambitions, of activities and interests, of barbecues. God put the sun in the sky to make us happy and, when we remember, we thank and bless Him for His goodness and gifts.

Night comes, as in pain, or grief, or loneliness, or searing questions and life is bereft of sunshine. We learn that happiness and busyness were surface activities and they die with darkness. In the night realities and memories come to birth, sometimes in dreams, sometimes in wakefulness, sometimes in panic and we pray for light and comfort. Then in the night and darkness, God comes Himself and we know Him. He has been there Himself and comes to us as He came to a garden and, if we watch Him we shall know that 'joy comes in the morning'. He says, 'I put the sun in the sky to keep you happy, but

when it gets dark I come Myself.' And that is joy.
Tears give place to joy, we see the stars again, and
know that joy is knowing God and that both are
eternal.

Today I believe.

Noel Bevan

July 25

Psalm 61:1-5, 8   Job 23:3-6   Luke 7:7
Revelation 3:20-21

'Though You be silent now
today I believe.'

Lord, I have nothing,
    help me to give even what I do not have.
Lord, I feel nothing,
    help me not to be jealous, that you may
    use me to touch others' hearts.
Lord, I am weary,
    help me to remember that you
        have been weary, too.
Lord, I need refreshing,
    help me to refresh others and to forget
    about my own needs.
Lord, I can't see the way ahead,
    help me not to get in the way
    of those who can.
Lord, I am disappointed,
    help me not to bring disappointment to others.
Lord, I have no one to help me,
    help me to trust in you.
Lord, I can't see you, yet you see me,
    help me to remember that.
Lord, I am not worthy to receive you,
    but only say the word and I shall be healed.

Hugh Barney

July 26

Psalm 8:5-8   Genesis 1:26   Revelation 4:1-11

**'All whom I love into Your safe keeping
All that I am into Your tender care.'**

When God looked at me, long before I ever saw Him, He knew all that I was, all that I might be. He knew me. He saw me.

Me, looking for Jesus, in a desperate, crumbling wreck of life, devastated by divorce, death, lies, cheating. He showed Himself, battered, beaten, dying on a cross. Dying my death, carrying my pain and despair.

He took, I gave: I gave, He took. He took the foundation of all that I was, and smashed it. I asked why I hurt so very much. He said, 'I love you, Steve', over and over again. I lost it all. I was ended, with nothing. When I had nothing, He said, 'I will repay the years the locusts have taken.' The cost of the new design? – the blood of Jesus. I have life, and in abundance. It has been painstakingly built with tender, loving care, to a new design.

For me, my wife and children, Jesus is everything. Coming to that place where He can hold you and you can trust Him, never, ever, to let go, is just so precious. I know His tender, loving care is tenderizing me into the man I must be. All He has given I share with Him. In 1 Peter 5:7 it says 'cast all your care on Him, for He cares for you.' I know, I *know* this to be true.

Steve Hartley

July 27

Psalm 122:8-9   *Genesis 1:27*   *Revelation 5:1-5*

**'He's touched something inside of me that's
now reaching out for Him, and I know that I
must go.'**

My Christian life had become like an old pair of
slippers; comfortable, unattractive, easily slipped on
or off. The fire, dedication, passion had been slowly
squeezed and faded into the past, apart from odd
flickerings. Then, I not only met 'the team' from the
Community, but through them, God met me, and I
rediscovered the life that Christ wants us to enjoy.
I saw, experienced, real Christian love and affection
once more and within my heart, found myself
getting excited about God (and His people) again.

I found a release in worship; God awakened gifts
I thought had died, my Christian heart began to
beat again regularly.

I do not know what God will have me do in the
future, in fact life has become more uncertain,
sometimes more difficult to cope with (the old
slippers have seemed attractive on fleeting
occasions), but I know God is real and is leading me
somewhere. All I want to do is follow, and on the
way, hopefully, point others to the reality of life
with God.

'To whom shall we go? You have the words of
eternal life.'

Paul Brain

July 28

Psalm 128:1-4   Isaiah 30:15   Matthew 19:20-22

'Do you seek Him with all your strength?'

It is easy seeking God when everything is going
fine, not so easy when decisions have to be made
that are life-changing, even harder when the cost is
letting go and handing over relationships and
situations to God. It is only in handing over we can
have any chance of contentment and peace.

'I quit my struggles, contentment at last. Jesus is
Lord of all.'

Kev Grimley

July 29

Psalm 19:7-11   Genesis 1:28-30
                        Revelation 7:9-17

'In this attitude of complete dependence, I become useful again.'

When my daughter began to walk her steps were
faltering and she often fell. She cried and shouted
until I ran to pick her up, and she expected me to
kiss it better and make everything all right again. As
she got better at walking, she was justifiably proud
of her achievements, and looked to me for approval
and encouragement. Her confidence grew, and she
started to toddle further and further from me.
Sometimes she walked out of sight and got
frightened. Sometimes she fell over. She still called,
and I came to make it better. As a Christian, I guess I
have been walking rather than toddling for some
time. I often run off with great confidence in my

own abilities – until I fall over, or get tripped up, or run out of sight of God, and find myself alone with my monsters. Then I am left calling out to God to save me, expecting Him to make it better again. It is right for me to be independent in some things. But how much better for me to know that God is the ground of my being, and that walking with Him is all the security I need! God has given me the world to play and work within, but one day I will stand in Heaven before Him, and want to know that I can look Him in the face and say, I did what I saw You doing, I went where I saw You going, and I depended on You through it all.

Dana Beney

July 30

Psalm 71:5-8   Isaiah 43:1-2   1 Peter 1:6-7

'So through my hurt Your love may shine.'

Seventeen months ago I broke my arm,
At a netball practice, playing well.
A shoot of goals could do no harm,
When all of a sudden I collided and fell.

Operations left me dazed.
Two steel plates so the bones would be strong.
Such a complicated break, I was amazed.
I had four more operations – my trial was long.

Life ever since has been such a struggle,
But kind friends and family pulled me through.
Physiotherapists taught me to juggle.
My recovery helped by the prayers and cards
     from you.

School was much harder, one arm in a sling.
Friends who once cared drifted apart.
Unkind words and stares, they sting,
But I knew God loved me deep in my heart.

A change in schools was a great idea.
New subjects and teachers; Ms Bowmer, Herr Weir.
I made lots of new friends who helped me get by,
When I found something hard they'd push me to try.

Coping alone would not have been easy,
But the prayers and support were always there.
I have the love and grace of Jesus,
And when I'm down he hears my prayer.

The dance at a christening was worded right for me:
Be strengthened by the things He brings you
through.
Spoke to me powerfully.
God loves me, that I knew.

On Easter day of 95,
My brother and I were baptized,
With all those who loved me by my side,
I wanted once more to be seen and not to hide.

Although it's still tough, I've had some great news,
A plate removed and mobility's fine.
Don't give up, you'll only lose,
Remember, through darkness God's love will shine.

Jessica Searle

July 31

Psalm 74:17   *Genesis 1:31*
Revelation 22:12-14, 16-17, 21

'He is able . . . only to bring the ones He wants to have there for His purposes.'

Hindsight would be a wonderful thing if it were possible to have it at the time when you feel you really need the knowledge. Sometimes we go through so much anguish because we are trying to control our circumstances. God often provokes, cajoles or puts us into situations so we go in a particular path. At times we are convinced that we see the picture clearly as to why we are doing something or going in a certain direction. At the end of the day through whatever path we may have been given, we arrive at the place where God wants us, and more importantly where God knows will be best for us. God provides us with our seat at His table.

Martin Frost

August Readings
What Gives You the Right?

August 1

Psalm 27:7-10   Deuteronomy 5:16   Mark 7:9-13

God's laws are there to protect us. Whether we have good or bad parents or, like most of us, something in between, it is important for us to honour and bless them. Sometimes it is necessary for a person to forgive a parent who has already died, and, even if it *is* only from one side, to make their peace.

No person can be to us *all* that we need, and only God is able to be A and O and all in between, to fill in the gaps where other people fail or disappoint us.

He is never a disappointment.

Judgements we have made against our parents may condemn us, and resentment can tie *us* up and cause us all kinds of damage as well as not freeing *them*. Often physical healings can be held back until resentments and bitterness are dealt with. Also, if you try to bless someone and they refuse to accept that, the worst thing that can happen is that you get more blessed instead! (Luke 10:5-6)

God can walk with us through all our memories until they become the peaceable Kingdom.

August 2

Psalm 44:1-7   Judges 1:8-13   Romans 8:14-18

Othniel already knew Achsah - they were cousins, and if he had not wanted to marry her he would not have taken the city for Caleb. To take the city was to ask for her hand. We know from Judges 3:8-11 that later Othniel would rise up and rescue his people, and finally be made the first judge over them.

We cannot know God to be our Father until we are adopted. He wants to adopt us, and accept us in His family, but that cannot happen unless we agree. It is the Spirit of God who brings us the assurance that the transaction is complete, that we are accepted in the beloved, one of His, and heir to all He has.

God is wealthy and willing, but we must help also to dispel the lie put about by the enemy telling people: 'We are *all* God's children.' It is not true, and believing that it *is* may prevent people from ever truly becoming a child of God.

August 3

Psalm 126   *Joshua 15:17-19*   *Luke 11:5-13*

Caleb had given his daughter Achsah a dark land for her dowry, a desert. It was not enough. She had confidence in her father, and she had become an asker. She got off her ass, and came to her father and said, You've given us this land; now give me also springs of water that the land might be irrigated. The father gave her upper springs and nether springs.

If we ask our Father to give us the gift of the Holy Spirit, we need not have any anxiety that we will receive some counterfeit gift. How can it be serpent or scorpion we receive, if it is God Himself we are asking? We ask with confidence: enough that by simple faith we can claim what He is more than willing to give, and begin to thank Him.

August 4

Psalm 146:5-7   Genesis 27:1-36   Luke 15:25-31

In the familiar prodigal story the father turns to the
elder son, and says, effectively, 'You are always with
me, and all that I have is yours. All you had to do was
ask. Have you been with me this long, and still you
don't know me?'

And Jesus says to us: 'Extravagance to a wild and
careless degree is the characteristic of my Father and
Me. I was never precise, calculating and sensible when
it came to giving life and love for you on that dark hill.
That is why I have the reputation (in Heaven anyway!)
of being the most extravagant person ever to walk the
dust paths on this planet ... You cannot hoard yourself
up for a rainy day, son, and justify it in the light of my
teaching. You must give yourself extravagantly, for
security in the wisdom of your own economic
prowess is directly opposite to the extravagance of
my Father who revels in feeding birds, cultivating
grass and inventing flowers simply because ...
because ... because He enjoys doing it.'

Phil Streeter

August 5

Oswald 605–642 (see Oswald liturgy, p. 28; May 23;
November 21)
Psalm 105:4-8   Genesis 32:22-32   Matthew 11:12

Jacob wrestled with someone, probably with
God Himself. He would not let the one he was
wrestling with go - unless He blessed him. He
wrestled with God and found his own identity in
the process.

Perhaps what God really requires is not so much an

upright man as one who is reckless, and determined to press into Him whatever the cost.

This is probably the meaning of the verse in Matthew 11 (and also in Luke 16:16) about the violent gaining of the Kingdom.

Jacob emerged a broken man, but with a whole new identity, and all of Israel is called by his name to this day. The name means prince with God, or prince of God, soldier of God or God-wrestling.

Do we prevail with God? Have we wrestled with Him enough to have also embraced who He says we are able to be? Do you seek Him with all your strength?

August 6

Psalm 51   *2 Samuel 11*   *Mark 2:3–12*

David stayed behind at home, when his place was with his men. This created the opportunity for the temptation. Each wrong step made the next more inevitable. And Joab was dangerously aware of what David was about. It is important to realize that through all this time the extraordinary worship David had instituted in Israel continued. There was continuous praise before the ark of God with no veil between. This happened twenty-four hours a day for well over thirty years. Everything did not grind to a halt because of David's sin. And eventually David would go and sit in God's presence, waiting for answers in his self-inflicted predicament.

The same God is worthy of all our devotion, He who alone has power to forgive sin, and who can say, 'Gather up your bed, and walk again.'

August 7

Psalm 40:9-14   *2 Samuel 2:13-32*
Matthew 5:21-6

Rivalry and jealousy and party-spirit, all these things can easily lead to unpleasantness and violence. When all of this escalates it is hard for it to stop, and it seems the only way is for someone to speak out for non-violence as Abner did. The fruit is peace, a cease-fire, for a time, until the need to retaliate re-emerges, and the focus of the anger is an Abner or a Martin Luther King or an Oscar Romeo.

Joab used his position of power as security, and assumed he would go unpunished. David curses him, but lets it pass. Joab after all is family, and was defending his own family honour. This story happens before David's adultery with Bathsheba, but both have something in common. Joab and David think themselves in such positions of power that they are outside the law, and need pay no heed to consequences!

Read 2 Samuel 3:27

August 8

Psalm 119:129-36   *2 Samuel 20:4-13*
Hebrews 4:14-16

Joab has no right to remove a man just because he is in his way, but relies on the fact that David is unable to point the finger, having requested Uriah's death in the same way.

Jesus when He died caused a veil between people and God to tear from top to bottom. (It was fastened at the top, so it even ripped the hard way!) This means we can come boldly into the presence of God to confess our failure and difficulties. We have the *right* to enter boldly because of trust in His death, His dying love. He has the right to say to us, 'I know what you feel like, I know how hard it is,' because God did not cheat: He was born as one of us, and experienced trials like our own.

He has every right to say, 'Hold on, it's possible for you to make it through.'

August 9

Psalm 72:1-14   1 Kings 2:1-6   John 14:27-30

David is dying and entrusts his throne to Solomon. Chief among his unfinished business is the task of holding Joab accountable for his murders.

Jesus can truthfully say that Satan had nothing on him, since he consistently has made right choices, all the way along. Satan has no legal right over him – no one takes his life from him, he even co-operates with the betrayal that has been engineered to bring about his death.

There is a traditional story in which Death gloats to the Prince of Hell that he has captured Jesus of Nazareth. Now finally he will take revenge on the one who released Lazarus from his clutches. 'Oh no,' screams his colleague. 'Don't you know what that means? He will come here, and none of our prisoners will be able to be secured. He can even preach to them if he wants to!' The Old Testament men of faith in their place of waiting begin to feel restless and excited …'Lift up your heads, your gates,' they say, 'that the King of glory may come in.' (See 1 Peter 3:19.)

August 10

Psalm 62:5-8   Joshua 20:1-6   John 8:3-11

In God's provision, places were to be set up for the protection of those who had killed someone without it being pre-meditated murder. There they could find sanctuary from anyone who wanted to avenge the death. There they could be secure.

When David was fleeing from Saul for his life, he and his followers hid in a cave called Adullam. Other people hurried to join him there: 'all those in debt, all those who were discontented, all those who were in distress'. These became David's mighty men who did great exploits (1 Sam 22:1-2).

We all need places where we can feel safe, where past misdeeds can be put behind us, where no one will condemn us. Then maybe we can go and do exploits, and maybe we can even go and sin no more.

Jesus did not pretend the past had never happened, but He seemed to find ways of not letting it be the end.

Now is where we are standing, and today is, obviously, the first day of the rest of our lives.

August 11

Psalm 25:7-14   Hosea 3:1-3
1 Corinthians 6:15-17

The prophet Hosea was married to Gomer whom he loved dearly, but who was often unfaithful to him. Out of this experience, Hosea was able to speak to the people about how God feels when they run away from His love, and how He remains faithful.

God made us, and for us to function as intended we should consult the Manufacturer's instructions.

Sometimes the handbook is out of reach, but it holds the answers, the explanation, anyway. God's intention (Genesis 2:24) for sex was that it be part of the bonding of a permanent relationship, that one body and one spirit go together.

When a person gives themselves to a number of partners that person is joined to each of them, and as they walk away the person feels more and more fragmented.

God can heal that fragmentedness, release the bonds of the past. These can be cut right through. His laws are there for our protection.

August 12

Psalm 53:1-4   *Genesis 5:21-31*   *John 2:1-11*

Enoch is known as a prophet, and the Scripture tells us that he walked with God from the time his son was born. This was obviously a turning-point in his life. Perhaps the naming of his son was his very first prophecy. The name he gave his son means 'After him it shall come', and his son was Methusaleh. The 'it' would seem to be speaking of judgement. God had spoken through Enoch that this must come. God is so reluctant to bring that judgement that the guy with the prophetic name saw his own son die of old age, and was the oldest man who ever lived. The exact year he died, there came the great flood. The delaying of it was certainly extreme, but then God rarely does anything by half-measures.

No, Jesus. You are by no means economical. Even the picnic on the hill resulted in twelve basketfuls of left-overs. It wasn't six bottles of well-water that You changed into wine, but SIX THIRTY-GALLON stone jars full! Once again, sheer extravagance!

Phil Streeter

August 13

Psalm 139   *Malachi 3:16-17*
                      Matthew 13:24-30

While we were still sinners Christ loved us. He sees
potential in the most unlikely lump of stone. But that
potential cannot even begin to be released until we
acknowledge Him. He has paid the price for the
whole quarry! Will we surrender to His purpose? and
allow Him to wash us clean, then chip away at all that
would get in the way, and hone the surfaces until He
can see His own reflection in the jewel of our lives?

We need to desire the uncomfortable process, not
only for ourselves, but for those who live in areas we
are responsible to pray for.

When He returns to make up His jewels, what will
He find? Stones, resistant, hard and rough? or gems,
prepared and radiant with His glory? The final day will
reveal it all. Willing and unwilling remain side by side
until then. In the field which is the world (Matthew
13:36-43), and also in the ground of my heart, wheat
and weeds grow together.

Without Walls

A hurting world is around us, and we hide behind our freshly decorated walls, and pretend it does not exist, or that we do not know what it is to hurt. We are challenged to come out and be *without walls*.

August 14

Psalm 50:2   Hosea 10:12b   2 Corinthians 4:6–7

'We are called to intentional, deliberate vulnerability.'
(The Rule of the Northumbria Community)

I had a vision of a house. Every time a crack appeared in the wall, or damage in the house, I dashed out to repair it as quickly as I possibly could, like most of us do, so that the inside of the house was protected and kept safe from the weather and the storms. And the Lord said to me, 'This is what your Christian life is like. Whenever any cracks appear in the wall that has been built up around about you over the years by the world and by yourself you dash out and you fill in the cracks so that no one is able to see what is inside. But I want the world to be able to see what is inside. I want to be able to come in through the cracks into your life and I am not going to fill them up either, I am going to flow in and out of these cracks. So when you see the cracks appear in your life, do not rush out and fill them in. Let Me come in.'

David Mattches

August 15

Psalm 18:49   Job 34:2-8   Matthew 9:10-11

The accusation made about Jesus is that He mixes
with the wrong kind of people. He has friends that
respectable people would be ashamed to be seen
with. It is not even as if He can keep these friends
hidden away in a different world; some of them follow
him around, and the circles begin to overlap. He
recognizes that how rich and successful, how
presentable someone is, how much 'street-cred'
someone has, does not matter: the rich can be very
needy, and the poor can be selfish. Inside we are all
weak and prone to failure; it would be unwise for any
of us to cast the first stone. Jesus was a friend of
sinners, and we need to be, too. He made Himself of
no reputation, and we need to be a little less
protective of our own.

August 16

Psalm 104:34   Exodus 4:2-3a
Colossians 3:17, 23-4

God asks the question, What is that in your hand? We
respond incredulously. Surely He knows, so why need
He ask the question? He draws our attention to the
very thing in our reach, and asks us to lay it at His feet,
our ability or treasured possession all at His disposal.
But then little can become much when we place it in
the Master's hands. In the book of Acts we read of a
woman called Dorcas (or Tabitha) who had won the
hearts of all around by her use of the gift she had for
sewing. It may be that God will make use of our
cooking or baking or hill-walking or love of sports or
whatever … to glorify Him. Remember the picture of

the juggler who would practise his juggling and
gymnastics before the altar in the church. A favourite
Christmas song tells the story of a little drummer boy:

I have no gifts to bring,
   to lay before the King,
Shall I play for Him?

Then He smiled at me,
   me and my drum.

August 17

Psalm 24:1   Ecclesiastes 10:19   Matthew 9:9-10

Matthew had met Jesus and he wanted all his friends
to meet the Master, too. What could he do? He could
do the one thing he really knew how to do well – he
could throw a party. People always enjoyed his
parties. So he threw a big party and invited everybody
– Jesus could do the rest.

   Why can we not just do the same, lay aside time-
consuming religious activities, and spend time with
people we like, instead?

August 18

Psalm 15:1-2, 4   Proverbs 11:24-5
John 13:7, 15, 14:26

We have sought not to supply the Holy Spirit with a
time-table and a specification of what we require.
He has a way of dealing with such impudence, and
invariably has the last laugh. What, then, are to be
our priorities? To be available. To be accepting
without being sentimental. The demands made
upon us are only possible to meet if matched by
openness to the Spirit. In the power of the Spirit,

therefore, we make ourselves available. We are
prepared to be vulnerable, to be sensitive enough
to try to protect others who may not understand
what we understand, and to be willing to spend and
be spent in the service of Christ the King.

Norman Motley, Letters to a Community

August 19

Psalm 18:49   *Esther 4:10-16*   *John 15:15*

The story of Esther is a remarkable picture to us of
what it is to be a bridge of peace. Esther took the
opportunities that came her way, and as a result was in
a position of particular influence.

The famous Irish legend is that if you ask anyone for
directions they will reply, 'The way to K——, that's
very easy, *but you wouldn't start from here!'*

Suddenly Esther is made to realize that she, and only
she, is in the very place the directions start from. She
is in a unique position.

Esther identifies with the people she has come
from. She speaks their language, knows their hearts,
but also can speak on their behalf. She is prepared to
risk her very life to do so.

Each of us has a position of influence no one else
could occupy but it is essential that we identify
ourselves with people.

'Sometimes we build up walls instead of bridges of
peace and we ask Your forgiveness, O Lord.' (*Carey
Landry*)

August 20

Oswin, King of southern Northumbria after the death
of his cousin Oswald. Greatly loved by Aidan.
Murdered at Oswy's order in 651.

Psalm 86:9   Proverbs 9:13, 15, 17   John 4:27-30

The woman came running into town shouting,'I've found a man! I've found a man!' What was new about that? This woman was partial to men, had been married four or five times. Her reputation never seemed to cause her any difficulty in finding a new replacement.'This man is different from any I've ever met – he told me all about me. Come on, everybody, I want you all to meet him. He's a prophet, no, more than that ...' She ran around shouting and calling out until everyone came out of their houses to see this man, and hear him speak. And no one spoke like this man. He told stories that made you feel that Heaven itself had opened and God Himself was near. Life would never be the same again.

August 21

Psalm 15:1-3   Proverbs 12:15   Luke 18:9-14

There is an over-used joke which tells of the man being shown around heaven by St Peter. He sees a small group of people sitting in a circle in one corner facing inwards. Who are they? he asks. Shhh, says Peter, they are the Baptists (or Catholics or Pentecostals, depending on who is telling the joke) – and they think they are the only ones here!

Perhaps C. S. Lewis was thinking of this joke when he described the dwarves in *The Last Battle*. In the story they also went through the stable door that led into Aslan's country, but instead of the beautiful sunshine they saw only darkness; instead of fresh flowers they smelt filthy stable-litter. The proverb says that there is none so blind as those who will not see. Sometimes our eyes can become so damaged we are unable to see even if we tried. If we want Him to, Jesus can make us see again – maybe tentatively at first, so that we see people who only look like trees walking, then eventually so we can see all people clearly – with His help.

August 22

Psalm 40:15   *Proverbs 25:6–7*   *1 Peter 2:9*

We are 'peculiar'. We have chosen not to go with the majority. We shall pray and reflect on the life of Christ: most people don't do this. We shall worship and receive God's gifts in His sacraments: most people don't do this. We shall be in a minority: we shall be odd. There will be no danger for us in that, as long as we don't begin actually to *like* being odd. We can see there, of course, the danger of wanting to withdraw into the small group of like-minded people, and to build the barricades to keep out those who are not sufficiently odd in *our* variety of oddness. That is the way to create sects and divisions, in which each is sure of his own chosenness and pours scorn on that of the others. In fact we have to find a balance. It is our faith that God loves all, and all to Him are welcome. But there has probably never been a time in history when the majority of people were seriously seeking Him!

Kate Tristram

August 23

Psalm 104:34   *Proverbs 15:31–2*
                    Matthew 9:11–13

A hospital exists for the benefit of its patients. It is nonsense to complain that having patients admitted interrupts the smooth running of the hospital. The church exists for the benefit of its non-members, to be salt for the earth, not for the sake of impressing more salt. Why is it, then, that so much of the church's activities are designed to be as off-putting as possible to the casual unchurched observer? At best they are user-friendly only to the initiated. Jesus said He did not come to call those who already thought they were right, but He came to call those who knew they were bad and selfish to be turned upside down.

August 24

Psalm 18:25   2 Samuel 22:30   Hebrews 11:30

There is an invisible line that is crossed when someone gives their heart to the Lord and passes from darkness to light, from being close to the Kingdom to being a subject of the King of kings. At the time someone crosses this line it may be so invisible they do not notice it at all, until afterwards they look back and see the distance they have travelled. Gratitude is appropriate, awareness of how momentous this transition has been is also appropriate. What is not appropriate is the building of a monument to that moment of remembered or unremembered transition, especially if this monument is a wall running the length of a friendship or a marriage. When a wall does appear we should be the ones who can reach over it, or leap over it, and affirm those relationships.

If the love inside is real it will break through any dividing wall and embrace those we care for, without needing to deny or defend what we have experienced.

August 25

Psalm 15:1-3   *Proverbs 17:17, 18:24*
                    Matthew 11:19

Who are my friends? Are they Christians or not? Or
some of each? If my friends are mostly Christians I am
in danger of disappearing into a little Christian ghetto
which will not be good for me.

My contact with non-Christians should not remain
superficial – friendship, when it happens, comes from
a mutual liking, beyond having just interests in
common. It means being glad to spend time together;
it means developing trust.

Friendship requires honesty. Friends do not need
you to be 'up' all the time – instead they enable you to
be more vulnerable.

August 26

Ninian (See November 10, 11)
Psalm 40:15   *Nehemiah 2:12*   *1 Peter 2:11-12*

**There has probably never been a time in history
when the majority of people were seriously
seeking God.**

Our Bible set before us the idea that God may use a
minority to serve the majority. Church history says
the same. It is because of the faithfulness of the few,
not the many, that the Christian faith has come
down the ages to us and we have the chance to
know God in this way. It has always been so. If God
has called us and we want to respond to Him, then
we must be faithful to our own vision, whatever the
many think. But we must do it with open hearts and
open arms, not safeguarding our fewness, our

specialness. And we must do it in healthy laughter directed at ourselves, because really it is so ridiculous to think that God has chosen us for anything at all, even though it is true.

Kate Tristram

August 27

Psalm 24:1   *Proverbs 20:12*   *Mark 7:24–8*

What we are called to do is be. Our whole being should be saturated with the presence of God. People who choose to be around us become familiar with this. They will not have unrealistic expectations of us, since we do not pretend to be anything we are not. We are simply ourselves, distinct individuals who have an awareness of the reality of God. That fact of His reality has affected our lives in various ways that are contagious, but do not need defending. We can include our friends in our normal activities and conversation of which God is a natural part. This need not and must not be self-conscious in any way. Any distancing or request for discretion on our part will come from our friends. We must only exercise the sensitivity necessary to relate to any person, not assume there are barriers in place which do not necessarily exist. Children will often be our teachers in this regard. They have no artificial concepts of spiritual or secular, Christian or 'worldly' – they are happy to love God and get on with it, and talk freely with whom they please.

August 28

Psalm 18:29, 36   Proverbs 27:9   2 Corinthians 4:2

Do not have ulterior motives. We must be prepared to
love someone as they are, not in the hope that
eventually they will become a Christian. Obviously if
we love them we want the best for them, and so
desire that they have a relationship with God
themselves, but if we could not go on loving them just
the same, even if they never 'came through', our love
is conditional and inadequate. Suppose we help our
neighbour with his garden 'because it's a good
witness.' That is not really good enough. We should do
it because we want to, because we care, and that is a
practical way of caring (then it *will* be a good
witness). The neighbour is surprised and questions in
himself why you are doing this. If it is because you
want to, that may impress him. But if next day you
invite him to church, he concludes that the garden
was an excuse to get under his defences and make it
difficult for him to say no when you invited him to
church, since he then feels under an obligation to you.
His initial delight that you should be so unselfish turns
instead to distaste. What a disappointment – he
thought just for a while that you might care about him
or be wishing to be friendly. Obviously he was wrong.

August 29

Psalm 131:1-2   Proverbs 20:24, 27   Matthew 6:5

If someone really does not care whether they live or
die it is hard to threaten them. If our identity lies in
Whose we are, and not just *who* we are, then even loss
of reputation will only be a temporary set-back. The
need to be someone, to have clout, to command

respect, to have prestige or position, these are shackles every bit as strong as those of materialism.

To be seen as holy, or spiritually mature, someone of depth, having a quiet authority: are these not also ambitions, or bolsters of our status?

If we can only reach the true poverty and yieldedness of not 'needing to be' anything (even a humble nothing), then we will truly be invisible. We will be unable to be bought by any pressure.

August 30

Psalm 24:1, 6   Proverbs 15:23   Matthew 5:13–16

Jesus talked of Christians as the salt of the earth, and as a light for the world. The salt is not good if it loses its flavour; the light is not good if it is hidden. To be effective, salt must not be separate, but amongst the food where it is invisible, but its influence pervades the whole. Light must not be blocked by anything, but set apart where it can be clearly visible. We are given two analogies that are almost opposite in their strategy – to show that there are times and situations which require one or the other approach. On the whole it seems there are two kinds of situation when we are required to actively set our light on a lampstand and avoid it being hidden. One of those is a direct confrontation in which the world insists upon us conforming to their standards (of darkness) but we refuse to compromise the truth we know. The second kind of situation is one where an encounter is not sustained, but a clear witness can still be given (like a person walking down a darkened street holding a candle). A light and darkness polarization is not usually desirable in long-term situations where we can instead build friendships, where people see how we really are on a day-to-day basis. Here we must be salt.

August 31

Aidan (see Aidan liturgy, p. 32; May 19, 22, 23, 25; July 15; November 22; September 1, 9; see also introduction to Oswald liturgy, p. 27)

Psalm 16:6   Proverbs 11:12   Matthew 13:18–23

Imagine a long line running from -100 to +100 with a zero point somewhere in the middle.

    -100_____0_____+100

At one end, -100 is the most hardened sinner that ever lived, who is coincidentally an out-and-out atheist. At the other, +100 is the most saintly believer you could meet. Everybody else is on the line somewhere. Zero represents the point of initial surrender to Christ. Often we think that evangelism is about moving someone we meet from -40 to +10 in twenty minutes! Even when someone makes a commitment abruptly they may have already been at -2 and only needed a nudge over to +5. A nudge at the wrong time could have shot them back to -18. When I use this analogy I am interested to see how people react. Some immediately apply it to the impact they have on friends or acquaintances. Others personalize it: 'Before what happened this week I must have been about -3, now I'm around +4.' 'I don't know where I am, -10 maybe.' What we must not do is judge someone else's position. All that matters is that through being with us each person is drawn along the line, closer to Christ, and not knocked farther back.

September Readings

This month's notes are divided into three sections. The first section is about intercessory prayer, and is called **Standing in the Secret**. The second is about meeting God in everyday life, and is called **Broken Gold**. The third is about insights from the Celtic church and is called, accordingly, **Celtic Insight**.

Standing in the Secret

September 1

Psalm 97:1, 3   Esther 7:9-10   Matthew 8:2-27

Once, when Aidan of Lindisfarne was praying on the island that is known as the Inner Farne, he looked out across the short stretch of water that separated him from the mainland and saw that a fire had been lit close to the gates of the city of Bamburgh, where his friend the King had his home and throne.

The ruthless Penda had been gathering forces against him for some time, so Aidan would be alarmed more than surprised. As the flames rose and threatened to devour Bamburgh, Aidan prayed, 'Lord, see what evil Penda does!' and in an instant the wind rose up and turned the fire away from the castle, wreaking havoc instead upon the perpetrators of the attack.

September 2

Psalm 5:1–3; 149:4–9   *Daniel 10:2–21*
Matthew 18:18   *Revelation 12:7–9*

The implication in this story about Daniel and the angel is that Daniel's prayers made the difference, and by him remaining constant in prayer until the answer came through, the blockage put up by the enemy was broken through.

Sometimes Satan will do all that he is allowed to thwart the purposes of God. We under-estimate the contribution that our prayers can make in defeating the devices and schemes of the enemy. Territorial spirits do have influence on, or by default have jurisdiction over, areas and their inhabitants. But the faithful prayer of even one person can swing the balance in spiritual conflict in which they are involved.

We only *begin* to understand the significance and secret power of prayer, but the mystery is this: God is more than willing to act on our behalf, but our prayerlessness so often impedes His intervention.

God heard and answered Daniel's prayer immediately, but the enemy intercepted and delayed the answer. His persistence in prayer won the day.

'But I am not defeated and I will not be; God sends
His angels, and they fight for me.'

An ancient prayer says:

St Michael the Archangel,
defend us in battle;
be our safeguard against
the wickedness and snares of the devil.
May God rebuke him, we humbly pray,
and do thou, O Prince of the heavenly host,
by the power of God, cast into hell

Satan and the other evil spirits
who prowl through the world,
seeking the ruin of souls. Amen.

September 3

Psalm 53:2   Isaiah 55:8-9   2 Corinthians 10:5

Too often when we come to pray we have fixed ideas
as to what the subject for our intercession will be – or
if God gives us the subject we again lapse into our
own thoughts, ideas and preconceptions instead of
letting the Spirit teach us what to pray. We need to
take authority over our own thoughts, however good,
in case they are an impediment to God's directives
and burden.

Wordless prayer can often be effective, too. Some of
the times when we 'worry' about a person for hours
on end for no apparent reason, who normally we
rarely think of, may turn out to be the closest to real
intercession we have ever come.

September 4

Psalm 62:8   1 Samuel 7:5-9   Mark 14:35-41

Sometimes it is important to pray and keep praying
until we feel released to stop. It may be that at that
precise time the breakthrough has come and our
prayer is answered or the answer set in motion. Often
if the date and time is logged in an intercession diary,
it can be confirmed that this was exactly when prayer
was needed. On other occasions the burden may be
given us to carry only for a little while and then put on
someone else in their turn.

Jesus in Gethsemane said, 'Could you not watch
with me for one hour?' An hour may often seem an

eternity, but at the end of that night He was to say 'The hour is come'; His disciples had slept at the crucial hour when He needed their support.

One man did watch with Him from a distance, a young man who had followed so hurriedly he had only had the chance to wrap a sheet around him and not lose sight of Jesus and the others. When Jesus was arrested he left in even more of a hurry, without even his sheet!

That young man who watched as Jesus prayed is usually believed to have been John Mark, the gospel writer.

September 5

Psalm 63:3   *1 Samuel 12:23-4*
1 Corinthians 7:3-5

Columba's friend, Lugne, had a problem in that his wife refused to share his bed any longer, so much had she come to find him and his attentions repulsive. She was prepared to care for all his other physical needs, or, if Columba so advised, to leave him and become a nun altogether. Columba would not hear of it, but instead suggested that all three of them fast from eating, and pray for the next twenty-four hours.

She agreed to try it, since the impossible or difficult might be altered by the prayer of faith. Accordingly all three prayed, and Columba stayed awake all night also, interceding for them.

She must have been well satisfied, on this occasion at least, for when next morning Columba asked Lugne's wife if she was willing to go to a convent she would on no account hear of it, and stayed happily with her man till the end of their days.

September 6

Psalm 63:4   Exodus 17:8-16   1 Timothy 2:8

It was as if he was the conductor. When Moses raised his stick the Israelites were advancing loudly; if he let it fall they pulled back.

I wonder how gradually or how soon he realized the connection.

They could not afford to take a hammering, so soon Aaron and Hur came to his rescue! The arms still are raised, and the rod; but now they will see it through together, and the stone can support his weight.

Often, we are the only one who can stand in our place of relationship and responsibility, but to know the support and prayer of others makes it bearable, and possible. There may be others, especially leaders, who need our support and loyalty, or who need our prayers, just to hold their arms up, because how they hold out greatly affects what happens for lots of people and their lives.

September 7

Psalm 25:5-9   Haggai 2:9   Romans 12:9b

From generation to generation the same problems may dog a particular area in a way that defies physical or sociological explanation – it is as if the place has a memory. Often in praying for a place the themes of its significant history will provide clues, keys to throw off all kinds of bondage. A trifling series of events may happen that unknowingly repeat a pattern, and it is as if there is a resonance with what parallel events have been before, and the effects are out of all proportion in consequence.

A prosperous city may owe its wealth, for example,

to slave trading – an injustice that could be repented for vicariously.

A place with a long-ago history of sectarian rivalry will often have disproportionate difficulty in setting up contemporary inter-church projects.

Today's oppressive atmosphere may have causes in what has happened before anything in living memory. Because this has often been found to be the case, we can anticipate this and do research, but it is important not to look just for negatives. There are positive and spiritually powerful events and places whose significance we can explore. This is part of our spiritual inheritance. There may even be prayers, and prophetic words waiting to be fulfilled – waiting for us to experience the reality of them in our generation.

September 8

Psalm 110:7   Jeremiah 31:21   2 Peter 1:12–15

What do we mean by 'memory-stones'?

Joshua had stones placed by the edge of the Jordan river which God had parted to let his people cross dry-shod. The intention was that future generations could ask the meaning of the stones and be taught of God's faithfulness.

Celtic preachers would often set up a stone cross as their preaching point, and there the people would gather to be taught the word of God. Some of these crosses have carved pictures of a number of the Bible stories as part of their design.

Memory-stones can be landmarks, signposts, waymarks to guide the lost, to point them to tried and proven paths. The ruined remains of ancient buildings also are memory-stones – like the Western Wall of the Temple of Jerusalem, often called the Wailing Wall.

Often the physical stones show us approximate sites, especially in Celtic Christianity where the original structures were almost always wooden. But the ancient ruins we are called to repair, and broken altars to restore, may not be of any concern to the Department of the Environment or National Trust.

The stones, like us, cry out for a renewal of the faith that first secured their presence on 'this small earth of sea and land, this small space on which we stand'.

September 9

Psalm 48:12-13   Joshua 14:6-12   Acts 16:6-10

To walk and pray predisposes us for all kinds of things to happen. We may be led to a place or building and claim its use for God. We may pray healing in an area that has known great distress. We certainly can pray quietly for the people who live and work in that area, even at the same time as we are exposed to new impressions of it. Two walking together gives the opportunity to pray aloud in turn, discreetly giving the impression of talking one to the other. Often God's heart for a place will come upon us under these circumstances, and we become aware of the needs of the people round about, and what can be done to be part of meeting such a challenge.

Sometimes such a walk enables us to be in the path of an event, encounter or difficulty. Praying does not exempt us from involvement – remember Jesus' story of the man set upon by thieves, and the ones who saw and passed by! Aidan and his companions walked, saying the psalms or reading Scripture as they went, but whoever they met he would challenge to love God more or, if they did not yet know Him, to believe and be baptized as His follower.

September 10

Psalm 5:11-12
Genesis 13:11-13; 18:17-33; 19:27-9
Ephesians 2:2

Abraham is not frightened to bargain with God and agree a fair arrangement – the figures are perhaps negotiable, the terms may be made more favourable, perhaps?

God proves willing to bend a little, or even a lot, but at the end of the day the justice of His judgement is all the more vindicated.

Can we reason with God in such a way? and plead mercy for those in danger of well-deserved disaster?

Do we care enough to try? and do we believe it could make any difference at all?

God relies on our prayer to take the limits off His activity in our world. We are not called to prayer in order to cater to His vanity, but in order to make a real difference in the earth.

September 11

Psalm 111:2, 10   Amos 3:7   2 Corinthians 10:3-5

Sometimes we will be led to pray things that make no sense to our natural mind. Later events could eventually help us to understand why it was necessary for us to pray the way we did.

For our own reference it will usually help to keep a record of these things, a kind of intercessory diary. If we pray and get it wrong, then, at least we have begun to be in motion and can be more easily redirected than if we made no move at all!

God's government is a moral government; its directions are partially determined by people's free choice. It is as if the will of God is the path down a ski-slope with much twisting and turning necessary to negotiate a clear run to the finishing line. Many of the obstacles only appear when the descent is already in process.

We need to listen to the Holy Spirit who can activate us to pray and intercede. Our prayers are part of the process of removing obstacles or alerting other skiers.

September 12

Psalm 3:8   *Proverbs 10:22*   *Romans 15:2*

We are called to bless even our enemies. How much more should we pray a blessing on others in the Body of Christ! – especially those we disagree with, or who hold a different view from our own.

If we ask a blessing on them it is up to God to decide what He can and cannot bless in what they are and what they are doing.

We are not asked to understand each other first. If there are some elements in the church who really aggravate us it may be more useful to pray a blessing on them than to interact with a critical spirit. As we pray we begin to realize just how much God cares about them.

We can pray blessings on non-Christian folk, too. It is like pouring glitter over a home-made Christmas card – wherever the glue-stick has prepared the card the glitter will stick, the rest only rolls off, and even a little of the glitter can be enough to spell out a clear message.

September 13

Psalm 68:17-19, 28   *Judges 13:15-18*
                Matthew 18:10-14

The book *Angels on Assignment* suggests that the
prayers of a believer can have powerful effects upon
the life-circumstances of their family members who
have no knowledge of God or love for Him. If the
believer does not pressurize their family, but prays
instead, angels of God can contrive all kinds of
situations which independently challenge the person
prayed for and create opportunity for them to
respond to Jesus. Prayer can often accomplish this
much, but no prayer, no angels, not even God Himself
can force that person to surrender – God will not
overrule another person's will, without their
permission. He can only begin the process again.

Augustine who so strongly stresses God's power to
intervene in the life even of so unwilling a convert as
he, was actually able to be so arrested because of the
persistent prayer of a believing mother.

September 14

Psalm 45:6   *Isaiah 9:6-7*   *Luke 23:26, 38*

In 1983 a core-group of leaders and other
representatives met in preparation for the next Easter
Workshop. Amongst other things it would be the first
time we would have substantial numbers of Catholics
and non-Catholics all together, and we were anxious
to smooth the way for those not used to mixing with
people from such a different background.

This first meeting was not going well – several
people were acting defensively. Alan Andrews picked
up a guitar and began to sing his song:

The King is among us
and His glory shall be seen
as we learn to ...touch each other.

Later in the day we would sing it again, and cry,
holding hands; but now we sat thoughtfully in a circle
staring at the coffee-table. I reached behind me for a
small wooden figure that was on the mantelpiece
above the fireplace and put it in the centre of the
coffee-table. It was a figure of Christ carrying his
cross, painfully stumbling along the road to Calvary.

Alan still was singing, but now I heard the words as
if for the first time:

And the government shall be *upon His shoulder;*
His kingdom shall never cease.

Christ still intercedes for us, and feels the pain of our
sin and division: the cross which was always on the
heart of God is still the throne He rules from.

September 15

Psalm 36:5   Jeremiah 33:3   Revelation 3:8

A number of years ago, my friend Nigel painted a
beautiful picture of a boy shooting lots of paper
aeroplanes into the sky. They are all being directed at
the same place high in front of him, and each falls to the
ground again. The ground is covered with snow, and the
sky with thick cloud, but in one place only a clearing
has appeared and the deep blue of the night sky can be
seen through it. It has become a gateway to heaven.

So often our prayers, and other initiatives taken in
blind obedience to the Spirit, seem as pointless as
shooting paper aeroplanes into the sky – but the eyes
of faith know that it is no coincidence that that will be
the place where the clouds clear and heaven
penetrates earth's concerns.

The following readings and prayers are about meeting God in everyday life, and offering that life to Him.

September 16

Psalm 65:8-13   Leviticus 27:30   1 Corinthians 16:2

Man offers the first-fruits of his labour to the creator of everything in the universe, stars and cornstalks and grains of dust. This is not to say however that man is simply a brutish breaker of furrows, but he labours well in a variety of trades also, with stone and with loom and with oar and with harp and with law-book and with sweet ordering of words and with prism, towards some end which is likewise a kind of harvest. Well he knows that he could not call himself man at all unless he labours all his time under the sun to encompass the end for which his faculties were given to him. This end, whatever the nature of his occupation, is his harvest time; and he would be a poor labourer that would not wish, among all that broken gold, to offer back a tithe or a hundredth into the hands that formed the original fecund dust.

George Mackay Brown, Magnus

September 17

Psalm 63:1   *Isaiah 55:1*   *Mark 9:24*

I am an emptiness
    for Thee to fill;
my soul a cavern
    for Thy sea.
George MacDonald

September 18

Psalm 51:1-2   Proverbs 18:10   John 14:1-6

A prayer from a tenth century poem called 'Manchan of Liath's desire':

O Father everlasting,
With house of many rooms,
With You may I live.
With You may I live.

Son of the living God,
Ancient and eternal King,
In You may my dwelling be.
In You may my dwelling be.

Holy Spirit of power,
In that clear pool of grace,
Wash away my sins.
Wash away my sins.

September 19

Psalm 72:6-7   Proverbs 3:7-8   1 John 5:20

God to enfold me,
    God to surround me,
God in my speaking,
    God in my thinking.

God in my sleeping,
    God in my waking,
God in my watching,
    God in my hoping.

God in my life,
    God in my lips,
God in my soul,
    God in my heart.

God in my sufficing,
  God in my slumber,
God in mine ever-living soul,
  God in mine eternity.

September 20

Psalm 63:6-7   *Ezekiel 36:26-7*   *John 8:12*

An old man, whom Carmichael described as 'poor,
aged and lonely', explained his night ritual:

I do now as my mother was doing when I was a
child. Before going to bed I place the bar upon the
leaf of the door, and I make the cross of Christ on
the bar and on the door, and I supplicate the great
God of life, the Father of all living, to protect and
comfort me this night ... After that I put out my
light and then I go to bed, and when I lie down on
my pillow I make the cross of Christ upon my
breast, over the tablet of my hard heart, and I
beseech the living God of the universe:

  May the Light of lights come
    To my dark heart from Thy place;
  May the Spirit's wisdom come
    To my heart's tablet from my Saviour.

September 21

Psalm 115:13   *Micah 5:2, 4*   *Luke 2:16-20*

        May God's blessing be yours,
        And well may it befall you.

The rest of the readings for this month are variously about the Celtic church or the everyday culture of Celtic Christians, mostly from the Western Isles of Scotland. Their way of seeing can teach and inspire us.

September 22

Psalm 24:7   Isaiah 53:12 John 14:3   Acts 1:9-12

Martin Reith in his 1991 lectures on Celtic Spirituality at Bishop's House, Iona, cites a quotation from O'Laoghaire in *Irish Spirituality* (ed. Maker, Veritas Publications, 1981). The words are originally in Irish and date from around AD 700; the subject is the Ascension of Christ:

WHEN THE PEOPLE OF HEAVEN WELCOMED
THEIR HEART-LOVE, O MARY, YOUR
BEAUTIFUL SON BROKE INTO TEARS
BEFORE THEM.

September 23

Psalm 119:66-7, 71   *Isaiah 40:3-4*
Matthew 3:1-2, 5-6; 4:12-17

From the Rule of Comgall:

If anybody enters the path of repentance
it is sufficient to advance a step every day.

If you practise repentance,
if your heart is meek,
your way will be straight
to the King of the Kingdom of heaven.

September 24

Psalm 127:3   Isaiah 11:1; 7:14; 11:2   Luke 1:41-8

The Christ-Child's Lullaby

There was once a shiftless laddie in the isles who
had lost his mother, and that is a sad tale, but had
got a stepmother in her place, and that is
sometimes a sadder ...

One evening he brought the cattle home for the
milking, and when they gave little milk that time, it
seemed to his stepmother that it was the poor
orphan who was to blame.

In the heat of anger she declared he brought
them only ill-luck that would never be gone from
their house as long as he remained with them.

...But leave the shiftless laddie did, and that of
his own will, and ere the full moon rose at night, he
was on the other side of the ben.

That night the stepmother could get neither
sleep nor ease; her bed was like a cairn of stones in
a forest of reptiles. 'I will rise', she said, 'and see if
the night outside is better than the night inside.'
She rose and went out, with her face towards the
ben; nor did she stop until she saw and heard
something which made her stop.

What was this but a Woman, with the very heat-
love of Heaven in her face, sitting on a grassy knoll
and song-lulling a baby-son with the sweetest music
ever heard under moon or sun; and at her feet the
shiftless laddie, his face like the dream of the Lord's
night. 'God of the Graces!' said the stepmother, 'it is
Mary Mother and she is doing what I ought to be
doing – song-lulling the orphan.' And she fell on her
knees and began to weep the soft warm tears of a
mother; and when, after a while, she looked up,

there was nobody there but herself and the shiftless laddie side by side.

And that is how Christ's Lullaby came to the Isles.

My love, my dear, my darling thou,
My treasure new, my gladness thou,
My comely beauteous babe-son thou,
Unworthy I to tend to thee.

Hosanna to the Son of David,
My King, my Lord and my Saviour!
Great my joy to be song-lulling thee –
Blessed among the women I.

Kenneth McLeod

September 25

Psalm 100:2-3   Jeremiah 23:4   John 21:16

The Waiting Crook

There was once a saint in Moidart who was always putting taunt upon himself as being the least of all the brethren, and the most useless. And one day he said within himself: 'No work that I am fit for has ever come to me; I will now take me to the hill, and let the Good Being himself choose a track for me.' On the third day he came to a great wooden cross partly decayed, standing on the edge of the peat moss. He knelt at the foot of the cross, and when he opened his eyes again, what saw he there but a shepherd's crook lying on the heather, as if it had dropped out of a hand. He took up the waiting crook, and, hurrying on, he now came to a *clachan**
here and a *clachan* there which had waited long for the man with the crook.

Kenneth McLeod, The Road to the Isles

* *clachan* – a stepping stone, village, hamlet where a church is, a kirk-town.

September 26

Psalm 71:6-7, 18-19, 23   *Isaiah 58:10-11*
     Deuteronomy 34:8, 10   *Acts 20:24-5, 28*

Lines from the poem of keening for Columcille (Columba of the Church), high saint of the Gael, by Blind Dallan Forgaill, Chief Poet of Ireland.

It is not a little story, this is not a story of a fool.
It is not one district that is keening, nor grief of one
     harpstring.
He, our rightful head, God's messenger, is dead.
The teller of words who took away our fear, does
     not return.
The learned one who taught us silence is gone
     from us.
Good his death: he went to God: angels met him.
He knew the way he was going.
He gave kindness for hatred, he broke the battle
     against hunger.
Healer of hearts, satisfier of guests.
Shelter of the naked, comfort of the poor.
Their soul's light, a perfect sage who believed Christ.
Nor went any from this world who more steadfastly
     bore the Cross.
IT IS HIGH HIS DEATH WAS . . .

September 27

Psalm 38:9   *Isaiah 40:3-4; 35:1-2a*   *Matthew 6:6*

As church and state in the Roman empire got married after the toleration edict of 312, heroic virtue was exchanged for compromise with the world, and the inevitable result was insipid mediocrity. Men, and women, finding no challenge in the cities, began to flock to the Egyptian and other deserts. This was a bold encounter with the realities of existence, a challenge to all accepted norms in society, a facing of the shadow side of the human personality, and ultimately confrontation with objective evil.

The desert Fathers were essentially solitaries, expressing their love for their neighbours by total self-oblation to God, by continuous prayer, and by handcraft work for the poor. Their lives reveal an extraordinary humility, gentleness, tenderness, sensitivity and compassion ... And a firm grasp of Bible teaching seems to have been based on the principle that you don't ignore what you don't like.

Martin Reith 'Celtic Spirituality'

September 28

Psalm 31:3-6, 14-19   *Proverbs 22:24-5, 28*
Mark 9:35-42,   Jude 20-3

The theology and observances of the ascetics of the Syrian and Egyptian deserts brought new choices for Christians. People could opt for an 'ordinary' life in the world, living the faith within the normal structures of human and political life, or could withdraw from everyday concerns and pursue their Christian vocation either as a solitary or as a member of an intentional community. This radical new alternative was obviously particularly attractive in a time of social upheaval.

The Eastern monastic tradition took hold among the Celts, many by this time living in the western parts of Britain and in Ireland, and linked by a common group of languages. From it emerged a very distinctive and dynamic form of Christian life and expression.

The faith of the Celtic Church was orthodox, and differed from the Continental Church only in matters of emphasis. They would have no difficulty in recognizing each other as fellow Catholic Christians. Where they differed was in priorities, style and organization. The Celtic Church inhabited a monastic ethos which shaped its life, and gave it a different 'feel' from the mainstream Continental Church.

What had happened was that while the Benedictine form of Christian organization was directly under the authority of the Pope, Celtic Christianity, though entirely orthodox, had developed its own distinctive style, untouched by continental influences. New arrangements for the dating of Easter and styles of tonsure had bypassed the Irish and Scots, who were the conservatives in the matter.

Chasing the Wild Goose

September 29

Psalm 27:11   *1 Kings 12:13*
           1 Corinthians 3:9–15, 20–23

Computing the date of Easter had been a perpetual problem for the Church since the first century. In AD 541 at the Synod of Orleans, new Easter tables were adopted but in the chaos of the times (there was a century and a half when migrating barbarian hordes had cut the Celtic Churches off from contact with Rome), no word of the change had reached Ireland. But when communications were restored Rome tried to insist that the clergy of the universal Church used the same identifying tonsure and the same date for Easter. Old habits die hard and the Celtic clergy would not conform.

At the Synod of Whitby in AD 664 King Oswy and the Northumbrians accepted the Roman system. Unfortunately Wilfred of York, who argued the Roman cause, had spent much time in Gaul and picked up, it seems, some of the acrimony which had been directed against St Columbanus. Wilfred won the argument but in such a way that the Iona missionaries felt slighted and they withdrew from England and many English monks went with them. They finally settled in the West of Ireland forming an English Community in Mayo. The Britons of Strathclyde and the Picts soon followed Northumbria's example and most of Ireland also accepted the new dating. But Iona clung to the old way.

The ninth Abbot of Iona was Adomnan MacRonan and in AD 688, after visiting Jarrow and talking to Bede's Abbot Ceolfrid, he accepted the Roman practice. But many of the Iona monks refused to follow him, denouncing him as a traitor to the Founder. It was this bitter controversy which led him to write his master work *The Life of St Columba* to show his devotion to him. So perhaps we should be grateful.

After Adomnan died a faction set up a counter-Abbot and for decades there were two Abbots, two tonsures and two Easters on the Island. Finally it was an Englishman, St Egbert, who brought them to celebrate Easter together again in AD 729. Iona was the last Scottish abbey to conform.

Reginald B. Hale, The Magnificent Gael

September 30

Michael and all angels (see September 2, 13)
Psalm 126:3, 5–6   *Ecclesiastes 3:1–2*
              1 Corinthians 3:6–8

'The making of the bread, is it not the gladsome thing!'

And yet the reaping-song of the Gael has never been the purely joyous gladness of the young mavie which has never known the sorrow of the empty nest or of the deserted wood. To the singing of the harvest-song goes the life of a year, or of all the years – the summer that is gone, the winter that is coming; the ones who have sown but are not here to reap; the ones who will sow when the reapers that are have been forgotten; the Good Being who makes the sun shine and the corn ripen. There may be the breath of a sigh in that song, but there is also in it a whole storm of rapture.

Gladness must come to its own some time; for the sorrows, there are all the times. To the harvest-field go we, then, for life as it ought to be. The sickle is fate, the hand that holds it is ours, and for once we will be the conqueror. Cut we down a sorrow here and a pain there, bind them, and make them our slaves. Sure, then, this is the glad day, and the beautiful world, and the brave life – what we shall afterwards dream of in the long winter night.

Kenneth McLeod, The Road to the Isles

October Readings
The Book of the Law

October 1

Psalm 1:1-3   *Exodus 20:2-17, 22a, 23-6*
                        Matthew 19:17

The Celtic Christians lived in the Psalms, praying,
memorizing and reciting them. They tried also to
delight in the Law and meditate on it.

The *Liber ex Lege Moisi* was prepared with
selections from Exodus, Leviticus, Numbers and
Deuteronomy, and these passages were painstakingly
copied and circulated, having a profound influence on
the way they lived.

This month we will look at these same passages in
The Book of the Law.

The purpose is not just to obey it, but to study it
also, and see how it shapes our thinking.

October 2

Psalm 2:10-12   *Exodus 21:1-36*   *Luke 17:7-10*

Thy measure of prayer shall be until thy tears come;
or thy measure of work or labour till thy tears come;
or thy measure of work or labour, or of thy
        genuflections,
until thy perspiration come often, if thy tears are
        not free.

                        From the Rule of St Columba of Iona

October 3

Psalm 3:2-5   Exodus 22:1-31   James 1:27

The collection of instructions in Exodus 22 make very
interesting reading! They say that people must suffer
consequences for carelessness as well as for
deliberate malice. It is important not to betray
another's trust.

We should also show care towards the
disadvantaged and to strangers. Those who are
strangers to us are known to God.

One Celtic brother called Cronan moved his whole
establishment to Roscrea after a royal visitor had been
unable to find him in Sean Ross.

'I shall not remain in a desert place,' he said, 'where
strangers and poor folk are unable to find me readily.
But here, by the public highway I shall live, where
they are able to reach me easily.'

This urge to dispense hospitality to the wayfarer
and the indigent led to the founding of the Christian
settlements along the main roads of Ireland.

October 4

Psalm 4:5-8   Exodus 23:1-19   Luke 17:11-17

Remembering to say thank you is important, not just
at special Feasts and Festivals but in our everyday
work and prayer.

Writing about monasticism in Egypt at around AD
390, Palladius reports:

Some toiled in garden and field, sowing and tending
the vineyards; others worked at building, cutting
logs and shaping stones; still others went quietly
about the tasks of weaving, cooking and
maintaining the machinery of the settlement. Then

at 3 o'clock each afternoon, one might stand and
hear how the strains of psalmody arise from each
habitation, so that one believes that one is high
above the world in Paradise. They occupy the
church only on Saturday and Sunday.

October 5

Psalm 5:3-7, 11-12   *Exodus 31:14*
                   Luke 13:10-17

Work is not always required of a man. There is such
a thing as sacred idleness, the cultivation of which
is now fearfully neglected.

George MacDonald

Exodus 31:14 tells us that Sabbath is holy to us,
set apart for us, not just to honour God, but for our
good also.

The Celtic church seems largely to have observed
Saturday as the Sabbath, and broken bread on Sundays
in honour of the resurrection of Jesus, but otherwise
treating it as a normal working day. Slowly the
preference for Sunday observation took root instead.

Each day is a day for prayer, and we should not give
up meeting together for worship whenever that may
be, but how do we safeguard some kind of Sabbath or
day for rest?

Its importance still stands in Scripture, not as an
excuse for legalism, but because God has said it is
important for His people.

How then shall we live?

October 6

Psalm 6:5-9   *Leviticus 5:1*   *Matthew 27:21-4*

Psalm 26:6
'I wash my hands in innocence, and go about your
altar, O Lord.'

First they came for the Jews
and I did not speak out
because I was not a Jew.
Then they came for the Communists
and I did not speak out
because I was not a Communist.
Then they came for the trade unionists
and I did not speak out
because I was not a trade unionist.
Then they came for me
and there was no one left
to speak out for me.
                    Pastor Martin Niemöller

Am I my brother's keeper?

October 7

Psalm 7:3-5   *Leviticus 6:1-6a*   *Luke 19:1-9*

The references printed for the Old Testament readings
this month (not the Psalms) refer to the passages
copied in the Celtic church's *Book of the Law
of Moses*.

The Law is clear in its insistence upon restitution
being made to someone who has been wronged or
cheated. Feeling remorse, or saying you are sorry, is
not enough, because repentance means a practical
change in behaviour.

Zacchaeus willingly and voluntarily admits he has

been wrong, and makes restitution beyond what the law requires.

Matthew 12:34 tells us that 'out of the overflow of the heart the mouth speaks'. Zacchaeus' words show us that in one day (as surprisingly as Ebenezer Scrooge!) he has undergone a conversion of the heart.

October 8

Psalm 8:4-8   *Leviticus 7:19-20, 11-33, 35-6*
2 Corinthians 6:14-18

These passages deal with uncleanness, and its importance. Sometimes having contact with something unclean 'infected' a person for the rest of that day. But tomorrow is a new day.

Someone who has already been washed may only need the dirt that has gathered on their feet removed. This is the teaching of John 13:10-11.

Sadly, if we put something clean and something dirty together it is usual for the unclean to infect the clean and not the other way round!

Something may be given to God, as a voluntary thank you present or peace-offering, and then enjoyed by the whole family in celebration.

October 9

Psalm 9:9-12   *Leviticus 12:1-5,6b*   *Luke 2:22-3*

Exodus 13:2,12, speaks about the first-born.

The following is quoted from notes prepared by a woman involved in the World Health Organization, commenting on Leviticus 18:19.

'It should be remembered that during menstruation the lining of the uterus (womb) is shed, leaving the empty uterus like a 'raw wound' which can easily be infected with 'germs' (bacteria and viruses) introduced during intercourse.'

'God made man and woman in his own image, as moral responsible human beings. God made man and woman as different sexes, complementary to each other and equal in His sight. God planned partnership between the sexes (marriage) for companionship, for sexual union and for having children and forming family units, so that mutual love, care, respect and understanding should be the basis of the family unit.'

October 10

Psalm 10:13-15   *Leviticus 17:10-11,13-15*
              Hebrews 9:20-22

Only parts of verses 11, 13 and 14 from Leviticus 17 are copied in *Liber ex Lege Moisi* (11a, 13c, 14b) but these are difficult to designate because of the order of the wording in different translations!

Two sentences stand out from the readings for today.

'There is no forgiveness without the shedding of blood' and 'The life is in the blood'.

All the Old Testament sacrifices say the same distasteful thing, that sin means death, and there can be no forgiveness without the shedding of blood. His Blood, the Blood of Jesus cries out from the ground where it fell. The price is paid!

There is life in the Blood.

October 11

Psalm 11:4
Leviticus 18:2b,5-13,15-21,22b-4,29
1 Corinthians 5:1-5,9-12

Many of the regulations concerning sexual
behaviour in Leviticus 18 have particular resonance
for the late twentieth century reader. Acutely aware
of HIV and AIDS as we have become, we cannot fail
to observe that many of the practices prohibited
here carry a high risk of spreading sexually
transmitted diseases. Such observations, however,
do not excuse us from behaving with compassion
towards those infected with HIV/AIDS. Aside from
preventing the spread of physical disease, these
regulations are designed to prevent the emotional
and psychological damage caused by sexual abuse
of children, adultery, sexual betrayal and
exploitation.

C.S. Lewis writes: 'He enjoins what is good, because He
is good. Hence His laws have "truth", intrinsic validity,
rock-bottom reality, being rooted in His own nature,
and are therefore as solid as that Nature which He has
created. The Psalmist's delight in the Law is a delight in
having touched firmness, like a walker's delight in
feeling the hard road beneath his feet after a false short
cut had long entangled him in muddy fields.'

October 12

Psalm 12:2-6
Leviticus 19:11-19b,20,21a,26-8,31-6
James 3:2-5

Truth is truth, whether from the lips of Jesus or
Balaam

George MacDonald

We must learn to listen with our ears, our minds and our hearts, embrace and co-operate with truth wherever we find it!

On our part, we should be known as people of our word.

A 'yes' should mean yes, without need of an oath or guarantee as surety. Where people do not mean what they say it is easy to lose a grip on reality. The liar cannot be relied upon; he does not even consistently tell lies, but mixes lies with truth.

But the words of the Lord are flawless, like silver refined in a furnace of clay, purified seven times.

Your word, Lord, have I hidden in my heart, so I might not sin against You. Teach me Your ways, Lord, help me to say what I mean, and mean what I say.

October 13

Psalm 13:2-3
Leviticus 20:6-7,9-12,14-19,21,23,27
1 Corinthians 6:9-12,18-20

Whoever did the work of editing the verses for the Celtic churches has consistently omitted the references to 'when you come into the land'. For them there was already a land to live in, and the Law is an expression of kingdom life.

Amongst the laws of affinity we have one verse emphasizing the importance of not cursing parents, but honouring them.

There is a Jewish proverb, found in the Apocryphal book of Ecclesiasticus, which echoes the same sentiments when it says: 'A son who respects his father will be made happy by his own children; when he prays, he will be heard.'

1 Corinthians reminds us that in Christ we can all begin again, living as new people.

October 14

Psalm 14:2-3 *Leviticus 22:8a,14,21-2*
1 Peter 1:18-20

O Son of God, do a miracle for me, and change my
heart; Thy having taken flesh to redeem me was
more difficult than to transform my wickedness.

Irish, Fifteenth century

O God, and Spirit, and Jesu, the Three,
From the crown of my head, O Trinity,
To the soles of my feet mine offering be;
Come I with my name and my witnessing,
Come I with my contrite heart, confessing,
Come unto thee, O Jesu my King –
O Jesu, do thou be my sheltering.

from South Uist

October 15

Psalm 15:1-5 *Leviticus 24:15a,16,18-22a*
Matthew 5:38-45

What is this perfect word of love?
Can I confess to you the truth?
– I want an eye for an eye
and a tooth for a tooth.
You tell me, 'Turn the other cheek ...'

Love your friends and hate your enemies
– well, that seems reasonable to me.
But You say, 'If that's true, the pagans
do as much as You. My Father lets the
sun rise on the evil and the good.'

Well, here I am again,
knocking at Your door.
You say,
   'Go brother ...
      go woman ...
         sin no more.'
           Ann Liddell

October 16

Psalm 16:2-6   *Leviticus 25:37*
            Matthew 15:32-5

The man to whom little is not enough
will not benefit from more.
                Columbanus

It is important that we hold lightly whatever
possessions and wealth are ours. It should never
be that we are eager to profit from another's
distress.

Aidan was uneasy to be King Oswald's guest at a
feast, with all the rich food before them; but when the
poor came to his door, the King ordered all the food to
be gathered up and distributed to them instead. Aidan
was overjoyed.

As it says in the song, 'Hard Times':

Let us pause in life's pleasures
and count its many tears,
for we all have sorrow with the poor.

October 17

Psalm 17:2-6   *Leviticus 27:1-20,25,30-34*
            Matthew 15:3-6

Giraldus Cambrensis in the twelfth century said that
Germanus and Lupus had introduced tithing into
Britain:

> They give the first piece broken off from every loaf
> of bread to the poor ...They give a tenth of all their
> property, animals, cattle and sheep.

A tithe is the first ten per cent of income, and where
that tithe is directed to is less important than the
understanding that this money in particular is God's
money and He must not be robbed.

One many may say, 'I can't afford to tithe,' but
another replies 'I can't afford not to!'

O we have gladly heard
your Word, your holy Word,
and now in answer, Lord,
our gifts we bring.
Our selfish hearts make true,
our failing faith renew;
our lives belong to you,
our Lord and King.

            Kevin Nichols

October 18

Psalm 18:30-33   *Numbers 27:7b-11a*
            Galatians 3:26-9

When Paul tells us that there is no more male or
female in Christ, he is not denying the distinctive gifts
of our sexuality, but saying that in Him we can come
to know God as our Father; that when we are adopted

into His family each one becomes heir to all that is
His, like the chosen son who would normally have
inherited. In that sense a woman becomes a 'son'.

Father God,
I wonder how I managed to exist without
the knowledge of Your parenthood
and Your loving care;
but now I am Your son,
I am adopted in Your family
and I can never be alone,
'cause, Father God,
You're there beside me.

October 19

Psalm 19:7-11   *Numbers 35:30b,31*
Matthew 18:15-17

Here in Numbers (and in Deuteronomy 17:6) it is
stressed that no one should be killed as a
consequence of the testimony of one witness,
who may be lying, or mistaken.

Jesus introduces an even more searching criterion
into the responsible task of making a judgement
(John 8:7-11). Only he who is faultless could begin
the stoning! Jesus is the only truly sinless One and He
chooses not to condemn, and only to command us to
walk free in obedience.

The other question raised by these scriptures is that
of the validity or otherwise of capital punishment. Our
own views only the subject are mostly in place, some
deeming it to be moral and expedient, others, to be
barbaric. But it is hard to remove the cultural
spectacles through which we read these scriptures –
are our views only a 'spiritualized' version of those held
by others of our own age, politics and culture, anyway?

Sin means death – and someone must pay.
Jesus paid, will forgive the whosoever, but
consequences of sin often remain to be dealt with.

October 20

Psalm 20:7-9   *Deuteronomy 1:16b,17a,b,c*
                    James 3:17-18

From the Old-Irish Penitential:

> Anyone who is himself conscious of any falsehood
> or unlawful gains, let him confess privately to a
> confessor, or to an elder who may be set over him. If
> there be none such, let him make his own
> confession to God, in whose presence the evil was
> done, so that He shall be his confessor.

Those whose positions were high and whose
knowledge was great were judged to have deeper
guilt. This was very different from the legal view of
the time, which often permitted a king to go free,
while his slave would be slain for the same crime.

October 21

Psalm 21:1-2   Deuteronomy 6:4-9,13b,16;13:1-4a
                    Luke 17:20-21

For morning prayer all orthodox Jewish males over
13, and some of the more reformed or liberal
tradition, bind tephilin (or philacteries), one to
the arm close to the heart, and the other to the
forehead.

These are small black boxes with scrolls inside, on
which are written Deuteronomy 6:4-9 and 11:13-21,
and Exodus 13:11-16. The Deuteronomy passages are
the same as those written in the mezuzah to be fixed

to the doorpost of a Jewish home, or often to that of each room.

In our Celtic tradition, we can also bind the Name of the Lord to us in our morning prayer, the Name which is lowly and meek, yet all-powerful:

I bind unto myself the name,
the strong name of the Trinity ...
the Three in One and One in Three;
Eternal Father, Spirit, Word:
praise to the Lord of my salvation.

October 22

Psalm 22:12–15   *Deuteronomy 14:21–2*
1 Corinthians 15:30–34

It is the words of Psalm 22 that Jesus calls out from the cross, and He would know them by heart. Like the Celtic saints, young Jews were taught to memorize psalms. The words would come immediately to Him ...

He could not see,
could not feel HIM near;
and yet it is 'My God' that He cries.

Thus the Will of Jesus, in the very moment when His faith seems about to yield, is finally triumphant. It has no feeling now to support it, no beatific vision to absorb it. It stands naked in His soul and tortured, as He stood naked and scourged before Pilate. Pure and simple and surrounded by fire, it declares for God.

George MacDonald

October 23

Psalm 23:3-3   *Deuteronomy 16:19b;17:1,6*
Luke 21:1-4

Psalm 119:11 says: 'I have hidden Your word in my heart, so I might not sin against You.'

The words of Scripture assume different values from those held by the world around us. They restore a sense of proportion.

Accepting bribes is not acceptable; accepting gifts from interested parties distorts the fairness of our perspective, or makes us dubious of our own lack of bias.

Second best is never good enough for God, and all is always more than a little, even when a little is a lot and all is not very much. Little becomes much when you place it in the Master's hands. (John 6:5-9)

October 24

Psalm 24:3-4   *Deuteronomy 18:10-12a*
1 Timothy 4:1

The Old Testament passage for today prompts us to look at the extremes of human life, from before the cradle to beyond the grave. The condemnation of those who sacrifice the lives of children challenges us to confront the issue of abortion in our own age. Is a society which permits abortion on demand one we can be proud of?

This passage also condemns those who talk with spirits that claim to be the spirits of the dead. As George MacDonald has written, such activity is the opposite of the religious faith by which we entrust our lives to God's mercy.

'Offered the Spirit of God for the asking ... they

betake themselves to necromancy instead, and raise the dead to ask their advice, and follow it, and will find some day that Satan had not forgotten how to dress like an angel of light ...What religion is there in being convinced of a future state? Is that to worship God?

It is no more religion than the belief that the sun will rise tomorrow is religion. It may be a source of happiness to those who could not believe it before, but it is not religion.'

George MacDonald

October 25

Psalm 25:1-3,20   *Deuteronomy 19:4-5,11-13a*
Hebrews 13:6

The monasticism of the Celts can also be better understood from the standard of Old Testament ways. Modelled on the cities of refuge, the monastery consisted of a walled village in which the mixed society of a Christian community lived lives of virtue and devotion separated from the evils of their heathen neighbours. Hospitality was dispensed. Man and woman and children, single and families, lived under the guidance of a leader who might be a clergyman or layman, and was called an abbot ...

Leslie Hardinge

There are differences between the cities of refuge and Christ our refuge. They protected only the innocent. Christ died for the guilty, for the deliberate sinner. He is nearer than any city of refuge. A runner could fail, but someone who looks to Christ can never fail. (John 6:37)

F. A. Schaeffer

October 26

Cedd – Abbot and bishop, brother of Chad. He was trained with his brothers by Aidan, on Lindisfarne. He founded the abbey at Lastingham and the monastery at Bradwell-on-Sea, where the present-day Othona community is based. Cedd died in 664.

Eata – one of the original twelve boys trained by Aidan, he was sent to Melrose to be its first Abbot. He became Abbot of Lindisfarne after the Synod of Whitby, and subsequently Bishop. He then swopped appointments with Cuthbert, and so became Bishop of Hexham.

Psalm 26   Deuteronomy 19:15–19   John 8:42–7

In Psalm 26 the good man is not only free from falsehood, but has not even been on intimate terms with those who are false. Instead he has hated them and their ways. C. S. Lewis points out that in contrast in our society we operate a double-standard that can disapprove of the ruthless, the liar, the womanizer who is a public figure, yet would be surprised if someone refused to meet any of these people or did not behave towards them in the friendliest and most cordial manner.

It is important not to consent to what we know to be false; important that, instead, we quietly, firmly, abstain or withdraw.

Lord, help me to believe the best about other people, and may I never pass on stories which are unkind, or which I do not know to be true.

October 27

Psalm 27:13-14   *Deuteronomy 22:6-8,28-9*
                          Luke 17:1-3

God requires that the vulnerable be protected. Even birds should not be wilfully killed or a species become extinct. A protective wall should edge the flat roof of a house to avoid accidents.

There are laws to discourage rape, to protect women from abuse and from loss of reputation. In Jewish Law, divorce was not part of God's original intention, but was provided for because of the people's hardness of heart. The Law states that the man who rapes an unmarried woman must marry her. It goes on to insist that he cannot divorce her and thus escape the consequences of his selfish actions.

October 28

Psalm 28:2-3   *Deuteronomy 23:19,20a,c,21-3*
                          Acts 4:32-4:10

Ananias and Sapphira are judged because they let people think they were making a sacrifice when in fact they were not. God did not tell them to give the money - it was theirs to give or keep. But they should do what they say. Promises are made to be kept.

Leslie Hardinge tells us that, in Celtic monasticism,

> marriage was permitted to all classes, although celibacy later came to be regarded as the mark of deeper devotion. Poverty was not insisted upon. Individuals and families might grow wealthy. The community consisted, on occasion, of many persons who pooled their abilities and resources for the common goal.

October 29

Psalm 29:11   *Deuteronomy 24:16-17;25:13-16a*
                          2 Timothy 3:13

One thing leads to another. One lie necessitates
another. One injury can lead to retaliation, or involve
whole families in a vendetta.

Here, the law sets a restriction: that each man's
crime is his own, and no one else should have to pay
for it. Of course, it also reminds us that each of us has
sins of his own to be held accountable for; all of us
have gone wrong, and turned to follow our own
desires.

Of course, we can be damaged by others' mistakes
and wrong decisions, and these may set us at a
disadvantage; but we are not held responsible by God
for their actions. He only holds us responsible for our
reactions to their damaging behaviour, and for wrong
actions of our own.

His love is powerful enough to free us from all the
past (Isaiah 53:6), and let us walk free (Joel 2:25a).

October 30

Psalm 30:1-10   *Deuteronomy 27:15-27*
                 James 2:10-13

No matter how ruined man and his world may
seem to be, and no matter how terrible man's despair
may become, as long as he continues to be a man his
very humanity continues to tell him that life has a
meaning ...

Nothing at all makes sense, unless we admit, with
John Donne, that:

No man is an island,
entire of itself;
every man is a piece
of the continent,
a part of the main.

We can help one another to find out the meaning of
life, no doubt, but although people have a common
destiny, each individual also has to work out his own
personal salvation for himself, in fear and trembling.

October 31

Psalm 31:19
Deuteronomy 28:1-11,12b-25,26c-33a,34-45
James 1:22-5

God is present in the blessing, He hems us in behind
and before (Psalm 139:5,8) – and even when our
choices mean that we walk into a curse we find He
has been there too before us (Deuteronomy 21:23;
Galatians 3:13).
He challenges us to trust in Him.

Son of God,
be at the outset,
Son of God,
be surety, friend;
Son of God,
make straight my way yet,
Son of God
at my seeking's end.
from Morar

November Readings
The House that John Built

November 1

Psalm 94:17   Exodus 20:18-21   John 14:1-4

At the Council of Whitby in AD 664 Colman readily
acknowledged not only the fidelity of the brothers
from Lindisfarne and their disciples to the teachings
of Columba, but that the apostle John had fathered the
branch of the church to which they owed allegiance.
The same easy familiarity and respect is present
amongst many of us especially in this community
when such names as Columba, Brigid, or Cuthbert are
mentioned.

This is Jesus, the Carpenter King
who came from God to show us His heart.
He died, but returned from the jaws of the grave
and promised His friends He would always be
    with them.
The fire of His love would remain in their heart
and this is the House that God built.

November 2

Psalm 25:14   Jeremiah 31:20   Revelation 1:12-18

This is John the beloved one
who followed Jesus as the Way,
embraced the Truth and shared His life;
and at the supper of the Lord
leaned closer to Him, heard His words;
for those who lean on Jesus' breast
hear the heart of God.
And this was the heart that John heard

When years had passed, and he was old,
on Patmos island he was held
a prisoner for his love of Christ;
but watching in his lonely cave
he saw the shape of things to come,
of things in heaven and on earth
a Revelation!

Sweet punishment to him – the solitude
that drove him deeper into God,
enfolded by the Spirit till he saw
the Lord with eyes of fire, and hair like wool,
and heard His voice like thundering waterfall:
and this was the heart that John heard

November 3

Psalm 26:1-2   *Jeremiah 31:21*   *Mark 1:16-18*

Repentance

Great Light, thank you for waking me
from my long, selfish sleep.
Lead me, my King.
I am ready to follow.

Stephen Lawhead, Merlin p. 445

November 4

Psalm 25:6   *Jeremiah 31:3*   *Mark 1:19-20*

The Seeking of Love

It is possible to search for love and find it. More
often, I think, love finds us when we are not even
searching ... Love has found us ... we cannot turn
it away.

Stephen Lawhead, Merlin p. 156

November 5

Psalm 26:3   *Jeremiah 31:22*   *John 13:23*

When a man whose marriage was in trouble sought his advice, the Master said, 'You must learn to listen to your wife.'

The man took this advice to heart and returned after a month to say that he had learned to listen to every word his wife was saying.

Said the Master with a smile, 'Now go home and listen to every word she isn't saying.'

Anthony de Mello, One Minute Wisdom

November 6

Martin of Tours (c. 315–97) Illtyd, fifth- to sixth-century Welsh hermit and scholar. (see November 9)

Psalm 45:10–11   *Micah 4:2–4*   *Luke 7:44–6*

This is an Amma, Desert mother,
one who left the city's crowds
to find a place of solitude
to seek God only, face to face,
to know her God and to be known
and truly seen, yet loved and claimed
as His, a warrior who has faced herself
and lived to tell the tale
of love that frees and draws and heals.

She is not alone, for many others
seek the desert and its wisdom, and
as others showed the way of Christ to *them*
so *they* each will show to each who seeks
the Way, by leaning, like beloved John,
on Jesus' breast and listening for His heart.

So many come; so many learn;
so many come to love and lean;
they say,
This is the house that love built.

November 7

Psalm 45:12-15   *Micah 4:5-8*   *Luke 8:1-3*

To a woman who complained about her destiny the
Abba said, 'It is you who make your destiny.'

'But surely I am not responsible for being born a
woman?'

'Being a woman isn't destiny. That is fate. Destiny
is how you accept your womanhood and what you
make of it.'

Anthony de Mello, One Minute Wisdom

November 8

Psalm 45:16-18   *Micah 2:12-13*   *Luke 8:11-21*

The Abba, while being gracious to all his disciples,
could not conceal his preference for those who
lived in the 'world' – the married, the merchants, the
farmers – over those who lived in the monastery.

When he was confronted about this he said,
'Spirituality practised in the state of activity is
incomparably superior to that practised in the state
of withdrawal.'

Anthony de Mello, One Minute Wisdom

November 9

Psalm 111:1-5   *2 Kings 6:1-4*
Matthew 25:37-8, 40

This is Martin, a soldier's son
who chose to follow Christ instead
and not the gods of war.
He tore his cloak in half, one night,
to wrap some poor uncared-for soul
in warmth and care against the bitter cold.
Next night, in dreams, he heard *in singing*
the voice of heaven saying,
'Martin, you have clothed Me with this cloak.'

At twenty-six he built his first community of hermits,
living simply, loving God;
and this was the life that Martin taught,
and this was the house that love built;
and this was the heart that John heard;
and this was the way that God made.

November 10

Psalm 139:4   *Daniel 12:10*   *Matthew 3:8-11*

Ninian returned to Scotland from his travels and
studies in Europe. At Whithorn he and a team of
skilled builders built a gleaming white stone
monastery which was famous throughout the land for
education and learning, prayer and mission.

   Sometimes he liked to visit the shepherds and
herdsmen who tended the flocks and cattle belonging
to the monastery. Once he had all the animals
gathered into one place so he could pray a blessing on
them. Last of all he came to the cattle and with his
staff drew around them a circle of protection.
Everyone ate, listened to Ninian, then went off to their

sleep. The cattle remained, and were noticed by thieves. No wall. No hedge. No ditch. No barking dogs! Just lots of cattle waiting to be carried away!

The thieves rushed inside the circle Ninian had drawn. The bull of the herd rushed at the men, and attacking their leader, pierced his belly with its horns so that the life was torn from him, and so were his entrails. The bull's hoof tore at the earth and dug its imprint into a stone there, so that place became known as 'The Bull's Print'.

Meanwhile, Ninian finishing his prayer came past that place and saw the man lying dead and the other thieves running hither and thither nearby. He prayed to God to restore the man to life and then to health, and ceased not his tears and entreaties till it was so. The other men, his companions, had found themselves unable to leave the confines of the circle, until begging Ninian's forgiveness and being scolded by him he bade them depart. And only then could they cross the circle.

November 11

Psalm 139:5   *Daniel 7:9*   *Matthew 5:14–16*

This is Ninian who went to Rome
to study the faith, but on his way home
to Britain visited Martin at Tours,
and was greatly encouraged, and learnt from his love.
He raised up in stone a Scottish foundation
called Candida Casa, the 'White House' no less!
It gleamed like a beacon, and so did its message
as Ninian travelled to preach to the people
the message of love and the kindness of Christ.
He taught them, as well, to seek God's protection
by drawing around them a circle of prayer;
and this was the circle that Ninian drew,

and this was the life that Martin taught;
and this was the house that love built;
and this was the heart that John heard;
and this was the way that God made.

November 12

Psalm 139:1   Daniel 11:33-5   Matthew 5:33-7

To the disciples' delight the abba said he wanted a
new shirt for his birthday. The finest cloth was
bought. The village tailor came in to have the abba
measured, and promised, by the will of God, to
make the shirt within a week.

A week went by and a disciple was despatched to
the tailor while the abba excitedly waited for his
shirt. Said the tailor, 'There had been a slight delay.
But by the will of God, it will be ready by
tomorrow.'

Next day the tailor said 'I'm sorry it isn't done.
Try again tomorrow and, if God wills, it will
certainly be ready.'

The following day the abba said, 'Ask him how
long it will take if he keeps God out of it.'

Anthony de Mello, One Minute Wisdom

November 13

Psalm 126:1   Exodus 3:2-6   Luke 15:20

This is Patrick, of Cumbria born,
his father and grandfather Christians and priests;
but God has no grandchildren, no hangers-on.
Faith must be *more* than, 'O yes, *I* know *that*.'
Patrick was captured and taken for slavery
to Ireland, where always he still dreamed of home

and the prayers of his family, Christ's cross
    and protection.
And now Patrick prayed like he'd never before!
God heard; he escaped, and came safely to Britain.
Now when he dreamed it was Ireland he saw
and he knew God had called him to go with
    the gospel,
to redeem from the darkness her people for God.
The presence of Christ would be his protection:
Christ under, above him, before and behind,
between him and each eye, between him and
    each word.
He *challenged* the *druids* (and some received Jesus)
then family by family won Ireland for Christ.
And this was the prayer that Patrick made;
and this was the circle that Ninian drew,
the life that Martin taught,
that love built,
the heart that John heard,
the way that God made.

November 14

Psalm 127:3-4   *Exodus 4:13*   *Luke 15:28-9, 31*

To a visitor who claimed he had no need to search
for Truth because he found it in the beliefs of his
religion the abba said:

> There once was a student who never became a
> mathematician because he blindly believed the
> answers he found at the back of his maths book –
> and, ironically, the answers were correct.

Anthony de Mello, One Minute Wisdom

November 15

Psalm 131:1-3   Exodus 4:29-31   John 14:8-9

'Every word, every image used for God is a
distortion more than a description.'
   'Then how does one speak of God?'
   'Through Silence.'
   'Why, then, do you speak in words?'
   At that the abba laughed uproariously. He said,
'When I speak, you must not listen to the words, my
dear. Listen to the Silence.'

Anthony de Mello, One Minute Wisdom

November 16

*Psalm 146:7-8   1 Samuel 25:18, 20, 32
                    1 John 4:19-21*

This is Brigid who loved the poor,
   and gave away all she could spare
and would have given everything
   if everything was hers to share.
She gave her *love* to God as well.
   In her community at Kildare,
all souls were welcome there to feast
on simple food, and ale, and love of Him
who gave unstintingly for us
his love, his heart, his dying blood.
Her *utmost* love was love *returned*.
And this was the way that Brigid lived,
the prayer that Patrick made,
the circle Ninian drew,
the life that Martin taught,
the house that love built,
the heart that John heard,
the way that God made.

November 17

Hild (see Hild liturgy, p. 39; November 23, 24, 26, 29; May 30)
Psalm 119:24   Isaiah 45:15   Romans 8:15, 17, 19

Our work in creation

I have not lost my way – it is just that so many ways open before me that sometimes I hardly know which way to choose. To decide for one is to decide against another. I never imagined it would be this hard.

Now you know. The higher a person's call and vision, the more choices are given them. This is our work in creation: to decide. And what we decide is woven into the thread of time and being for ever. Choose wisely, then, but you must choose.

Stephen Lawhead, Merlin p. 345

November 18

Psalm 119:26-31; 120:7   Isaiah 48:17-20
Romans 5:1-5

This is Columba who followed the Lord,
and chose to be monk instead of High King;
but when wronged against let his clan become angry,
and bloodshed and war followed swiftly in slaughter.
So, sailing from Ireland, at least he determined
to win for his Lord as many in lives
as the deaths he had caused.
Iona was his harbour, foundation and shortmooring
as tirelessly he laboured to win souls for his Master.
Columba now the gentle, Columba of the church.
And this was the peace Columba found, the peace
    of Christ,
the way that Brigid lived,

the prayer that Patrick made,
the circle Ninian drew,
the life that Martin taught,
the house that love built,
the heart that John heard,
the way that God made.

November 19

Psalm 119:32-3   *Isaiah 45:18*   *Romans 8:31*

My All-in-all

Great light, Mover of all that is moving and at rest,
be my Journey and my Destination, be my Want and
my Fulfilling, be my Sowing and my Reaping, be my
glad Song and my stark Silence. Be my Sword and
my strong Shield, be my Lantern and my dark Night,
be my everlasting Strength and my piteous
Weakness. Be my Greeting and my parting Prayer,
be my bright Vision and my Blindness, be my Joy
and my sharp Grief, be my sad Death and my sure
Resurrection!

Stephen Lawhead, Merlin p. 220

November 20

Psalm 119:67, 77   *Isaiah 49:15-17*
Romans 6:1-2, 5

One of the disconcerting – and delightful –
teachings of the abba was: 'God is closer to sinners
than to saints.' This is how he explained it:

God in heaven holds each person by a string.
When you sin, you cut the string. Then God ties it
up again, making a knot – and thereby bringing

you a little closer to him. Again and again your
sins cut the string – and with each further knot
God keeps drawing you closer and closer.

Anthony de Mello, One Minute Wisdom

November 21

Psalm 5:3   Isaiah 55:4   2 Thessalonians 2:16–17

This is Oswald, who learned to pray
that God would *be* with him in each new day
and when, as King, Northumbria was his,
back to Iona he sent messengers with speed,
to help him win his people for the Lord.
And this was the work that Oswald loved,
the peace Columba found, the peace of Christ,
the way that Brigid lived,
the prayer that Patrick made,
the circle Ninian drew,
the life that Martin taught,
the house that love built,
the heart that John heard,
the way that God made.

November 22

Psalm 112:2, 4–5   Isaiah 58:10–11   Matthew 7:26

This is Aidan, strong and good,
who challenged all to love God more,
believe, and truly follow Him with generous heart;
and this was the message that Aidan lived,
and this was the work that Oswald loved,
the peace Columba found, the peace of Christ,
the way that Brigid lived,
the prayer that Patrick made,
the circle Ninian drew,

the life that Martin taught,
the house that love built,
the heart that John heard,
the way that God made.

November 23

Columbanus (c. 540–615), Irish missionary to Europe.
Known for the strictness of the Rule of Life observed
by him and his followers. His letter to a young disciple
forms the headings for the commentary for May in
this book.

Psalm 18:46   *Isaiah 6:8*   *Matthew 13:45–6*

This is Hild who Aidan challenged
to found a rule and live its power,
and influence leaders, and care for the humble,
and be just where God called her to be.
And this was the Yes that Hild said,
the message that Aidan lived,
the work that Oswald loved,
the peace that Columba found, the peace of Christ,
the way that Brigid lived,
the prayer that Patrick made,
the circle Ninian drew,
the life that Martin taught,
the house that love built,
the heart that John heard,
the way that God made.

November 24

Psalm 19:1–3   *Isaiah 11:2–3*   *Matthew 13:35*

One of the marks of the apostolic is to call out the
gifts of others. The wise leader recognizes the

importance of being aware of what God is doing and co-operating with it. Aidan had done just this with Hild, challenging her to return to Northumbria and trusting God in her to be equal to any eventuality she might face.

When Caedmon suddenly exhibited the ability to compose wonderful songs celebrating God as Saviour and Creator, Hild was eager to encourage, release and commission him to instruct the people through his songs. God in him, and the Spirit upon him, would be equal to the task.

November 25

Psalm 19:4a   Isaiah 27:2-3, 6   Matthew 13:34

The Language of the Heart

The surest way to the heart is through song and story ...I do not know why this should be, but I believe it to be true ...Perhaps it is how we are made; perhaps words of truth reach us best through the heart, and stories and songs are the language of the heart.

Stephen Lawhead, Merlin, pp. 158-9

The shortest distance between a human being and Truth is a story.

Anthony de Mello, One Minute Wisdom

November 26

Psalm 17:10, 18:37   Isaiah 5:1-4   Matthew 13:33

Hild and Wilfrid were both intelligent, able and devout Christians. Both had been exposed to Christian teaching and usage more in the Roman tradition before encountering its counterpart in the vibrancy and simplicity of the Celtic church.

Hild was more than happy to acknowledge her indebtedness to all who had shown her the way of Christ, but openly embraced and sided with the Celtic way. To her way of thinking Wilfrid had been schooled by the best, learning even from Aidan himself on Lindisfarne, but used them only as a stepping stone on his own journey that led him to embrace the Roman way. He sneered at the Celtic church's 'ignorance' and 'awkwardness', misrepresenting the issues involved to the king at the Whitby synod, and effectively betrayed those who had raised and sought to nurture him. Hild as a Christian may have had to forgive Wilfrid, but nonetheless did all she could to thwart his further aggrandizement and to block his influence.

November 27

Psalm 115:17–18   2 Kings 2:10–12   Hebrews 13:7

This is Cuthbert, who watching sheep,
saw light in the sky as Aidan died.
He dedicated his life to God
in prayer,
in love and solitude.
He sought to reconcile his brothers,
    protecting in his prayer
the house that John built,
    and Columba taught,
and the *yes* that Hild said,
which was the message Aidan lived,
       the work that Oswald loved,
       the way that Brigid lived,
       the prayer that Patrick made,
       the circle Ninian drew,
       the life that Martin taught,

the house that John built,
that love built,
that God made.

November 28

Psalm 36:7–9   *Proverbs 17:1*   *Matthew 7:25*

King Oswy needed the Whitby synod to settle once
and for all which way Easter should be calculated.
A small enough matter, but emotive because of
conflicting loyalties involved and declared.

Colman spoke with pride for the Celtic side
declaring their loyalty to John the apostle who had
ruled that Easter continue to be calculated in accord
with Jewish reckoning. It had always been so, and
Columba and others before and since had not seen fit
to question this. It would do well enough.

Wilfrid, instead of arguing for the expectancy of
united practice of some kind, spoke rudely of
Columba and deprecatingly of the entire Celtic
tradition. His six years on Lindisfarne had apparently
not taught him to respect his betters, nor his time
away taught him manners.

Instead he employs an ingeniously simplistic
argument:

Peter holds the keys to the kingdom of heaven, yes?
And you suggest that the king today make a decision
that will honour John in precedence over Peter?

Oswy the king felt left with no choice. It was not
wise for someone who had lived a life that was at best
only intermittently holy to risk the displeasure of the
door-keeper of heaven itself.

Wilfrid thus in Northumbria brought devastation
on much that had been built by Oswald and Aidan in
the name of John and Columba. What would remain or
be built again in the same spirit of the gospel?

November 29

Psalm 88:8-9   *Proverbs 15:18, 20, 33*
                Hebrews 12:14-15

So in Northumbria the church had officially fallen to Roman control and usage. Those who left travelled to Iona and on to Ireland where the Celtic ways persisted in places for hundreds of years.

But those like Hild and Cuthbert who had supported the Celtic side at the Whitby council but chose to remain in Northumbria had difficult tasks ahead. For the sake of peace and unity all must conform to the rulings now being introduced. Cuthbert especially would persuade those under his care to embrace ways and regulations he had no innate sympathy for, either.

It is amusing to notice the characteristically uncontrollable aspects of Celtic Christianity appearing through the cracks even after the reorganization. In later years, for example, Cuthbert is finally persuaded to leave his hermitage on Inner Farne to be a bishop. But he agrees only because it is in line with unfulfilled prophecy in his life. Even then, he has a quiet word with his friend who is Bishop of Lindisfarne, and without consulting anyone else the two men swap bishoprics to keep Cuthbert closer to home. In their generation at least, Roman standardization may have triumphed, but had certainly not won.

The Wild Goose still flew.

November 30

Psalm 119:65   Proverbs 3:13, 17   Colossians 3:15

So, is there a house that John built – today? Is it being built again? If so, it will be through leaning as beloved John did on the breast of Jesus, through hearing His heartcry and uniting our hearts with His. It will not be through the establishing of some radical alternative structure that breeds schism or becomes another fast-decaying denomination awaiting fossilization. It may be through living in a way that is recognizably different as Hild and Cuthbert and the others did, working in and alongside the structures presented to them – with simplicity and fervour. If the structures fall, so be it – whatever is of lasting value will endure.

As Columba said to his community when he was dying:

> 'See that you be at peace among yourselves,
> my children, and love one another.
> Follow the example of good men of old,
> and God will comfort you and help you
> both in this world
> and in the world which is to come.'

And this was the peace Columba found,
the peace of Christ.

December Readings
Enter In

December 1

Psalm 27:8, 31:16　　　　　*Isaiah 41:17-20,43:19*
　　　　　Mark 6:31b-32

The notes this month are taken from *Poustinia* by
Catherine de Hueck Doherty, used with permission of
Fr Robert Wild, Madonna House, Combermere,
Ontario. Copies of the book may be obtained from
that address or from Madonna House, Thorpe Lane,
Robin Hood's Bay, North Yorkshire YO22 4TQ.
　(Please note: One or two of the words of the
original text may have been changed to enable the
quotes to stand alone, or a small amount of
explanation may have been added in brackets.)

May the risen Lord lead each of you into the desert
of your heart, and speak to you there in his Spirit,
and show you there the radiant mercy of his
Father's face. Then may he lead you to his brothers
and sisters who are everywhere awaiting your love.

December 2

Psalm 138:1-5　　　　　*Deuteronomy 32:10-14*
　　　　　Hebrews 11:38

The word 'poustinia' is Russian meaning 'desert'. It is
an ordinary word. If I were a little Russian girl, and a
teacher during a geography lesson asked me to name
a desert, I might say 'Saharskaya Poustinia' – the Sahara
Desert. That's all it really means. It also has another
connotation, as so many words have. It also means the
desert of the Fathers of the Desert, who in ages past
went away from everything and settled there. In the

Western sense of the word, it would mean a place to which a hermit goes and, hence, it could be called a hermitage. The word to the Russian means much more than a geographical place. It means a quiet, lonely place that people wish to enter, to find God who dwells within them. It also means truly isolated, lonely places to which specially called people go as hermits, and would seek God in solitude, silence and prayer for the rest of their lives.

However, a poustinia was not necessarily completely away from the haunts of men. Some people had reserved, in their homes, a small room to which they went to pray and meditate, which some might call a poustinia. Generally speaking, however, a 'poustinik' (a person dwelling in a poustinia) meant someone in a secluded spot.

It was considered a definite vocation, a call from God to go into the 'desert' to pray to God for one's sins and the sins of the world. Also to thank him for the joys and the gladness and all his gifts.

December 3

Psalm 57:7-11   *Song of Songs 4:12,15; 8:6-7*
Revelation 7:7-15

It seems strange to say, but what can help modern man find the answers to his own mystery and the mystery of him in whose image he is created, is *silence, solitude - in a word, the desert*. Modern man needs these things more than the hermits of old.

If we are to witness to Christ in today's market places, we need silence. If we are always to be available, not only physically, but by empathy, sympathy, friendship, understanding and boundless 'caritas', we need silence. To be able to give joyous, unflagging hospitality, not only of house and food, but of mind, heart, body and soul, we need silence.

True silence is the search of man for God.

True silence is a suspension bridge that a soul in love with God builds across the dark, frightening gullies of its own mind, the strange chasms of temptation, the depthless precipices of its own fears that impede its way to God.

True silence is the speech of lovers. For only love knows its beauty, completeness, and utter joy.

True silence is a garden enclosed, where alone the soul can meet its God. It is a sealed fountain that he alone can unseal to slake the soul's infinite thirst for him.

December 4

Psalm 89:1-2   Lamentations 2:19   Matthew 6:16

There was no big fuss about going into a poustinia. From some village, from some nobleman's house, from some merchant's house – from any part of our society in Russia – a man would arise. (Of course only God knows *why* he did arise.) He would arise and go into the place (as the Russians say) *where heaven meets earth,* departing without any earthly goods, usually dressed in the normal dress of a pilgrim. In summertime, this garb was a simple hand woven shift of linen of the kind ladies wore these days, only it came down to his ankles. It was tied in the middle with an ordinary cord. He took along a linen bag, a loaf of bread, some salt, a gourd of water. Thus he departed, after, of course, taking leave of everyone in the household or in the village. Some didn't even do this. They just stole away at dawn or in the dark of the night leaving a message that they had gone on a pilgrimage and maybe would find a poustinia to pray

to God for their sins and the sins of the world, to
atone, to fast, to live in poverty and to enter the great
silence of God.

December 5

Psalm 16   Isaiah 58:6-12   Revelation 21:1-7

True silence is a key to the immense and flaming heart
of God. It is the beginning of a divine courtship that
will end only in the immense, creative, fruitful, loving
silence of final union with the Beloved.

Yes, such silence is holy, a prayer beyond all prayers,
leading to the final prayer of constant presence of
God, to the heights of contemplation, when the soul,
finally at peace, lives by the will of him whom she
loves totally, utterly and completely.

This silence, then, will break forth in a charity that
overflows in the service of the neighbour without
counting the cost. It will witness to Christ anywhere,
always.

Availability will become delightsome and easy, for
in each person the soul will see the face of her Love.

Hospitality will be deep and real, for a silent heart
is a loving heart, and a loving heart is a hospice to
the world.

December 6

Psalm 48:1-3,8-14   Isaiah 6:1-9
Jeremiah 1:4-9   Mark 9:9-27

Who were these men and women of Russia? Why did
they go into 'the desert'? Who were they spiritually?

They were people who craved in their hearts to be
alone with God and his immense silence.

The mountain of God's silence - covered with the

cloud of his mysterious presence – called these future poustinikki in that awesome yet loving way.

To go into the poustinia means to listen to God. It means entering into *kenosis* – the emptying of oneself. This emptying of oneself, even as Christ emptied himself for us, is really a climbing of this awesome mountain right to the very top where God abides in his warm silence. It also means to know 'how terrible it is to fall into the hands of the living God' . . . and yet how delightful, how joyful, and how attractive! So attractive, in fact, that the soul cannot resist. That is why the Russians say that he who is called to the poustinia must go there or die because God has called him to this mountain to speak to him in that awesome silence, in that gentle, loving silence. For God has something to say to those whom he calls to the poustinia, and what God says to them the poustinikki must repeat as a prophet does.

Humanly and psychologically speaking he is reluctant to speak, as every prophet was reluctant; but to him too comes the angel with the coal of fire, that invisible angel that cleanses his mind, his mouth, and his lips (symbolically speaking) and watches that man or woman arise and start on this awesome pilgrimage.

December 7

Psalm 107:4-5   *1 Kings 19:9-13*   *Mark 1:35*

Silence is not the exclusive prerogative of monasteries or convents. Simple, prayerful silence is everybody's silence – or if it isn't, it should be. It belongs to every Christian who loves God, to every Jew who has heard the echoes of God's voice in his prophets, to everyone whose soul has risen in search of truth, in search of God. For where noise is – inward noise and confusion – there God is not!

Deserts, silence, solitudes are *not necessarily places but states of mind and heart*. These deserts can be found in the midst of the city, and in the every day of our lives. We need only to look for them and realize our tremendous need for them. They will be small solitudes, little deserts, tiny pools of silence, but the experience they will bring, if we are disposed to enter them, may be as exultant and as holy as all the deserts of the world, even the one God himself entered.

For it is God who makes solitude, deserts, and silences holy.

December 8

Psalm 19:7-11; 119:97-106   *Ezekiel 3:3*
Daniel 2:1-23   *Luke 2:19*

Into the poustinia the poustiniks brought one book only – the Bible. They read it on their knees, impervious to or even perhaps uninterested in any purely academic question. To them the Bible was the incarnation of the Word and they felt a lifetime wasn't enough in which to read it. Every time they opened it they believed with a tremendous deep faith that they were face to face with the Word.

Yes, the poustinik reads the Bible on his knees. He doesn't read it with his head (conceptually, critically) except in the sense that the words pass through his intelligence, but the intelligence of the poustinik is in his heart. The words of the Bible are like honey on his tongue. He reads them in deep faith. He doesn't analyse them, he reads them and allows them to stay in his heart. He may read only one or two sentences or maybe a single page in one day. The point is that he puts them all in his heart like Mary did. He lets them take root in his heart and waits for God to come and explain them which inevitably he will do when he finds such deep and complete faith.

December 9

Psalm 89:8-16   *Lamentations 3:40-41a*
              Galatians 5:18-35

Deserts, silence, solitude.

For a soul that realizes the tremendous need of all three, opportunities present themselves in the midst of the congested trappings of all the world's immense cities. But how, really, can one achieve such solitude?

By standing still!

Stand still, and allow the strange, deadly restlessness of our tragic age to fall away like the worn-out, dusty cloak that it is – a cloak that was once considered beautiful. The restlessness was considered the magic carpet to tomorrow, but now in reality we see it for what it is: a running away from oneself, a turning from that journey inward that all men must undertake to meet God dwelling within the depths of their souls.

Stand still, and look deep into the motivations of life.

Stand still, and lifting your hearts and hands to God pray that the mighty wind of his Holy Spirit may clear all the cobwebs of fears, selfishness, greed, narrow-heartedness away from the soul: that his tongues of flame may descend to give courage to begin again.

December 10

Psalm 63:1-7   Isaiah 61:8-9   Matthew 6:5-6

From the moment their poustinia was built, from the moment of their closing its door upon themselves, not only they but the whole of humanity entered into that cabin with them.

When he closed the door for the first time he entered the very essence of the novitiate of God's love, for in this wondrous, extraordinary, awesome, beautiful, tremulous silence of God he would learn to know who God is.

God would reveal himself to the poustinik in a fullness that he rarely communicates even to those who live in a religious community.

Every man is a pilgrim on the road of life. Some – and there are more than we know of – are like the poustinikki, truly seeking the Absolute – God!

So I think the poustinia will begin slowly to attract many such people who will arise now here, now there ... and go seeking to find a place where they can enter into the silence of God and meet his Word – Christ – in that silence.

December 11

Psalm 5:4-5,8-12   Exodus 19:1-9, 17-20
Romans 16:25-7

Thus the hermit, the poustinik, learns to know God. Not learn *about* him, but learn *of God himself through God himself.*

For in the tremendous silence into which this poustinik entered, God reveals himself to those who wait for that revelation and who don't try to 'tear at the hem of a mystery' forcing disclosure.

Now the poustinik lies prostrated, waiting for God to explain, as God did to the disciples of Emmaus, whatever God wants to explain to him. All he knows is that his heart too will burn within him as did that of those disciples.

December 12

Psalm 127:1   1 Chronicles 17:4-10   Mark 1:17

The person who follows the call to the poustinia and who leaves everything behind relies on the help of his fellow men. He becomes in reality a beggar. In Russia, when a village knew that a hermit was going to dwell in some abandoned hut or one that he would come to beg them to help to build, they were glad. It meant that there was someone praying for them.

So the poustinik usually selected a secluded spot in a clearing in the woods. The hermit really sought the hidden places of his world – mountains, forests, woods – places where he was really alone with God.

Thus his human horizons were somewhat limited so that his spiritual horizons could grow without distractions.

December 13

Psalm 118:19-29   1 Kings 17:7-16
Matthew 7:8   Revelation 3:8

The poustinik also occupied himself with some work, like weaving baskets … People came to visit him.

For a Russian hermit has no lock or latch on his door except against the wind. Anyone at any time of day or night can knock at his door. Remember, he is in the poustinia not for himself but for others. He is a connecting bridge between men and God and God and men, and God speaks through him ... The East believes that the poustinik is such a channel so they come to him and he must always be available.

He also must share food with anyone that comes. They may refuse, but it must always be offered. He may just have a piece of bread, but he will break it in half or into as many parts as there are people. Thus the second aspect of this strange life is hospitality ... the sharing of what he has ... the offering of it at any moment.

Hospitality above all means that the poustinik is just passing on whatever God has put into his empty hands.

He gives all that he has and is.

Words, works, himself, and his food.

December 14

Psalm 34:6   *Deuteronomy 15:16-17*

             Matthew 25:5-7

He gives of his works

(The poustinik lives not far from a village. It is hay making time, the weather turns stormy, and his help is asked.)

Immediately the poustinik drops everything or anything he might be doing – prayer, garden, reading, whatever it may be – and spends all his time on the hay.

For we believe in Russia that if I touch God I must touch man, for there is really no distinction. Christ incarnated himself and became man, so I must, like Christ himself, be a person of the towel and the water. That is to say, wash the feet of my fellow men as Christ did, and washing the feet of my fellow men means service.

I cannot pray if I don't serve my brother. I cannot pray to the God who incarnated himself when my brother is in need. It is an impossibility. It would be like the priest, the Levite, who passed the man beset with robbers, and that one cannot do.

So sometimes a poustinik might spend a month, six weeks, working for the various needs of the villagers and never think even for one minute about the fact that he is supposed to be in a poustinia, reading the Bible, or praying, because *he is in the poustinia of his heart always*, especially when serving his fellow men.

December 15

Psalm 132:16   *Micah 6:6–8*   *Matthew 18:1–5*

If you ever see a *sad* hermit or poustinik, then he is no hermit at all. The most joyous persons in Russia are the ones who have the eyes of a child at 70 and who are filled with the joy of the Lord, for they who have entered the silence of God are filled with God's joy. Yes, the life of a poustinik should be truly joyous with the quiet joy of the Lord and this will be visible. He will have the eyes of a child even if his face is old. You cannot fool people as to such things as the presence of love and joy in a human being.

December 16

Psalm 4:8   *Genesis 28:10–22*   *Matthew 8:20*

The poustinia must be almost stark in its simplicity and poverty. It must contain a table and a chair. On the table there must be a Bible. There should also be a pencil and some paper. In one corner area a basin and pitcher for washing up. The bed, if bed there be, should be a cot with wooden slats instead of a mattress, a couple of blankets or quilts and a pillow if absolutely necessary. This is all that should be offered in the way of bedding. Drinking water, a loaf of bread, which will be divided into three parts, one for breakfast, one for lunch and one for dinner. For those not accustomed to eating their bread with water, there are the makings for tea and coffee.

Prominent in the poustinia is a cross without a corpus, about six feet by three feet, which is nailed to the wall, and an icon of Our Lady in the eastern corner with a vigil light in front of it. The cross without a corpus is a symbol of one's own crucifixion on it, for those of us who love Christ passionately want to be crucified with him so as to know the joy of his resurrection.

December 17

Psalm 139:15-16   *1 Kings 9:1-3*
        Proverbs 3:7-8   Hebrews 8:10-11

The poustinia can never simply be a place of rest – sleeping, recreation, a 'change of pace'. The poustinia is a holy place, so holy that one trembles when one enters. It is not an eating place, nor a sleeping place. It is God's place.

The desert, of course, is the symbol of austerity, poverty, and utter simplicity. It is God who leads the soul to the desert and the soul cannot remain in the desert long unless it is nourished by God. Therefore, it is a place where we fast from bodily food and even spiritual food, such as reading all kinds of books, for we enter there to meet our God with the only book in which he is fully accessible: the Bible.

Let your poustinia be a quiet, secret garden enclosed, for it is a hallowed place, a holy place where the soul enters to meet its God.

December 18

Psalm 131   *Ezekiel 11:5*   *2 Corinthians 3:12-16*

The one who goes to the poustinia for the first time
…will experience a certain amount of interior noise.

The first time one of the staff went she said to me
on returning,'Boy, that was a terrible experience! You
know what happened to me?'

I said,'Yes, I think I do. But tell me anyway.'

She said,'All my thoughts buzzed in me like flies. I
was thinking that my jeans needed stitching, that the
garden needed weeding. I thought about everything
except God.'

I said,'Oh, that's perfectly natural.'

It takes a long time for modern man to close
the wings of his intellect and to open the door of
his heart.

December 19

Psalm 95:8-9   *Deuteronomy 7:17-24*
Hebrews 2:14-18

At all costs the desert must be a place of utter
simplicity. No books, no curtains, no pictures, except
for an icon. And don't let us kid ourselves into
thinking a poustinia must always be in the country,
must always be a log house, or a shingled farmhouse
…No this would be a false idea of the poustinia – the
desert – for the desert, the poustinia can be located
everywhere, for fundamentally it is interiorized. If
you have a spare room in the house or a large closet,
it will do.

Truly the desert will strip you. The Lord of the
Desert will do that too. Truly you will be tempted
even as he had been tempted. You will suffer as he has

suffered, but you will also be filled with tranquillity –
the tranquillity of God's order.

December 20

Psalm 17:17   *Proverbs 3:3-6*   *John 13:23-5*

For those of you who go into the poustinia . . . this is
the essence of it:

to fold the wings of your intellect.

In the civilization of the West everything is sifted
through your heads. You are so intellectual, so full of
knowledge of all kinds. The poustinia brings you into
contact first and foremost with solitude. Secondly, it
brings you in contact with God. Even if you don't feel
anything at all, the fact remains that you have come to
have a date with God, a very special rendezvous. You
have said to the Lord,

'Lord, I want to take this 24, 36, 48 hours out of my
busy life and I want to come to You because I am
very tired. The world is not as you want it, and
neither am I. I want to come and rest on your breast
as St John the Beloved.
   That is why I have come to this place.'

December 21

Psalm 132:7-9   *Leviticus 25:17*
            John 13:33-4, 14:25-7

The West values itself for its ability to produce things.
Priests, nuns and lay people tend to evaluate
themselves interiorly by what they *produce*. Priests
especially do not realize that their presence is
enough. I often tell priests who work in parishes that

one of the best things they can 'do' is simply walk around their neighbourhoods and be present to their people. If they don't do something, they feel that they are wasting their lives away. So it is with the poustinik. There is an inability to realize that the presence of a person who is in love with God is enough, and that nothing else is needed. That doesn't mean that the poustinik's assistance in definite ways cannot be helpful to the community. But it does mean that one should be perfectly at peace even (should I say especially?) when one hasn't got 'something to do'.

December 22

Psalm 37:4-7a   *Song of Songs 8:6-7*
1 Thessalonians 3:6-10

Prayer is the source and the most intimate part of our lives. The life of prayer – its intensity, its depth, its rhythm – is the measure of our spiritual health and reveals to us ourselves. With the ascetics, the desert is interiorized, and signifies the concentration of a recollected spirit. At this level, where man knows how to be silent, true prayer is found. Here he is mysteriously visited.

There should be no break in our prayer. Why should my heart be removed from God just because I am talking to you? When you are in love with someone, it seems the face of the beloved is before you when you drive, when you type and so on. Prayer is like that. If you fall in love then it is impossible to separate life and breath from prayer. Prayer is simply union with God. Prayer does not need words. When people are in love they look at each other, look into each other's eyes, or a wife simply lies in the arms of her husband. Neither of them talks. When love reaches its apex it cannot be expressed anymore. It has reached that immense realm of silence where it pulsates and reaches proportions unknown to those who haven't entered into it. Such is the life of prayer with God. You enter into God and God enters into you, and the union is constant.

December 23

Psalm 119:105   Proverbs 6:23   Revelation 4:4–10

The call to be a poustinia in the marketplace.

> 'Go into the market place and stay with me. Be a light to your neighbour's feet. Go without fear into the depth of men's hearts. I shall be with you. Pray always. I shall be your rest.'

The face of this apostolate (call) would be Nazareth. Nazareth, where he spent his hidden life. Nazareth, where the days were humdrum and ordinary, where no visible results were forthcoming except tables and chairs.

Nazareth, where the son of God was simply the son of Mary and Joseph to all the people around him. Nazareth, where he lived as we will have to live, in the company of Mary and Joseph, and from them learn the silence of the heart. Nazareth, the preparation of his entrance into the desert, which was already a kind of desert situated in a small village of Galilee.

It would continue to intensify its very ordinariness and simplicity, bearing with people who will not understand why they are *producing so little*. They will have to accept the fact that people will say of them what others said of Jesus,

> 'Can anything good come out of Nazareth?'

Through their prayerful, hidden and seemingly

unproductive life, God will prepare them for new contacts and new works according to *his* plan and not *theirs*.

December 24

Christmas Eve (see liturgies, pp. 62–3)
Psalm 22:24   1 Samuel 3:1–10   Acts 9:3–19

The poustinia in the market place begins with prayer, much prayer. It does not mean that you are not doing the work you have been doing: housing migrant workers, and so on. No. You must understand that the poustinia *begins in your heart*. It is not a place, a geographical spot. It is not first and foremost a house or a room. It is within your heart. It is implementing the prayer of St Francis. That is the work of the poustinik in the market place, to be hidden as Christ was hidden in Nazareth.

When this work of the Holy Spirit is really allowed to take place in a human heart, the person is utterly indifferent as to where geographically he is situated. It is possible to live in a lovely house while inwardly, spiritually, you are clad like John the Baptist in animal skins and eating locusts and wild honey.

If this inner poustinia, this stripping of oneself, this kenosis, is begun, it means that you kneel before the Lord and say,

'Here I am, Lord, do with me as you will. Speak for your servant is listening. Lord, I thank you for all you have given me, for all you have taken away from me, for all you have left me.'

When you have done that, you will have begun to understand the poustinia in the market place.

December 25

Christmas Day (see liturgies, pp. 63-4)
Psalm 86:1-12   Ecclesiastes 1:10-11   John 11:5-7

To achieve this kind of missionary activity (in the market place), we must follow Christ in the rhythm of his own life, the rhythm of solitude and action. What is needed today is to retire to solitude and silence, to hear the voice of God, to glorify him and pray to him, and then to return to the secular world. Tragically the West keeps brushing this aside and saying,

> 'Yes, these are the basic verities – but let's get down to action!'

December 26

Stephen – first Christian martyr
Psalm 145   Ezekiel 36:38   Luke 17:20-21

I don't know if I have succeeded in giving you a clearer idea of what this kind of poustinia of the market place is. It is not a matter of retiring to any basement! You live in the market place and carry the poustinia within you. That is your vocation. You are pregnant with Christ. You are Christ-bearers. You are poustinia bearers.

Where? In the market place.

To whom? To anyone whom you meet there, but especially to those you are mandated to be with.

This eliminates, I hope, all notions of being recluses, of withdrawing from the market place.

December 27

John – the beloved disciple
Psalm 105:42-5   *Nehemiah 2:17-18*
      Philemon 20-21

(In the poustinia you can – as the Russian poustinik –
live there for all your life, seven days a week; or as at
the Madonna House live there only part of your life,
three or four days a week; or you may just visit for an
hour or a day – living still in the 'market place'.) You
may feel guilty because you are not *part of the
community*.

But you should not think this. If a Russian built a
poustinia next to the village, he automatically knows
that he is part of that village. He doesn't have to be
told that he is now part of that community.

*Being part of the community is not a matter of
geography.*

If your spiritual director says that you should spend
three days in the poustinia, you spend three days. If he
thinks you should spend four, you spend four. If he
thinks you should come out of the poustinia for a
while altogether, you come out. *Wherever you are in
obedience, you are part of the community.* It is not a
matter of being inside or outside the poustinia.

December 28

Psalm 41 *Genesis 3:8-10* *1 Corinthians 13:12*

Poustinia in the Hospital – October 21 1973

A room, a bed, two chairs
Stark, naked room of pain
A room set all apart
For just that pain, in a desert more real

Than the deserts of sand and heat.
Poustinias indeed where man meets his God
   Face to face
      Both crucified.
Gone are all subterfuges, excuses, rationalizations.
Now man enters into the truth of God,
All his masks are torn and man becomes what he
    truly is.
Poustinias in a hospital of Golgotha
On which the crucified God is planted in the midst of
    crucified men.
Now is the moment of meeting,
Now is the moment of speaking.
But no words are needed in the poustinia of a
    hospital room.
Only the steps of the Father
And the light of the Spirit
That comes
Like a gentle breeze
In the spring,
Consoling,
Assuaging,
Making clear
All that was unclear
So that
In a stark,
Naked
Room of pain
Joy enters.
The sick arise
   And dance with Christ.

December 29

Psalm 23   *Genesis 5:21-4*   *Revelation 3:1-6*

As I sit here and try to rethink and meditate on what I

have written about the poustinia, I honestly wonder if I can say 'Amen' just yet. My purpose was to explain the poustinia vocation as found in Russia, in my own life and in the life of the Madonna House. But ... when you come right down to it, the poustinia is not a place at all - and yet it is. It is a stage, a vocation, belonging to all Christians by Baptism.

It is a vocation to be a contemplative.

There will always be 'solitaries', or should be. But the essence of the poustinia is that it is a place within oneself, a result of Baptism, where each of us contemplates the Trinity. Within my heart, within me, I am or should be constantly in the presence of God. This is another way of saying that I live in a garden enclosed where I walk and talk with God (though a Russian would say 'where all in me is silent and where I am immersed in the silence of God'). It's as if I were sitting next to God in complete silence, although there are always many other people around. (Like a husband and wife being in a private silence and solitude even though they are at a party and the room is filled with people.)

How stumbling words are! How inadequate the similes! Yet the poustinia is something like this to me: a state of contemplating God in silence.

December 30

Psalm 39:1-3   Deuteronomy 11:18   John 1:1-18

The poustinia is within, and one is forever immersed in the silence of God, forever listening to the word of God, forever repeating it to others in word and deed. Thus everything that I have said about the physical poustinia, about trying to adapt it to the West, can be said about every Christian everywhere. The poustinia is this inner solitude, this inner immersion in the silence of God. It is through this inner, total identification with humanity and with Christ that every Christian should be living in a state of contemplation. This is the poustinia within oneself.

I don't know if all this makes any sense. It does to me. It is only in identifying with Christ, it is only by plunging into the great silence of God within myself, that I can love and identify with others.

It is by listening to the great silence of God, and having this strange, passive dialogue in which I become aware of the silence which is the speech of God – it is only by listening to this that I am able to speak to my brother. It is only by listening to this silence that I can acquire the ingenuity of love, the delicacy of Christ in my human relationships.

In this silence I become identified with Christ, I acquire a listening heart.

December 31

Psalm 97:1-6   Exodus 3:1-6   Acts 2:1-11, 16-21

The poustinia is a state of constantly being in the presence of God because one desires him with a great desire, because in him alone one can rest. The poustinia is walking in this inner solitude, immersed in the silence of God. My life of service and love to my fellowman is simply the echo of this silence and solitude.

Inwardly I identify myself with God and with humanity. Jesus Christ himself conducts me into this inner silence, into that solitude which speaks so loudly to the Father under the guidance of the Holy Spirit.

Now I am immersed in the Trinity, in the fire of the silence of God (for the silence of God is always fire; his speech is fire). Now I become as one on fire with love of him and of all humanity across the world. Now it is not I who speak. I speak what God tells me to speak. When my immersion into this immense silence has finally caught fire from his words, then I am able to speak. I can speak because his voice is sounding loudly and clearly in my ears, which have been emptied of everything except him.

Now only his name is on my heart, constantly; it has become my heartbeat.

About the Northumbria Community

A Rule of Life

The Northumbria Community is bound together by our commitment to a common Rule of Life. We say, Yes to AVAILABILITY and to VULNERABILITY as our *way for living*. The Community has seen gradual development over the years, and so the Rule has grown out of our history and the values and emphasis which reflect what we hope is our character and ethos. We are responding to a call we believe to be from God: it is a call to risky living.

And what of poverty, chastity and obedience? We have mostly not been called to relinquish all our possessions. We are nearly all married or presently single, rather than committed to a permanent celibacy. We seek to be accountable to others rather than under strict vows of obedience. Yet our vows – of availability and vulnerability – are seriously taken and in this respect we are a monastic community, consecrated to God in our way for living.

A Rhythm for Living

As part of our rhythm of life in the Community one of our disciplines is to stop and be still long enough to 'say Office' at various points during the day. In *Celtic Daily Prayer* we made available to other people the form of Morning, Midday and Evening prayer used throughout the community by groups and individuals.

Each person has to struggle to find a rhythm of prayer in their life, regular time with God that is built into their pattern of daily activities and responsibilities. The more flexible and varied their schedule is, the more opportunity there is for prayer, but also the greater the danger of no life-giving discipline being established. If we are serious about going deeper in prayer and our relationship with God, we will be encouraged by the constant pattern which a discipline of prayer affords.

Our subjectivity often perceives God to be distant and uncaring just when it is important to hold fast and follow Him on unfamiliar paths. It is then we need to hear:

Lord, You have always lightened
this darkness of mine;
and though the night is here,
today I believe.

Relationship that is Life Giving

There are members of the Community across not only Northumbria, but throughout Britain and various places overseas.

For someone to be identified as part of the Community it is important that they be taught the Rule and incorporate the regular use of the Northumbrian Office into their rhythm of prayer. It is meaningless, however, to speak of community without relationship.

In some areas members and friends of the Community meet together on a regular basis. We are involved in praying for each other's needs, and also shouldering in whatever way we can the burden of the work of the Community. Everyone is encouraged to visit the Nether Springs, the mother-house of the Community.

It is our primary purpose to provide facility for those seeking God, as we draw on the richness of our inheritance in desert and Celtic spirituality. Hundreds of people each year experience the welcome of the

Nether Springs or hospitality in the homes of Northumbria Community folk in other places. Music, dance, drama, and story-telling have always had a significant place in the life of the Community, and are naturally used in teaching or in mission. Sometimes our own prayer and study results in writing and publications. Recently a trading company has even been established in the hope of easing the financial burden of all that maintaining and resourcing the Community presently involves.

We have a preferential commitment to involvement around ancient Celtic Christian sites. In particular, we have a special affection for Holy Island (Lindisfarne), Iona and Heavenfield; and will assist in the establishing or development of various houses which embody a kindred ethos and way for living – in places as diverse as Turkey, Ireland and Russia.

The Community is unashamedly Christian, Trinitarian in belief and nourished by the Scriptures which are the memory-book of the people of God. Our church involvements are differing and varied. We are committed to involvement in the real world rather than a segregated Christian environment.

Most take the insight and support they gain from the Community and seek to relate them to the ordinary situations of everyday life.

For more information, or details of other publications, music tapes etc., contact:

Northumbria Community
Nether Springs, Hetton Hall
Chatton, Northumberland
UK NE66 5SD
Telephone: 01289 – 388235/388242

In North America:
Northumbria Community
PO Box 1824
Keene
New Hampshire 03431

Invocation of the Holy Spirit

Most powerful Holy Spirit,
    come down upon us
             and subdue us.

    From Heaven,
    where the ordinary
is made glorious,
    and glory seems
            but ordinary,

    bathe us
      with the brilliance
        of your light
      like dew.

Acknowledgements

Like the wise merchant Jesus talked about, we have brought out from our storehouse treasures both old and new; some have been with us for so long we have forgotten quite where they came from! Permission has been sought for all copyright material (and sources are often acknowledged within the text) but any omissions or suggested amendments will be noted for future editions.

Adam, David, *The Edge of Glory*, Triangle, SPCK, 1985.

Brown, George Mackay, *Magnus*, London: Hogarth Press, 1973.

Buechner, Frederick, *Wishful Thinking - A Theological ABC*, New York: Harper & Row, 1973; *The Final Beast*, New York: Atheneum, 1965.

Cape, Dave, *On The Road With Jesus*, Kingsway Publications, 1993.

Card, Michael, 'The Basin and the Towel', from *Poiema*; 'Why' from *Scandalon*, Word Records.

Carmichael, Alexander, *Carmine Gadelica*, Edinburgh: Floris Books.

Carmichael, Amy, *Toward Jerusalem*, Dohnavur/SPCK, 1987.

Crabb, Kemper, 'The Vigil', Nashville: Starsong Records, Benson Corp.

Darnall, Jean, *Heaven here I come*, London: Marshall, Morgan & Scott, 1974.

de Foucauld, Charles, *Letters from the Desert*, Burns & Oates, 1977; *Meditations of a Hermit*, Burns & Oates, 1930.

de Mello, Anthony, *One Minute Wisdom*, USA: Doubleday Image, 1985.

Ferguson, Ron, *Chasing The Wild Goose*, London: Fount, HarperCollins *Publishers*, 1988.

Gillard, Richard, 'Servant Song', New Zealand: Scripture in Song, 1977.

Hale, Reginald B., *The Magnificent Gael*, Canada: World Media Productions, 1976.

Hawley, William A., 'A Light Came Out', *Salvation Army Songbook*, London: Salvationist Publishers and Supplies.

Hollis, Gertrude, *A Scholar of Lindisfarne*, SPCK.

Hunter, Charles & Frances, with Buck, Roland, *Angels on Assignment*, Houston: Hunter Books, 1979.

Hybels, Bill, *Honest To God?*, USA: Zondervan, 1991.

Lawhead, Stephen, *Merlin*, Lion Publishing, 1988.

Maclean, Alistair, *Hebridean Altars*, Moray Press, 1937.

McLeod, Kenneth, *The Road to the Isles*, Edinburgh: Robert Grant & Son, 1927.

Motley, Norman, *Letters to a Community 1970-1980*, Othona Community, 1986.

New Wine Magazine, 'A Physician Looks at the Crucifixion', Alabama: Mobile.

Norbet, Gregory, 'A Time to Gather' from *Spirit Alive*, Weston Priory, Vt 06161.

Nouwen, Henri, *Seeds of Hope*, London: Darton, Longman & Todd, 1989.

O'Fiannachta/Foristal, *Saltair Prayers from the Irish Tradition*, Dublin: Columba Press, 1988.

Paris, Twila, 'Cry for the Desert', 'You have been good', 'Keeper of the Door', Nashville: Starsong Records, Benson Corp.

Pickova, Eva, 'Fear', from *I Never Saw Another Butterfly*, Prague: State Jewish Museum; Word Music, 1989.

Rambo, Reba & McGuire, Dony, 'We're giving her back to You', 'Keep on Fightin'', RMR Records.

Redwood, Hugh, *God in the Shadows*, London: Hodder & Stoughton, 1932.

Roberts, Frances, *Come Away, My beloved*, California: Kings Press.

Rolheiser, Ronald, *Forgotten among the Lilies*, *The Restless Heart*, London: Hodder & Stoughton, 1990.

Six, Jean Francois, *Is God Endangered by Believers?*, New Jersey: Dimension Books, 1983. (Originally published as *L'incroyance et la foi ne sont pas qu'on croit*, Paris: Editions du Centurion, 1979.)

Slater, Richard, 'When Wise Men Came Seeking', *Salvation Army Songbook*, London: Salvationist Publishers and Supplies.

Taule, John & Bevan, Emma Frances, 'Belonging', Hymns Ancient and Modern Ltd.

Van de Weyer, Robert, *Celtic Fire*, London: Darton, Longman & Todd, 1990.

Wiesel, Elie, *The Testament*, London: Penguin, 1982.

Whitham, A. E., *The Discipline and Culture of the Spiritual Life*, London: Hodder & Stoughton.